"*Asia in International Relations* injects new dimensions into the ways that we think of contemporary world affairs, and encourages us to reflect upon our engagement in 'IR' as an academic discipline. This is a stimulating, vigorous, and exciting book to be read with sustained interest."

Kosuke Shimizu, Department of Global Studies, Ryukoku University, Kyoto, Japan

"A refreshing (re)introduction to Asia's international relations from a critical perspective that challenges much of the conventional wisdom about Asia's history, interactions, and identity. This volume is not only a valuable teaching resource, but it also opens up new avenues of research and thinking on Asia's place in the study of international relations and global order."

Amitav Acharya, American University, Washington, DC, USA

ASIA IN INTERNATIONAL RELATIONS

Asia in International Relations decolonizes conventional understandings and representations of Asia in International Relations (IR). This book opens by including all those geographical and cultural linkages that constitute Asia today but are generally ignored by mainstream IR. Covering the Indian subcontinent, Turkey, the Mediterranean, Iran, the Arab world, Ethiopia, and Central-Northeast-Southeast Asia, the volume draws on rich literatures to develop our understanding of power relations in the world's largest continent. Contributors "de-colonize", "de-imperialize", and "de-Cold War" the region to articulate an alternative narrative about Asia, world politics, and IR. This approach reframes old problems in new ways with the possibility of transforming them, rather than recycling the same old approaches with the same old "intractable" outcomes.

Pinar Bilgin is Professor of International Relations at Bilkent University, Ankara, Turkey.

L.H.M. Ling is Professor of International Affairs at The New School, New York, NY, USA.

RETHINKING ASIA AND INTERNATIONAL RELATIONS

Series Editor – Emilian Kavalski, Australian Catholic University (Sydney)

This series seeks to provide thoughtful consideration both of the growing prominence of Asian actors on the global stage and the changes in the study and practice of world affairs that they provoke. It intends to offer a comprehensive parallel assessment of the full spectrum of Asian states, organisations, and regions and their impact on the dynamics of global politics.

The series seeks to encourage conversation on:

- what rules, norms, and strategic cultures are likely to dominate international life in the 'Asian Century';
- how global problems will be reframed and addressed by a 'rising Asia';
- which institutions, actors, and states are likely to provide leadership during such 'shifts to the East';
- whether there is something distinctly 'Asian' about the emerging patterns of global politics.

Such comprehensive engagement not only aims to offer a critical assessment of the actual and prospective roles of Asian actors, but also seeks to rethink the concepts, practices, and frameworks of analysis of world politics.

Recent titles:

India–US Relations in the Age of Uncertainty: An Uneasy Courtship
B. M. Jain

One Korea: Visions of Korean Unification
Edited by Tae-Hwan Kwak and Seung-Ho Joo

Asia in International Relations: Unlearning Imperial Power Relations
Edited by Pinar Bilgin and L.H.M. Ling

Forthcoming titles:

Uncertainty, Threat and International Security: Implications for Southeast Asia
Zachary C. Shirkey and Ivan Savic

Theorizing Indian Foreign Policy
Edited by Misha Hansel, Raphaelle Khan and Mélissa Levaillant

Russia's Geoeconomic Strategy for a Greater Eurasia
Glenn Diesen

ASIA IN INTERNATIONAL RELATIONS

Unlearning Imperial Power Relations

Edited by Pinar Bilgin and L.H.M. Ling

Routledge
Taylor & Francis Group
LONDON AND NEW YORK

First published 2017
by Routledge
2 Park Square, Milton Park, Abingdon, Oxon OX14 4RN

and by Routledge
711 Third Avenue, New York, NY 10017

Routledge is an imprint of the Taylor & Francis Group, an informa business

© 2017 selection and editorial matter, Pinar Bilgin and L.H.M. Ling; individual chapters, the contributors

The right of Pinar Bilgin and L.H.M. Ling to be identified as the authors of the editorial material, and of the authors for their individual chapters, has been asserted in accordance with sections 77 and 78 of the Copyright, Designs and Patents Act 1988.

All rights reserved. No part of this book may be reprinted or reproduced or utilised in any form or by any electronic, mechanical, or other means, now known or hereafter invented, including photocopying and recording, or in any information storage or retrieval system, without permission in writing from the publishers.

Trademark notice: Product or corporate names may be trademarks or registered trademarks, and are used only for identification and explanation without intent to infringe.

British Library Cataloguing-in-Publication Data
A catalogue record for this book is available from the British Library

Library of Congress Cataloging-in-Publication Data
Names: Bilgin, Pinar, 1971- editor. | Ling, L. H. M., editor.
Title: Asia in international relations : unlearning imperial power relations / edited by Pianr Bilgin and Lily Ling.
Description: Milton Park, Abingdon, Oxon ; New York, NY : Routledge, 2017. | Series: Rethinking Asia and international relations | Includes bibliographical references and index.
Identifiers: LCCN 2016033420 | ISBN 9781472469045 (hardback) | ISBN 9781472469076 (pbk.) | ISBN 9781315576183 (e-book)
Subjects: LCSH: Asia--Foreign relations. | Asia--Strategic aspects.
Classification: LCC JZ1980 .A79 2017 | DDC 327.5--dc23
LC record available at https://lccn.loc.gov/2016033420

ISBN: 978-1-472-46904-5 (hbk)
ISBN: 978-1-472-46907-6 (pbk)
ISBN: 978-1-315-57618-3 (ebk)

Typeset in Bembo
by Taylor & Francis Books

CONTENTS

List of illustrations — x
List of contributors — xi
Preface — xiii
Acknowledgments — xv

Introduction: Learning anew: Asia in IR and world politics — 1
L.H.M. Ling

PART I
SECURITY — 11

1 Dialogue of civilizations: A critical security studies perspective — 13
   Pınar Bilgin

2 Cosmopolitan disorders: Ignoring power, overcoming diversity, transcending borders — 25
   Everita Silina

3 Dams and "green growth"? Development dissonance and the transnational percolations of power — 36
   Payal Banerjee

4 Latitudes of anxieties: The Bengali-speaking Muslims and the postcolonial state in Assam — 48
   Rafiul Ahmed

PART II
History 65

5 The nation-state problematic: South Asia's experience 67
   Binoda K. Mishra

6 The Diaoyutai/Senkaku Islands dispute: An ethos of
   appropriateness and China's "Loss" of Ryukyu 75
   Ching-Chang Chen

7 Sovereignty or identity? Significance of the Diaoyutai/Senkaku
   Islands dispute for Taiwan 86
   Boyu Chen

8 Stories of IR: Turkey and the Cold War 97
   Zeynep Gulsah Capan

PART III
Theory 107

9 The postcolonial paradox of Eastern agency 109
   John M. Hobson

10 Justification of trans-cultural international studies 121
    Gavan Duffy

PART IV
Articulations 135

11 Anti-colonial empires: Creation of Afro-Asian spaces of
    resistance 137
    Clemens Hoffmann

12 From territory to travel: Metabolism, metamorphosis, and
    mutation in IR 149
    Josuke Ikeda

13 Empire of the mind: José Rizal and proto-nationalism in the
    Philippines 160
    Alan Chong

14 The Korean Wave: Korean popular culture at the intersection
    of state, economy, and history 172
    Jooyoun Lee

15 Romancing Westphalia: Westphalian IR and *Romance of the Three Kingdoms* 184
   L.H.M. Ling

Conclusion: Uncontained worlds 195
Stephen Chan

Index *199*

ILLUSTRATIONS

Figures

10.1	Lakatos' epistemological typology	123
10.2	Aristotelian *aitia*	130

Tables

9.1	The four variants of generic Eurocentrism/Orientalism in International Theory	110
9.2	Alternative conceptions of Orientalism/Eurocentrism	111
15.1	Westphalia and *Romance* compared	190

CONTRIBUTORS

Rafiul Ahmed, Assistant Professor, Department of Geography, Sikkim University, Sikkim, India.

Payal Banerjee, Associate Professor, Department of Sociology, Smith College, Northampton, MA, USA.

Pinar Bilgin, Professor, Department of International Relations, Bilkent University, Ankara, Turkey.

Zeynep Gulsah Capan, Lecturer, Department of International Relations, Istanbul Bilgi University, Turkey.

Stephen Chan, Professor of World Politics, School of Oriental and African Studies, University of London, London, UK.

Boyu Chen, Lecturer, Department of International Studies and Regional Development, University of Nigata Prefecture, Nigata Prefecture, Japan.

Ching-Chang Chen, Associate Professor of International Politics, Department of Global Studies, Faculty of International Studies, Ryukoku University, Kyoto, Japan.

Alan Chong, Associate Professor, Centre for Multilateralism Studies, Institute of Defence and Strategic Studies, S. Rajaratnam School of International Studies, Nanyang Technological University, Singapore.

Gavan Duffy, Associate Professor, Department of Political Science, Maxwell School of Public Affairs and Citizenship, Syracuse University, Syracuse, NY, USA.

John M. Hobson, Professor of Politics and International Relations, University of Sheffield, Sheffield, UK.

Clemens Hoffman, Assistant Professor, Department of International Relations, Bilkent University, Ankara, Turkey. Lecturer in International Politics at the University of Stirling, Stirling, Scotland.

Josuke Ikeda, Associate Professor, Faculty of Human Development, University of Toyama, Toyama Prefecture, Japan.

Jooyoun Lee, Assistant Professor of Global Studies, School of Behavioral and Social Sciences, St. Edward's University, Austin, TX, USA.

L.H.M. Ling, Professor of International Affairs, The New School, New York City, NY, USA.

Binoda K. Mishra, Director, Centre for Studies in International Relations and Development (CSIRD), Kolkata, India.

Everita Silina, Assistant Professor, Julien J. Studley Graduate Program in International Affairs, The New School, New York City, NY, USA.

PREFACE

I can trace one of the beginnings of this book to a 2009 exhibition at the Guggenheim museum in New York, entitled "Third Mind: American Artists Contemplate Asia, 1869–1989," exploring the impact of "Asian art" on "American art." For those not aware of give-and-take, learning and mutual constitution of (what we choose to call) "civilizations," exhibitions such as these serve as eye openers. They highlight how much of "Asia" already is a part of "America" where "standard" approaches to International Relations (IR) orient us to think of "civilizations" as autonomously developed entities.

I chose to begin with this exhibition to highlight one of the beginnings of this book, in terms of my own train of thought. Over the years, my own train of thought was fed by postcolonial and other critiques of "standard" approaches to thinking about "civilizations" and developed over conversations with L.H.M. Ling. We first sat down to formulate our ideas in the form of a workshop proposal in the spring of 2009. That proposal did not get funded. We tried our luck three more times, with different professional organizations, failing three more times. When Turkey's Strategic Research Center (SAM, in its Turkish acronym) invited me in 2012 to organize an international conference, I offered them our proposal instead. I am grateful to SAM's then director Bülent Aras for his foresight in agreeing to fund our conference "Transcultural Asia." We would like to acknowledge generous monetary and human support provided by SAM in making our conference happen in Ankara in the summer of 2013.

The papers presented at the 2013 conference were published in a special issue of SAM's in-house journal, *Perceptions*, in 2014. I would like to thank SAM once again for allowing us to reproduce those papers. Yet this book goes beyond the papers presented at the Ankara conference. We added four new chapters and an introduction. I am grateful to Stephen Chan for agreeing to write a concluding chapter.

I was recently reminded of the Guggenheim exhibition when I went to see another art exhibit at the Danish Museum of Art & Design. This time the exhibition focused on a similar process of give-and-take, learning and mutual constitution between two countries, Denmark and Japan. It focused on more or less the same period, highlighting how Danish design, well-known for its minimalism, clear lines and functionalism, modeled itself after Japanese design in the late nineteenth and early twentieth century. The similarity between more contemporary works of art and design was so striking that the curators of the exhibition had chosen to mark the items by the flags to highlight their country of origin. As with our "standard" approaches to IR, the world of art also seems to have limited tolerance for (what we choose to call) hybridity, choosing to draw boundaries even as it showcases objects that transgress those boundaries. This book is yet another attempt to encourage the students of IR to re-think the very notions of "civilizations" and "boundaries," this time by focusing on "Transcultural Asia."

Pinar Bilgin
Copenhagen

ACKNOWLEDGMENTS

First and foremost, Pinar Bilgin and L.H.M. Ling would like to thank the following at SAM: Murat Yeşiltaş, Engin Karaca, Şaban Kardaş, and Bülent Aras (then head of SAM). As mentioned in the Preface, they made possible our conference that subsequently led to this volume. Titled "Transcultural Asia: Unlearning Colonial/Imperial Power Relations," our conference was held in Ankara on 27–28 June 2013. We are grateful to Bilkent University and TOBB-ETU Sosyal Tesisler for providing, respectively, accommodation for the participants and facilities for our meeting. We are thankful, also, to Everita Silina for offering her elegant photograph that graced our conference poster.

We are indebted to SAM's journal, *Perceptions*, for permitting us to reprint all of our articles from the conference in its 2014 special issue. Since then, however, the chapters by Banerjee, Ahmed, C. Chen, and Ikeda have new titles and have been substantially revised. We thank the following for joining this book venture at a later date: Zeynep Gulsah Capan, Alan Chong, Clemens Hoffman, and Jooyoun Lee.

And Stephen Chan deserves special thanks. His conclusion gives us a thoughtful summary of the volume that, dialectically, also begins it.

Lastly, I'd like to thank Pinar Bilgin for embarking on this adventure with me. We started out with an idea in spring 2009 that simply would not die, despite several rounds of rejection from all sorts of sources. Through Pinar, we were able to receive funding from SAM that revived our endeavors. It's been a long haul but our collaboration has finally borne fruit. Perseverance, indeed, furthers.

INTRODUCTION

Learning anew: Asia in IR and world politics

L.H.M. Ling

This volume provides a new narrative about Asia in International Relations (IR) and world politics. It begins with a basic premise: that is, borders in Asia – whether geographical, political, cultural, or epistemic – are and always have been fluid, mobile, and mutually enmeshed. Accordingly, mixings and their resultant hybridities characterize the continent (Ling 2002, 2016). This does not mean, as this volume shows, that the outcomes themselves are not mixed and mobile: they could vary from the positive to the negative, from the revolutionary to the conformist – and back again. Nor does this mean that issues of borders and security do not matter. They matter critically, especially given the region's experiences with colonialism and imperialism in the past and the horrors of terrorism, civil war, and genocide in the present. Nonetheless, we suggest in this volume that a larger context applies. It cannot be limited to Westphalian power politics only where "sovereignty" stops at the water's edge, bounded by physical space alone. Asia's larger context conveys alternative repertoires of thinking and doing, being and relating. Ignoring such epistemic richness not only sows ignorance; it also defies daily reality on the continent and in the world.

In brief, we need to "re-learn" IR. This means broadening "Asia" to include all those geographical and cultural linkages that make the continent what it is: for example, the Indian subcontinent, Turkey, and the rest of what European colonizers called "Asia Minor," the Mediterranean, Arab and Muslim "worlds," and Central-Northeast-Southeast Asia. Western colonialism and imperialism have tried to erase these linkages analytically but failed to do so substantively. As this volume shows, such linkages still account for currents of meaning, if not action, on the continent. We also draw on rich literatures that have emerged in the Humanities and other branches of the Social Sciences (including Area Studies) (Chan, Mandaville, and Bleiker 2001). Additionally, we heed a call from within the region to "de-colonize," "de-imperialize," and "de-Cold War" (Chen 2007).

Four themes

Four main themes resound in this volume:

1. *Security* intervenes critically and inevitably in IR. It could be articulated in terms of "civilization," "cosmopolitanism," "development," or "modernity." Nonetheless, security and its twin, insecurity, frame what transpires in Asia, specifically, and world politics, generally.
2. *History* explains why the insecurities play out the way they do. Postcolonial insecurities stem from a disruptive mismatch between pre-colonial and colonial governing institutions, reflecting unresolved contestations in not just ideology but also worldview, thereby leading to foreign policy ambiguities as well as complicit Western-centric narratives outside the West.
3. *Theory* offers a caution and an opportunity. Over the past three centuries, orientalists have "included" the agency of the "Eastern Other" but in a Eurocentric way. For this reason, mere calls for liberal universalism or cosmopolitanism do not suffice. We need to probe deeper. Here, social science as developed in the West offers a seemingly counter-intuitive yet demonstrable proposition: it bears the epistemological potential to *self-transform* into a truly trans-cultural discipline.
4. *Articulations* from Asia's own traditions and experiences ultimately give us the means, epistemically and practically, to globalize IR. These provide significant insights for not just problem-solving but also problem-framing for the region as well as the world.

Each chapter within substantiates one or several of these themes.

Chapter 1, "Dialogue of civilizations: A critical security studies perspective," invites advocates of "civilizational dialogue" to discourse with those most concerned with security, national, and otherwise. Pinar Bilgin calls for a critical interrogation of all the major concepts involved: "civilization," "dialogue," and "security."

Chapter 2, "Cosmopolitan disorders: Ignoring power, overcoming diversity, transcending borders," questions the notion of cosmopolitanism under globalization. It amounts to elitism, Everita Silina states, when identity's intimate dependence on security is not considered.

Chapter 3, "Dams and 'green growth'? Development dissonance and the transnational percolations of power," shows how the government of India today entwines energy resources with national security. Payal Banerjee examines the implications of this entwinement for people, society, and development at large.

Chapter 4, "Latitudes of anxieties: The Bengali-speaking Muslims and the postcolonial state in Assam," brings the analysis inside and from below. A "cartographic anxiety," Rafiul Ahmed finds, still besets the postcolonial state, leading it to violence against and repression of the internal Other.

Chapter 5, "The nation-state problematic: South Asia's experience," shows how the modern state in South Asia has always defined nationhood in terms of security.

Such twinning of concept and policy, argues Binoda K. Mishra, stems from Western colonialism and imperialism in the region.

Chapter 6, "The Diaoyutai/Senkaku Islands dispute: An ethos of appropriateness and China's 'Loss' of Ryukyu," addresses the escalating dispute between China and Japan in the East China Sea. We need to understand their pre-Westphalian history and norms, Ching-Chang Chen proposes, in order to find a post-Westphalian venue to peaceful resolution. A Westphalian approach can only postpone or, worse, aggravate the crisis.

Chapter 7, "Sovereignty or identity? Significance of the Diaoyutai/Senkaku Islands dispute for Taiwan," underscores that national identity is neither monolithic nor fixed. For a postcolonial state like Taiwan, Boyu Chen finds, multiple identities and loyalties apply, especially in reference to the Diaoyutai/Senkaku Islands dispute. Taiwan's ambiguity reflects a typical postcolonial conglomeration of pre-colonial, colonial, and postcolonial experiences.

Chapter 8, "Stories of IR: Turkey and the Cold War," problematizes the critique of Eurocentrism as another instance of Eurocentrism. As a remedy, Zeynep Gulsah Capan highlights a certain kind of agency by the Other: complicity with the West. She draws on accounts of the Cold War by Turkey's foreign policy and academic elites as an apt example. These conform consistently to US and European interests and rhetoric.

Chapter 9, "The postcolonial paradox of Eastern agency," notes that the East is *already* in IR. Eurocentric IR, John M. Hobson cautions, has always relied on such analytical sleight-of-hand to rationalize scientific and institutional racism in its past and continuing present.

Chapter 10, "Justification of trans-cultural international studies," highlights the seeds of self-transformation towards a trans-cultural IR *within* Western social science. As demonstrated by Gavan Duffy, this potential within contrasts with extremist views on either side of the ideological spectrum: that is, whether they tout "the West is Best" or incite "Death to America!"

Chapter 11, "Anti-colonial empires: Creation of Afro-Asian spaces of resistance," makes a rare connection: it compares Turkey and Ethiopia. Their common experiences with anti-colonial pan-Islamism and pan-Africanism, Clemens Hoffman argues, produces "AfroAsian *spaces of resistance* conceptually." These indicate a co-construction of world politics, rather than its single dominance and creation by the Westphalian West.

Chapter 12, "From territory to travel: Metabolism, metamorphosis, and mutation in IR," revisits the concept of a "road." To Josuke Ikeda, a revised notion of the road could serve as a metaphor for a post-Western, post-Westphalian IR. It entails a comparative study of ideas and how they travel.

Chapter 13, "Empire of the mind: José Rizal and Proto-Nationalism in the Philippines," shows attempts to decolonize the mind from early, anti-colonial struggles. Alan Chong reviews the novels of José Rizal, a Filipino nationalist from the late nineteenth century, and how he aimed to prepare Spain's colonized subjects in the Philippines for a post-revolutionary world.

Chapter 14 "The Korean Wave: Korean popular culture at the intersection of state, economy, and history," links the state, the economy, culture, and history. For Jooyoun Lee, the Korean Wave infers more than simply a successful media exportation overseas; rather, it offers a "third space" of border-crossing commonality among postcolonial peoples and cultures.

Chapter 15, "Romancing Westphalia: Westphalian IR and *Romance of the Three Kingdoms*," submits that what goes on "inside" and "outside" national borders does not necessarily align with colonially drawn geographies. Instead, L.H.M. Ling suggests, a more globalized, post-Westphalian IR could articulate world politics culturally and normatively by region. Doing so helps to curb Westphalian hegemony by (1) provincializing the West as one region among many, and (2) visibilizing the Rest in all its entwined complexities. Ling refers to the fourteenth-century Chinese epic, *The Romance of the Three Kingdoms*, as a way of signifying Asia in IR and world politics.

"Uncontained worlds," concludes with a caution: articulations of and by the Other must not "exoticize." To do so would fall into the same orientalist trap that comes with Westphalian, Disciplinary IR. But Stephen Chan also sounds a note of optimism: "[This volume] offers not a series of solutions but a series of insights and *inside* accounts of the variables that must go into a new IR. What emerges is not a paradigm of 'worlding' but a *program* of study for worlding to undertake." In this sense, Chan suggests world politics as *uncontainable* worlds.

These arguments depart markedly from current understandings of IR.

IR, the discipline

Elsewhere (Ling 2015), I characterize Disciplinary IR as the domain of Hypermasculine-Eurocentric Whiteness (HEW). It retains a Protestant-based, Realist/Liberal mode of interacting with the world. Stemming from North America and Western Europe as the "origin" of our contemporary world politics, HEW translates into one set of social, institutional, and epistemic legacies that Vitalis (2015) calls a "white world order." For an arena like world politics, where multiple traditions, practices, and worldviews pertain, such singularity and inflexibility can only lead to a warlike ultimatum: i.e., either you convert to become like us or we will annihilate you. In either case, the result is a losing one – for everyone.

Critical theories in IR have long called for emancipating the discipline (Brincat, Lima, and Nunes 2011). Postmodernists, poststructuralists, neo-Gramscians, and feminists have led the movement since the 1990s (Walker 1988; Pasha and Murphy 2002; Hobson 2007; Tickner and Tsygankov 2008). Constructivists and postcolonialists have joined these ranks more recently (Chowdhry and Nair 2002; Barkawi and Laffey 2006; Grovogui 2006). All have focused on cultural constructions of IR and its possibilities for reformulations. In this volume, we have participants whose personal backgrounds come from India, Japan, Korea, Latvia, Singapore, Taiwan, Turkey, United Kingdom, and United States, regardless of their current institutional affiliation. In terms of academic discipline, they represent Sociology, Urban Studies, Communications, and Philosophy, along with IR. In this sense, our authors reflect the world.

Much has happened along the civilizational front in world politics. In 1998, the United Nations (UN) resolved to name 2001 as the "UN Year of Dialogue among Civilizations." By chance (or not), that year was also when al-Qaeda operatives attacked the US in New York and Washington, D.C. on September 11. These attacks have hampered the UN's efforts to foster a dialogue among civilizations. At the same time, these events have highlighted the need for precisely such efforts. Since then, Spain and Turkey, under the auspices of the UN and supported by the European Union (EU) and the Vatican, have formed an "Alliance of Civilizations" to enhance exchanges between Islam and the West. While the discursive jump from "dialogue" to "alliance" is yet to transpire in policy practice, Track II efforts have flourished across the Mediterranean.

Nonetheless, IR remains hostage to notions of culture or civilization as pre-given and unchanging. Richard Ned Lebow's *A Cultural Theory of International Relations* (2008) offers the latest example. A work of magisterial scholarship, the book still fails to recognize the role and impact of "non-Western" cultures, societies, traditions, or philosophies on "the West." Instead, Lebow universalizes IR in classical Greek terms only. In this way, he eternalizes Disciplinary IR as a domain of Anglo-American-European *episteme*, leaving no room for alternative discourses, traditions, norms, and practices. Where Disciplinary IR may acknowledge civilizational encounters, these are seen usually as a "clash" only between two pristine sets of thought and behavior (Huntington 1996).

Most problematic about this "clash" scenario, as Amartya Sen (2006: 11) puts it, is "the presumption of the unique relevance of a singular classification." There is little appreciation of the interactive dynamism between worlds that lead, eventually, to a hybrid legacy. Indeed, it flowers abundantly in conflict resolution, business dealings, intervention and treatment of migrants, and even in the re-integration of the former East Germany into the "Western" fold (O'Hagan 1995; Doty 1996; Jackson 2006). Critical IR scholars have responded by tracing the continuities and disruptions between so-called civilized vs. barbaric divides, particularly how the "East" helped to make the "West" what it is today (Hobson 2004).

Still, Huntington's (1993) challenge to his critics rankles: "If not civilizations, what?" Seeking to replace "civilization" with another equally problematic category will not address the problem. Working through the notion of civilization may allow inquiry into the international politics of a category, its emergence and various uses in the worlds of policy and academia. But operating with the notion of civilization as currently conceptualized is too limiting. Not only does it reinforce the differences between civilizations, thereby marginalizing attempts to recognize centuries of integration across and within civilizations, but also the conventional take on civilizations tends to fix in place nationalist reactions outside the West to Orientalist impositions, typically by reproducing the violence of such in the process (Bilgin 2012).

Individual scholars, though, have long examined civilizational encounters. I mention only a small sample here. Research by Gerrit Gong (1984) and Shogo Suzuki (2009) brings to light some "non-Western" responses to the West's imposition of "standards of civilization" rhetoric. Antony Anghie (2003, 2005) points to the ways in which contemporary international law rests upon notions of sovereignty developed through interactions shaped by such "standards." Cemil Aydın (2007) connects "anti-Westernism" in Asia to Western policy-making, showing how admiration for the "West" eventually turns into disappointment and resentment, particularly given Europe's self-serving resort to "standards of civilization." And Brett Bowden (2009) tracks the evolution of the idea of "civilization" from its imperial/ist origins to the contemporary era.

Conclusion

"Asia" rivets the world today. The region contains some of the world's most densely-populated states, dynamic economies, and oldest spiritual/cultural/civilizational legacies. Currently, two developments further mark the Asian landscape: (1) China's $1 trillion Silk-Road initiative, announced in 2013 as the "One Belt, One Road" (OBOR) policy (Sibal 2014; Denyer 2015; Dollar 2015; Mansharamani 2016; Pentucci 2016); and (2) the creation of an Asian Infrastructure Investment Bank (AIIB), with a capital base of $50 billion just for building local infrastructures. Signed in 2014 by 21 states in the region, the AIIB will serve as a supplement to, if not substitute for, two pillars of post-war, Western-led world politics, the World Bank and the International Monetary Fund (IMF). With OBOR and the AIIB, tremendous structural and economic changes, along with cultural and political ones, loom on the horizon. Nonetheless, these represent but the latest of a series of institutional, normative, and epistemic challenges that have transformed the region, spurred most recently by Western imperialism and colonialism since the eighteenth century (Chan 1991, 1993; Ling 2002).

Yet the study of International Relations (IR) continues to treat "Asia" as a subsidiary of the "West"[1] and, by extension, its Westphalian inter-state system.[2] With Hobbes's State of Nature as template, Westphalia casts world politics as "solitary, poore, nasty, brutish, and short." States vie for power in ceaseless rounds of murderous competition, now formalized into an overarching structure or closed system (Waltz 1979). The only possibility for change comes from military power; however, it affects the position among individual states or "units" only. The structure itself remains immutable.

Culturally, normatively, and politically, this means continuation of a "white world order" (Vitalis 2015). It turns all Others into a dependent, degenerate Concubine, at best, or a servile, scraping Mimic, at worst; the West remains, as ever, dynamic, masterful, and virile (Said 1979). Those who refuse to stay put face disciplinary action. Today, for instance, the Obama Administration "pivots" towards Asia to contain what it considers a rising hegemon in the twenty-first century: China (Campbell and Andrews 2013). Everyone and everything else serve as mere pieces for the Great Game of power politics (Ling 2013). Convention dictates that the same logic endures even as the goals, norms, and nature of gaming mutate.

We clearly need a fresh take on civilizations in world politics. IR must recognize that not only do multiplicities and mixings apply in Asia but they also help to make the rest of the world. Accordingly, IR must learn new ways of thinking and doing, being and relating – and Asia's experiences with such is a good start. This kind of inquiry will probe into similarities, not just differences, and how the former may override the latter. Only in this way could we emancipate IR from its colonialist, imperialist, and Cold War foundations.

This volume presents a first step in doing so.

Notes

1 I place these terms in quotes to indicate their contingent, constructed nature. I refrain from using quotes throughout the text, though, to make it easier to read. See Bilgin (2008) and Ling (2015).
2 The Treaty of Westphalia (1648) settled the Thirty Years War (for some, it was the Hundred Years War) on the European continent. It formalized the concept of "national sovereignty" based on bordered territories and commerce as a venue for peaceful interactions. Carvalho et al. (2011) critique Westphalia as a founding myth in Disciplinary IR. I use the term here to serve as shorthand for our contemporary, state-centric and Western-led global order.

Bibliography

Anghie, Antony. (2003) *The Third World and International Order: Law, Politics, and Globalization*. Leiden: Martinus Nijhoff.
Anghie, Antony. (2005) *Imperialism, Sovereignty, and the Making of International Law*. Cambridge: Cambridge University Press.
Aydın, Cemil. (2007) *The Politics of Anti-Westernism in Asia: Visions of World Order in Pan-Islamic and Pan-Asian Thought*. New York: Columbia University Press.
Barkawi, Tarak and Mark Laffey. (2006) "The Postcolonial Moment in Security Studies." *Review of International Studies* 32(2): 329–352.
Bilgin, Pinar. (2008) "Thinking Past 'Western' IR?" *Third World Quarterly* 29(1): 5–23.
Bilgin, Pinar. (2012) "Civilisation, Dialogue, Security: The Challenge of Post-Secularism and the Limits of Civilisational Dialogue." *Review of International Studies* 38(5): 1099–1115.
Bowden, Brett. (2009) *The Empire of Civilization: The Evolution of an Imperial Idea*. Chicago: University of Chicago Press.
Brincat, Shannon, Laura Lima, and João Nunes. (2011) *Critical Theory in International Relations and Security Studies*. London: Routledge.
Campbell, Kurt and Brian Andrews. (2013) "Explaining the US 'Pivot' to Asia." *Chatham House*. August (https://www.chathamhouse.org/sites/files/chathamhouse/public/Research/Americas/0813pp_pivottoasia.pdf). Accessed: 18 April 2016.
Carvalho, B.d., H. Leira and John M. Hobson. (2011) "The Big Bangs of IR: The Myths That Your Teachers Still Tell You about 1648 and 1919." *Millennium: Journal of International Studies* 39(3): 735–758.
Chan, Stephen. (1991) "Small Revolutions and the Study of International Relations: The Problematique of Affiliation." *Political Science* 43(2): 67–77.

Chan, Stephen. (1993) "Cultural and Linguistic Reductionisms and a New Historical Sociology for International Relations." *Millennium: Journal of International Studies* 22(3): 423–442.

Chan, Stephen, Peter G. Mandaville, and Roland Bleiker (eds). (2001) *The Zen of International Relations: IR Theory from East to West*. London: Palgrave Macmillan.

Chen, Kuan-Hsing. (2007) *Qudiguo: Yazhou zuowei fanggao* (Towards De-Imperialization: Asia as a Method). Taipei: Flaneur Publisher.

Chowdhry, Geeta and Sheila Nair. (2002) *Power, Postcolonialism, and International Relations: Reading Race, Gender, and Class*. London: Routledge.

Denyer, Simon. (2015) "In Central Asia, Chinese Inroads in Russia's Back Yard." *Washington Post*. 27 December (https://www.washingtonpost.com/world/asia_pacific/chinas-advance-into-central-asia-ruffles-russian-feathers/2015/12/27/cfedeb22-61ff-11e5-8475-781cc9851652_story.html) (Accessed: 7 March 2016).

Dollar, David. (2015) "China's Rise as a Regional and Global Power: The AIIB and the 'One Belt, One Road'." *Brookings*. Summer (http://www.brookings.edu/research/papers/2015/07/china-regional-global-power-dollar) (Downloaded: 7 March 2016).

Doty, Roxanne Lynn. (1996) *Imperial Encounters: The Politics of Representation in North–South Relations*. Minneapolis: University of Minnesota Press.

Friedberg, Aaron L. (2011) *A Contest for Supremacy: China, America, and the Struggle for Mastery in Asia*. New York: W.W. Norton & Co.

Gong, Gerrit W. (1984) *The Standard of 'Civilization' in International Society*. Oxford: Clarendon Press.

Grovogui, Siba N. (2006) *Beyond Eurocentrism and Anarchy: Memories of International Oder and Institutions*. New York: Palgrave Macmillan.

Hobson, John M. (2004) *The Eastern Origins of Western Civilization*. Cambridge: Cambridge University Press.

Hobson, John M. (2007) "Is Critical Theory always for the White West and Western Imperialism? Beyond Westphlilian towards a Post-Racist Critical IR." *Review of International Studies* 33(1): 91–116.

Hung, Ho-fung. (2016) *China Boom: Why China Will Not Rule the World*. New York: Columbia University Press.

Huntington, Samuel P. (1993) "If Not Civilizations, What? Paradigms of the Post-Cold War World." *Foreign Affairs* 72(5). (https://www.foreignaffairs.com/articles/global-commons/1993-12-01/if-not-civilizations-what-samuel-huntington-responds-his-critics) (Accessed: 18 November 2016).

Huntington, Samuel P. (1996) *The Clash of Civilizations and the Remaking of World Order*. New York: Simon & Schuster.

Jackson, Patrick Thaddeus. (2006) *Civilizing the Enemy: German Reconstruction and the Invention of the West*. Ann Arbor: University of Michigan Press.

Jacques, Martin. (2012) *When China Rules the World: The End of the Western World and the Birth of a New Global Order*. New York: Penguin Books.

Lebow, Richard Ned. (2008) *A Cultural Theory of International Relations*. Cambridge: Cambridge University Press.

Ling, L.H.M. (2002) *Postcolonial International Relations: Conquest and Desire between Asia and the West*. New York: Palgrave Macmillan.

Ling, L.H.M. (2013) "Worlds beyond Westphalia: Daoist Dialectics and the 'China Threat'." *Review of International Studies* 39(3) July: 549–568.

Ling, L.H.M. (2015) "Don't Flatter Yourself: World Politics as We Know It is Changing and So Must Disciplinary IR." *Essay for the 50th Anniversary Celebration of IR Studies at Sussex University*, 10–11 December 2015.

Ling, L.H.M. (ed.) (2016) *India and China: Rethinking Borders and Security*. Ann Arbor: University of Michigan Press.

Mansharamani, Vikram. (2016) "China is Spending Nearly $1 Trillion to Rebuild the Silk Road." *PBS Newshour*. 2 March (http://www.pbs.org/newshour/making-sense/china-is-spending-nearly-1-trillion-to-rebuild-the-silk-road/) (Accessed: 7 March 2016).

O'Hagan, Jacinta. (1995) "Civilizational Conflict? Looking for Cultural Enemies." *Third World Quarterly* 16(1): 19–38.

Pasha, Mustapha Kamal and Craig N. Murphy. (2002) "Knowledge/Power/Inequality." *International Studies Review* 4(2): 1–6.

Pentucci, Rafaello. (2016) "China's New Silk Road is Designed to Cut Russia out of Eurasian Trade." *China in Central Asia*. 29 February (http://chinaincentralasia.com/) (Downloaded: 7 March 2016).

Said, Edward. (1979) *Orientalism*. New York: Random House.

Sen, Amartya K. (2006) *Identity and Violence: The Illusion of Destiny*. New York: W.W. Norton & Co.

Sibal, Kanwal. (2014) "China's Maritime 'Silk Road' Proposals Are Not as Peaceful as They Seem." *Daily Mail India*. 21 February (http://www.dailymail.co.uk/indiahome/indianews/article-2566881/Chinas-maritime-silk-road-proposals-not-peaceful-seem.html) (Accessed: 28 May 2014).

S.R. (2014) "Why China is Creating a New 'World Bank' for Asia." *Economist*. 11 November (http://www.economist.com/blogs/economist-explains/2014/11/economist-explains-6). Accessed: 18 April 2016.

Suzuki, Shogo. (2009) *Civilization and Empire: China and Japan's Encounter with European International Society*. New York: Routledge.

Tickner, J. Ann and Andrei P. Tsygankov (eds). (2008) "Responsible Scholarship in International Relations: A Symposium." *International Studies Review* 10(4): 661–666.

Vitalis, Robert. (2015) *White World Order, Black Power Politics: The Birth of American International Relations*. Ithaca: Cornell University Press.

Walker, R.B.J. (1988) *One World, Many Worlds: Struggles for a Just World Peace*. Boulder, CO: Lynne Rienner.

Waltz, Kenneth N. (1979) *Theory of International Politics*. New York: Random House.

Zhang, Yongjin and Teng-chi Chang (eds). (2016) *Constructing a Chinese School(s) of IR: Ongoing Debates and Critical Assessment*. London: Routledge.

PART I
SECURITY

1

DIALOGUE OF CIVILIZATIONS

A critical security studies perspective

Pınar Bilgin

In the fall of 1998, United Nations (UN) member states agreed on declaring the year 2001 the "UN Year of Dialogue among Civilizations."[1] One of the major players behind the proposal, then President of Iran Seyyed Mohammed Khātamī, described the UN initiative as an attempt to counter the primacy of Huntingtonian axioms in world politics. The 9/11 attacks against the US hampered the UN's efforts while at the same time created a new impetus for dialogue. That said, while President Khātamī's (2000) initial proposal portrayed the Dialogue of Civilizations initiative as a way for managing "chaos and anarchy" and seeking "harmony" in world politics, subsequent revivals of the project explicitly invoked the challenge posed by "terrorism" for world security in justifying the need for dialogue (Mestres and Lecha 2006). The point being is that civilizational dialogue initiatives have their origins in security concerns and have been offered by their proponents as responding to threats to world security.

Over the years, civilizational dialogue initiatives have received support from the scholarly world as well. For Richard Falk (2002: 323), civilizational dialogue is not merely a "normative effort to appreciate the relevance of the civilizational interpretation of the historical situation, but at the same time seeking to avoid reproducing the Westphalian war system in the emergent inter-civilizational context." Consider Fred Dallmayr (2002: 1), who views civilizational dialogue as contributing to efforts towards "strengthening ... the prospect of a more peaceful world and more amicable relations between peoples." More recently, Marc Lynch (2000) has explored whether civilizational dialogue constitutes an instance of an international public sphere in the making (in the Habermasian sense). Fabio Petito (2011: 762), in turn, has offered civilizational dialogue as an important alternative to those other discourses of world order that fail to consider the need for "reopening and rediscussion of the core of Western-centric and liberal assumptions upon which the normative structure of the contemporary international society is based."

Without wanting to underestimate the significance of such critical explorations for a peaceful world order amidst rampant fears of a "clash," this chapter presents a critical security studies perspective on civilizational dialogue initiatives. Critical security studies are concerned with insecurities as experienced by multiple referents, including individuals, social groups, states, and the global environment. This chapter argues that students of critical security studies and proponents of civilizational dialogue initiatives potentially have something to talk about between themselves. In presenting a two-step critique of civilizational dialogue initiatives, this chapter explores such potential, which could allow for further dialogue with a view to addressing insecurities of multiple security referents.

The growing literature on critical security studies has produced multiple ways to approach security critically (Krause and Williams 1997; Waever, Buzan, and De Wilde 1998; Aradau et al. 2006; Bigo 2008). In what follows, I will be building upon the insights of the Aberystwyth School of Critical Security Studies. From an Aberystwyth School perspective, thinking differently about security involves first challenging the ways in which security has traditionally been conceptualized by broadening and deepening the concept and by rejecting the primacy given to the sovereign state as the primary referent for, and agent of, security. Critical approaches also problematize the militarized and zero-sum practices informed by prevailing discourses and call for a reconceptualizing. Second, this perspective rejects the conception of theory as a neutral tool, which merely explains social phenomena, and emphasizes the mutually constitutive relationship between theory and practice. What distinguishes the Aberystwyth School from other critical approaches to security is an explicit commitment to emancipatory practices in addressing insecurities as experienced by multiple referents, including individuals, social groups, states and the global environment.[2]

The first section of the chapter argues that civilizational dialogue initiatives, in their current conception, overlook insecurities of referents other than those they are seeking to secure (i.e. states). The second section focuses on the notion of dialogue on which civilizational dialogue initiatives rest, and calls for approaching civilizational dialogue in a way that is dialogical not only in ethics but also epistemology as well.[3] The third section highlights untapped potential in civilizational dialogue initiatives as viewed from a critical security studies perspective.

Overlooking insecurities of non-state referents

From a critical security studies perspective, civilizational dialogue initiatives, given their primary concern with preventing a potential clash between states, come across as prioritizing state security to the neglect of other referents. The issue here is not only that they do not prioritize non-state referents' security, but also that they are not concerned with the potential implications such a state-focused approach would likely have for the security of individuals and social groups. What follows briefly highlights three such instances of insecurity.

One instance is that through focusing on the ontology of civilization and considering individuals and social groups insofar as they are members of this or that civilization, civilizational dialogue initiatives risk marginalizing other ways of engaging with people and social groups. This is because civilizational dialogue initiatives ultimately locate "the problem of difference" outside civilizations, with little consideration for differences inside. To paraphrase a point Naeem Inayatullah and David Blaney (2004: 44) made in another context, projects of civilizational dialogue constitute "a deferral of a genuine recognition, exploration, and engagement of difference" with difference being "marked and contained" as civilizational difference. In other words, through pursuing world security as peace between states belonging to different civilizations, "the problem of difference" would be "deferred." Such deferral, in turn, could potentially allow for insecurities inside civilizations, including marginalization of insecurities of those with "interstitial identities" – to invoke Homi K. Bhabha (1994).

Second, given prevailing conceptions of "civilizations" as having an unchanging "essence" (an assumption shared by Samuel Huntington and some of his dialogue-oriented critics) there will not be much room left for inquiring into power/knowledge dynamics in the (re)production of differences. Indeed, civilizational dialogue initiatives often fail to acknowledge that "identity is not a fact of society" but a "process of negotiation among people and interest groups" (McSweeney 1999: 73). More significantly, oftentimes such negotiations themselves are sources of in/security, while at the same time taking identities of people as "pre-given." As Bill McSweeney (ibid.) has argued when writing on insecurities in Northern Ireland, "the security problem is not there because people have separate identities; it may well be the case that they have separate identities because of the security problem."

Third, envisioning a world order structured around civilizational essences could potentially amplify the voices of those who dress their rhetoric in terms of cultural "essence." One concrete instance of such insecurity was observed when Pope Benedict XVI embraced civilizational dialogue initiatives and sought to re-define "Western" civilization along religious lines. This is not to reduce the former Pope's interest in dialogue to his "in-house" concerns, but to highlight how engaging in civilizational dialogue allowed Pope Benedict XVI to form alliances with like-minded leaders from other civilizations and justify various policies that overlooked women's insecurities (among others) (Halliday 2006).

Highlighting insecurities as experienced by myriad referents should not be taken as underestimating the potential contributions that dialogue between civilizations could make. Indeed, I join Fabio Petito (2011) in underscoring the need to acknowledge something like a fundamental ethical-political crisis linked to the present liberal Western civilization and its expansion, and recognize that dialogue of civilizations seems to enshrine the promise of an answer, or rather to start a path toward an answer.

However, what civilizational dialogue initiatives currently offer in terms of contributing to security is a potential, a potential that needs exploring, but with a view to what Friedrich Kratochwil (2005) referred to as "interpretative struggles" that are going on within civilizations, and the insecurities of myriad referents that follow.[4]

That said, it is important to note that the proponents of civilizational dialogue do not prioritize non-state referents' insecurities for a reason. Their thinking is that given the urgency of preventing a potential clash between states belonging to different civilizations, the current insecurities of non-state referents could be postponed until later (Dallmayr 2002). Without wanting to underestimate the potential planetary consequences of such a clash, what is also important to remember is, first, that such "short-termism" may not allow for the addressing of medium- to long-term consequences.[5] The steps we take here and now allow some future steps to be taken while disallowing some others. Second, focusing on the short-term as such betrays a non-reflexive approach to security. Non-reflexive approaches to security do not reflect upon insecurities generated as we put various security policies into effect (Burgess 2011). The point is that civilizational dialogue initiatives do not reflect on potential insecurities that may follow the adoption of state-focused security policies as such. Cold War policy-making is a scary but useful reminder of potential implications (for individuals, social groups and the environment) of adopting such short-termist, state-focused and non-reflexive notions of security (Bilgin, Booth, and Wyn Jones 1998; Bilgin 1999).

Dialogical in ethics but not epistemology

Civilizational dialogue initiatives, in their current conception, embrace dialogue as ethics but not as epistemology, which, in turn, limits their horizons. In making this point, I build upon Xavier Guillaume's explication of Bakhtinian notion of dialogue. Critiquing those approaches that adopt a narrow notion of dialogue, Guillaume writes:

> This discovery of the "other" within the "self" is a peculiar and narrow approach to dialogism since it only considers dialogue as a "possibility of conversation" between civilizational actors, and not as a general process underlying continuous active and passive interactions.
>
> (Guillaume 2000: 10)

Whereas Bakhtinian dialogism, argues Guillaume, underscores the need for adopting dialogue as ethics and epistemology:[6]

> Ethically, the completion and perfection of a self is determined by the reflexive and dialogical integration of otherness. This, in turn, is opposed to an unethical approach, which would understand otherness through monological lenses, and thus as an object. Epistemologically, dialogism enables us to tackle the identity-alterity nexus through the existence of a hermeneutical locus – a concept that draws on the three main characteristics of an utterance (expression, context,

and relation) and which I will develop further in the next section – by using its definition as an interweaving of mutually-responsive utterances. A dialogical approach, then, illuminates both the formation and performance of an identity.

(Guillaume 2000: 9)

An example of a monological approach to dialogue was exhibited by Pope Benedict XVI, notes Mustapha Kamal Pasha:

> Pope Benedict's recent remarks on the inextricable association between violence and faith as a durable feature of Islam offers a striking example of essentialism's immunization against modernity or globalizing currents, economic integration, cultural flows, or scientific exchange. The other's past, present and future are simply identical.
>
> *(Pasha 2006a: 26)*

In contrast, seeking sociological insights into civilizations would "afford sensitivity to differentiations and distinctions of locale, class, gender or ethnicity" among Muslims (Pasha 2006b: 71). Avoiding essentialism, then, needs to go hand in hand with efforts at avoiding monological epistemology. Adopting a dialogical epistemology to look at historical dialogue of civilizations amounts to – in philosopher Susan Buck-Morss's (2003: 74) words – "[rejecting] essentialist ontology and [returning] to critical epistemology."

While major proponents of dialogue recognize some give-and-take between civilizations, they consider such exchanges to have taken place at the margins, thereby leaving civilizations largely untouched.[7] As such, civilizational dialogue initiatives overlook historical dialogue between civilizations. What I mean by historical dialogue is the give-and-take between civilizations that has, throughout the ages, gone beyond surface interaction, as explored by John Hobson in his writings.

What Hobson means by "dialogue" is different from the conception of dialogue that civilizational dialogue initiatives rest upon. For Hobson, dialogue is

> a fundamental concept that underpins the non-Eurocentric global-dialogical approach, referring to the ways in which civilizations mutually shape each other as new ideas, technologies, and institutions invented in one civilization diffuse to another.
>
> *(Hobson 2009: 26)*

As such, Hobson adopts a dialogical epistemology toward imagining "the identity of the West along polycivilisational lines" (Hobson 2009: 17). That such give-and-take had taken place centuries ago does not render it a historical curiosity that is inconsequential for present-day world politics. What is at stake is recognizing multiple civilizations' contributions to what are popularly portrayed as "Western" ideas and institutions. Such acknowledgement, in turn, would potentially have significant consequences for averting a potential clash and allowing further dialogue.

Stated in less abstract terms, recognizing civilizations as dynamic, pluralistic, and co-constituted entities allows recognizing multiple agency in the emergence of ideas and institutions such as human rights, rationalism, and democracy, which are presently viewed by Huntington, as well as some of his critics, as exclusively "Western" inventions (Bilgin forthcoming). Indeed, the historical give-and-take between civilizations, Hobson reminds us,

> was vital in enabling not just the early phase of the rise of the West but in positively shaping Europe's cultural identity (especially through the Renaissance) ... the Muslims acted as "switchmen" in that they served to retrace the path that European development underwent, helping to put it on an eventual collision course with capitalist modernity. But while the Muslims were vitally important in making and remaking of the West between about 650 and 1500, the progressive baton of global power and influence was then passed on to the Chinese who ran with it right down to the early nineteenth century.
> *(Hobson 2007: 161)*

Even more relevant for the purposes of this chapter is Hobson's point that "the very term European 'Renaissance' is problematic, since it exaggerates its Ancient Greek foundations and denies its substantial Eastern heritage" (Hobson 2007: 159).[8] Nobel Laureate Amartya Sen concurs:

> There is a chain of intellectual relations that link Western mathematics and science to a collection of distinctly non-Western practitioners. For example, the decimal system, which evolved in India in the early centuries of the first millennium, went to Europe at the end of that millennium via the Arabs. A large group of contributors from different non-Western societies – Chinese, Arab, Iranian, Indian, and others – influenced the science, mathematics, and philosophy that played a major part in the European renaissance and, later, the Enlightenment.
> *(Sen 2006: 56)*[9]

Hobson makes a similar point about the Reformation and highlights how the idea of "man [as] a free and rational agent" was integral to the works of Islamic scholars and that "these ideas were also strikingly similar to those that inspired Martin Luther and reformation" (Hobson 2007: 177–178).

The point being, writing values and institutions such as human rights and democracy out of the history of civilizations other than "the West" do not only render invisible others' contributions to the making of (what is popularly referred to as) the "civilized way of life" but also ends up substantiating extremists' theses. For, it is based on the presumed absence of such values and institutions outside the "West" that Huntingtonians have called for strengthening their own vis-à-vis the rest; likewise Muslim extremists have warned against "Western" plots to export "alien" values (such as democracy or women's rights as human rights) to the land of Islam and have called for *jihad*.[10]

In contrast a dialogical approach to civilizational give-and-take would uncover a multiple beginnings of human rights norms. Among others, Zehra Kabasakal-Arat has warned against reading the history of the human rights norms through the categories of current debates:

> Although the current vocabulary of human rights has more easily detectable references in Western philosophical writings, this does not mean that the notion of human rights was alien to other cultures or that the Western cultures and societies have been pro-human rights.
>
> *(Kabasakal-Arat 2006: 419)*

Siba N. Grovogui has challenged assumptions regarding the "Western" origins of human rights, and pointed to other imaginaries that could allow expanded domains of human rights. Comparing French, American and Haitian revolutions' different formulations of human rights, Grovogui (2006) has maintained that

> human rights have multiple genealogies, and it is possible, as often happens in the Global South, to imagine protected human rights as existing outside of Western norms, without negating the possibility of universalism or universality, which is the appeal of the concept of human rights.

Meghana Nayak and Eric Selbin's *De-centering International Relations* (2008), in turn, has highlighted multiple authorship of the human rights convention.[11] Kabasakal-Arat (2006: 421) has provided further evidence:

> The Universal Declaration was formulated through debates that involved participants from different cultures. Although representation in the UN Human Rights Commission, which drafted the Universal Declaration, was not global, it was not limited to the Western states either. Two of three main intellectual forces in the drafting subcommittee, Charles Malik from Lebanon, and Peng-chun (P.C.) Chang from China, had their roots in the Middle Eastern and Asian cultures.

Finally, Gurminder Bhambra and Robbie Shilliam (2009) have pointed to the agency of social movements in different parts of the world who framed their struggles in human rights terms. Taken together, these writings point to multiple beginnings of what is popularly portrayed as the "Western" origins of human rights, and highlight potential for further and worldwide dialogue on human rights.

This is not to lose sight of the fact that the world has changed since 1948 when the human rights convention was written. Arab representatives to the United Nations at the time (Syria, Lebanon, Egypt and Saudi Arabia) are currently under different leadership. There are other state and non-state actors in the Arab world and beyond that vie for shaping Muslim minds. Aziz Al-Azmeh (2007) reminds us that whereas the late nineteenth and early twentieth century was characterized by

Muslim thinkers inquiring into "Reformist Islam," recent decades have witnessed marginalization of such efforts. As such, highlighting multiple beginnings of human rights norms is not meant to imply their universal acceptance in present-day politics. Rather, the point here is that what renders human rights a contentious issue is not a question of "origins" of ideas about human rights (for we know that there are multiple beginnings),[12] but present-day contentions of world politics. A dialogical approach to a history of civilizations would help uncover the historical dialogue of civilizations and allow further dialogue toward addressing insecurities experienced by multiple referents.

A critical security studies perspective on civilizational dialogue?

Students of critical security studies and proponents of civilizational dialogue initiatives potentially have something to talk about between them. Critical studies approaches (broadly conceived) are concerned with insecurities as experienced by multiple referents – individuals, social groups, states and the environment. Those critical approaches that originate from the Aberystwyth School tradition rest on a notion of security as emancipation, understood as the "political-ethical direction" of security scholarship (Wyn Jones 2005: 217).[13]

Emancipatory approaches are almost always criticized for their reliance on "Western" traditions of thought. Over the years, critics have pointed to the ideational origins of critical approaches to security and have argued that they are bound to be of limited use in analyzing insecurities in "non-Western" contexts (Ayoob 1995; Peoples and Vaughan-Williams 2010). What the critics sometimes overlook is that the notion of emancipation adopted by students of critical security studies pushes the term beyond its Western European origins and conceptualizes it as – in Hayward Alker's (2005: 201) turn of phrase – "political convergences on needs, not agreement on foundations." Indeed, reflecting on the Enlightenment roots of emancipation, Booth has maintained that "what matters is not where ideas come from but how well they travel" (Booth 2005: 181). Susan Buck-Morss's (2003: 99) remark, made with reference to the possibility of alliances between critical actors in the aftermath of 9/11, is highly relevant to the discussion here:

> [T]he rejection of Western-centrism does not place a taboo on using the tools of Western thought. On the contrary, it frees the critical tools of the Enlightenment (as well as those of Islam) for original and creative application.

Recently, Jürgen Habermas (2006) has identified dialogue between civilizations as a remedy to "Western" roots of our key concepts including emancipation. Indeed, a dialogue of civilizations could potentially help us find multiple beginnings of our key notions in different civilizations. However, to achieve such an end, civilizational dialogue initiatives would need to embrace dialogue not only as ethics but also epistemology as well. From a critical theory perspective, the goal, in Buck-Morss's (2003: 4–5) words, is not to "understand" some "other" discourse, emanating from a "civilization" that is intrinsically different from "our own." Nor is it merely organizational, to form pragmatic, interest-driven alliances among pre-defined and self-contained groups. Much less is it to accuse a part of the polity being backward in its political beliefs, or worse, the very key embodiment of evil. Rather, what is needed is to rethink the entire project of politics within the changes condition of a global public sphere – and to do this democratically, as people who speak different political languages, but whose goals are nonetheless the same: global peace, economic justice, legal equality, democratic participation, individual freedom, mutual respect.

Students of critical security studies, in turn, could adopt a twofold strategy. On the one hand, they could focus on highlighting how emancipation, to quote Booth (2007: 111),

[a]s an ideal and a rallying cry, in practice, was prominent in many nineteenth-century struggles for independence or for freedom from legal restrictions; notable examples included Jews in Europe, slaves in the United States, blacks in the West Indies, the Irish in the British state, and serfs in Russia.

This would also allow moving civilizational dialogue initiatives from their current focus on state security. On the other hand, students of critical security studies could inquire into multiple beginnings of their core ideas (as with human rights; see above) (Bilgin 2012a).[14] Towards this end, approaching civilizational dialogue as ethics *and* epistemology carries significant potential.

Conclusion

Civilizational dialogue initiatives are currently viewed as our best chance to prevent a potential clash between states belonging to different civilizations. Critical security studies are concerned with insecurities as experienced by individuals, social groups, states and the global environment. In this chapter, I have argued that students of critical security studies and proponents of civilizational dialogue initiatives potentially have something to talk about toward rendering possible further dialogue with a view to addressing insecurities of multiple security referents (including states).

Notes

1 Further information on this initiative is available at (http://www.un.org/Dialogue/) (Downloaded: 19 September 2011).
2 On the Aberystwyth School, see Booth (1991), Bilgin, Booth, and Wyn Jones (1998), Wyn Jones (1999), Bilgin (2005), Booth (2005, 2007).
3 For an earlier elaboration on these two points, see Bilgin (2012b). The present article builds on these points and presents a critical security perspective.
4 Also see, Pieterse (1992) and Narayan (2000).

5 A point made by Booth about the nuclear policies of great powers; see Booth (1999a, b).
6 Also see, Neumann (2003).
7 See, for instance, President Khatami quoted in Esposito and Voll (2003).
8 On Egyptian and Phoenician roots of what is popularly viewed as Greek heritage, see Bernal (1987) and Orrells, Bhambra, and Roynon (2011).
9 See also, Al-Khalili (2011).
10 On the parallels between George W. Bush and Osama Bin Laden's discourses, see Agathangelou and Ling (2004).
11 Also see, Prashad (2008).
12 On "origins" versus "beginnings," see Said (1975, 1993). For an elaboration, see Bhambra (2007).
13 Also see, Booth (1991, 2007) and Alker (2005).
14 On emancipation, see Booth (2005, 2007).

References

Agathangelou, Anna and L.H.M. Ling. (2004) "Power, Borders, Security, Wealth: Lessons of Violence and Desire from September 11." *International Studies Quarterly* 48(3): 517–538.
Al-Azmeh, Aziz. (2007) "Human Rights and Contemporaneity of Islam: A Matter of Dialogue?" In H.M. Neto (ed.), *The Universal in Human Rights: Precondition for a Dialogue of Culture*, 65–80. Rio de Janerio: Educam – Editoria Universitaria Candido Mendes.
Al-Khalili, Jim. (2011) *The House of Wisdom: How Arabic Science Saved Ancient Knowledge and Gave us the Renaissance*. New York: Penguin Press.
Alker, Hayward. (2005) "Emancipation in the Critical Security Studies Project." In Ken Booth (ed.), *Critical Security Studies and World Politics*, 189–213. Boulder: Lynne Rienner.
Aradau, C. et al. (2006) "Critical Approaches to Security in Europe: A Networked Manifesto." *Security Dialogue* 37(4): 443–487.
Ayoob, Mohammed. (1995) *The Third World Security Predicament: State Making, Regional Conflict, and the International System*. Boulder: Lynne Rienner.
Bernal, Martin. (1987) *Black Athena: The Afroasiatic Roots of Classical Civilisation*. New Brunswick: Rutgers University Press.
Bhabha, Homi K. (1994) *The Location of Culture*. London: Routledge.
Bhambra, Gurminder K. (2007) *Rethinking Modernity: Postcolonialism and the Sociological Imagination*. New York: Palgrave.
Bhambra, Gurminder K. and Robbie Shilliam. (2009) *Silencing Human Rights: Critical Engagements with a Contested Project*. New York: Palgrave Macmillan.
Bigo, Didier. (2008) "International Political Sociology." In Paul D. Williams (ed.), *Security Studies: An Introduction*, 116–129. London: Routledge.
Bilgin, Pinar. (1999) "Security Studies: Theory/Practice." *Cambridge Review of International Affairs* 12(2): 31–42.
Bilgin, Pinar. (2005) *Regional Security in the Middle East: A Critical Perspective*. London: Routledge.
Bilgin, Pinar. (2012a) "Civilisation, Dialogue, Security: The Challenge of Post-Secularism and the Limits of Civilisational Dialogue." *Review of International Studies* 38(5): 1099–1115.
Bilgin, Pinar. (2012b) "Continuing Appeal of Critical Security Studies." In Shannon Brincat, Laura Lima, and Joao Nunes (eds), *Critical Theory in International Relations and Security Studies: Interviews and Reflections*, 159–170. London: Routledge.
Bilgin, Pinar (forthcoming) "Do IR Scholars Engage with the Same World?" In Ken Booth and Toni Erskine (eds), *International Relations Theory Today*, 2nd ed. Oxford: Polity Press.

Bilgin, Pinar, Ken Booth and Richard Wyn Jones. (1998) "Security Studies: The Next Stage?" *Nacao e Defesa* 84: 137–157.
Booth, Ken. (1991a) "Security and Emancipation." *Review of International Studies* 17(4): 313–326.
Booth, Ken. (1999b) "Nuclearism, Human Rights and Constructions of Security (Part 1)." *The International Journal of Human Rights* 3(2): 1–24.
Booth, Ken. (1999) "Nuclearism, Human Rights and Contructions of Security (Part 2)." *International Journal of Human Rights* 3(3): 44–61.
Booth, Ken (ed.). (2005) *Critical Security Studies and World Politics*. Boulder: Lynne Rienner Publishers.
Booth, Ken. (2007) *Theory of World Security*. Cambridge: Cambridge University Press.
Buck-Morss, Susan. (2003) *Thinking Past Terror: Islamism and Critical Theory on the Left*. New York: Verso.
Burgess, J. Peter. (2011) *The Ethical Subject of Security: Geopolitical Reason and the Threat against Europe*. New York: Routledge.
Dallmayr, Fred (ed.) (2002) *Dialogue among Civilisations: Some Exemplary Voices*. New York: Palgrave Macmillan.
Esposito, John L. and John O. Voll. (2003) "Islam and the West: Muslim Voices of Dialogue." In Pavlos Hatzopoulos and Fabio Petito (eds), *Religion in International Relations: The Return from Exile*, 237–269. London: Palgrave Macmillan.
Falk, Richard A. (2002) "Revisiting Westphalia, Discovering Post-Westphalia." *Journal of Ethics* 6: 311–352.
Grovogui, Siba N. (2006) "Mind, Body, and Gut! Elements of a Postcolonial Human Rights Discourse." In Branwen Gruffydd Jones (ed.), *Decolonizing International Relations*, 179–196. London: Routledge.
Guillaume, Xavier. (2000) "Foreign Policy and the Politics of Alterity: A Dialogical Understanding of International Relations." *Millenium: Journal of International Studies* 31(1): 1–26.
Habermas, Jürgen. (2006) "Religion in the Public Sphere." *European Journal of Philosophy* 14(1): 1–25.
Halliday, Fred. (2006) "The End of the Vatican." (https://www.opendemocracy.net/globalization/benedict_4156.jsp) (accessed 8 May 2016).
Hobson, John M. (2004) *The Eastern Origins of Western Civilisation*. Cambridge: Cambridge University Press.
Hobson, John M. (2007) "Deconstructing the Eurocentic Clash of Civilisations: De-Westernizing the West by Acknowledging the Dialogue of Civilisations." In Martin Hall and Patrick Thaddeus Jackson (eds), *Civilisational Identity: The Production and Reproduction of "Civilisations" in International Relations*, 149–165. New York: Palgrave Macmillan.
Hobson, John M. (2009) "The Myth of the Clash of Civilisations in Dialogical-Historical Context." In Pinar Bilgin and Paul D Williams (eds), *Global Security, in Encyclopedia of Life Support Systems (EoLSS)*. Oxford: UNESCO, EoLSS Publishers.
Inayatullah, Naeem and David L. Blaney. (2004) *International Relations and the Problem of Difference*. London: Routledge.
Kabasakal-Arat, Zehra F. (2006) "Forging a Global Culture of Human Rights: Origins and Prospects of the International Bill of Rights." *Human Rights Quarterly* 28(2): 416–437.
Khātamī, Mohammed. (2000) "Round Table: Dialogue among Civilisations." *United Nations* (http://www.unesco.org/dialogue/en/khatami.htm) (Downloaded: 9 November 2013).
Kratochwil, Friedrich V. (2005) "Religion and (Inter-)National Politics: On the Heuristics of Identities, Structures, and Agents." *Alternatives* 30(2): 113–140.
Krause, Keith and Michael C. Williams (eds) (1997) *Critical Security Studies: Concepts and Cases*. Minneapolis: University of Minnesota Press.

Lynch, Mark. (2000) "The Dialogue of Civilisations and International Public Spheres." *Millennium: Journal of International Studies* 29(2): 307–330.
McSweeney, Bill. (1999) *Security, Identity and Interests: A Sociology of International Relations*. Cambridge: Cambridge University Press.
Mestres, Laia and Eduard Soler i Lecha. (2006) "Spain and Turkey: A Long-Lasting Alliance in a Turbulent Context?" *Insight Turkey* 8(2): 117–126.
Narayan, Uma. (2000) "Essence of Culture and a Sense of History: A Feminist Critique of Cultural Essentialism." In Uma Narayan and Sandra Harding (eds), *Decentering the Center: Philosophy for a Multicultural, Postcolonial, and Feminist World*, 80–100. Bloomington: Indiana University Press.
Nayak, Meghana and Eric Selbin (2008) *De-centering International Relations*. London: Zed Books.
Neumann, Iver B. (2003) "International Relations as Emergent Bakhtinian Dialogue." *International Studies Review* 5(1): 137–140.
Orrells, Daniel, Gurminder K. Bhambra and Tessa Roynon (eds) (2011) *African Athena: New Agendas, Classical Presences*. Oxford: Oxford University Press.
Pasha, Mustapha Kamal. (2006a) "Islam, 'Soft' Orientalism and Empire: A Gramscian Rereading." In Andreas Bieler and Adam David Morton (eds), *Images of Gramsci: Connections and Contentions in Political Theory and International Relations*. London: Routledge.
Pasha, Mustapha Kamal. (2006b) "Liberalism, Islam, and International Relations." In Branwen Grufydd Jones (ed.), *Decolonizing International Relations*, 65–85. Lanham: Rowman & Littlefield.
Peoples, Columba and Nick Vaughan-Williams. (2010) *Critical Security Studies: An Introduction*. New York: Routledge.
Petito, Fabio. (2011) "In Defence of Dialogue of Civilisations: With a Brief Illustration of the Diverging Agreement between Edward Said and Louis Masignon." *Millenium: Journal of International Studies* 39(3): 759–779.
Pieterse, Jan Nederveen. (1992) "Emancipations, Modern and Postmodern." *Development and Change* 23(3): 5–41.
Prashad, Vijay. (2008) *The Darker Nations: A People's History of the Third World*. New York: New Press.
Said, Edward W. (1975) *Beginnings: Intention and Method*. New York: Basic Books.
Said, Edward W. (1993) *Culture and Imperialism*. New York: Knopf.
Sen, Amartya Kumar. (2005) *The Argumentative Indian: Writings on Indian History, Culture, and Identity*. New York: Farrar, Straus and Giroux.
Sen, Amartya Kumar. (2006) *Identity and Violence: The Illusion of Destiny*. New York: W.W. Norton & Co.
Waever, Ole, Barry Buzan and Jaap De Wilde. (1998) *Security: A New Framework for Analysis*. Boulder: Lynne Rienner Publishers.
Wyn Jones, Richard. (1999) *Security, Strategy and Critical Theory*. Boulder: Lynne Rienner Publishers.
Wyn Jones, Richard. (2005) "On Emancipation." In Ken Booth (ed.), *Critical Security Studies and World Politics*, 215–235. Boulder: Lynne Rienner Publishers.

2

COSMOPOLITAN DISORDERS

Ignoring power, overcoming diversity, transcending borders

Everita Silina

The discourse on global governance invites us into a strange world of disassociation from time and space. Based on broadly Cosmopolitan principles, it invokes a global normative ethic, a kind of shared civic identity that ignores the burdens of history, obstacles of geography, and the diversity of peoples, uniting all under a set of identifiable global problems. As global problems are seen to multiply and persist, the Cosmopolitan models of governance proliferate. Yet, their indifference to vagaries of time and space means that they operate on a limited conception of power and present an under-theorized notion of identity.

In what follows, I focus on the dominant approaches to Cosmopolitanism and their critical alternatives. I suggest that both ignore the structural interpretations of global politics and therefore greatly underestimate the power of the global market and its effects on the relationships within and outside its economic sphere of influence. Consequently, they tend to reinforce rather than challenge the dominant power imbalance in the global sphere. I consider the implications of these dominant models for addressing the issues of power, identity, and agency in the globalized environment and explore whether global governance ought to be more than an analytical tool.

Cosmopolitanism in brief

Despite the proliferation of Cosmopolitan arguments and models of governance, it is not an easy task to present a succinct account of current Cosmopolitan theory. Every single text on Cosmopolitanism starts with an observation or recantation that there is nothing resembling a consensus regarding "what constitutes Cosmopolitanism, who can be described as Cosmopolitan or where Cosmopolitanism is to be found" (Rumford 2007: 1). And no less than a dozen strands of Cosmopolitanism exist.[1]

At its core, Cosmopolitanism believes that all people have equal worth and dignity as members of a common human family. This commitment to the bond of shared humanity leads Cosmopolitans to call into question the moral significance of national (or any other) borders and identities attached to them. At best, territorial boundaries have only derivative value (Brock and Brighouse 2005). The argument is traced back to the Greek Stoics and Cynics who are credited with coining the term "Cosmopolitan" to describe their new identity that transcends the boundaries of the *polis* to embrace the *cosmos*, the only true community. According to David Held (2005: 10), the Stoics believed that "[e]ach person lives in a local community and in a wider community of human ideals, aspirations, and arguments." Of these, humanity is the only moral identity and association, the former being merely an accident of birth (ibid.).

More recently, Cosmopolitans have taken inspiration from the writings of the eighteenth-century German philosopher, Immanuel Kant (McGrew 2000). He proposed the idea of a global civil society and an international order composed of republics or democracies "operating under the rule of a Cosmopolitan law" (Held and McGrew 2000: 413). Kant saw the emergence of such an order as a natural progression of history, an expression of "the fundamentally moral nature of humanity" (Boon and Delanty 2007: 21). He perceived the interactions between states to be driven by the same "state of nature" logic for which Hobbes had argued the necessity of a social contract in the domestic sphere. All states would strike a global social contract, Kant extrapolated, voluntarily entering into a binding agreement to limit their sovereignty and power. A global civil society would buttress from below and Cosmopolitan international law from above. The result would be nothing less than an end to all wars (ibid.).

Kant's recommendations seem particularly relevant in an era of rapid globalization and the perceived decline of the state. Eşref Aksu (2008) sees Kant's writings on "perpetual peace" as laying the conceptual ground for current theorizing on various global governance arrangements, both in their normative and institutional guises. The search for democratic structures and institutions beyond the state has led many writers to re-examine Kant's writings. At the same time, Kant's belief in the principles of reason and his emphasis on global consciousness and understanding appeal to many who seek "novel" solutions for "inter-cultural" problems in a post 9/11 world. Kant understood that a better international order could not rely on international law alone. Its success required the right attitudes and dispositions. Reason would be a way to escape from "dogma and unvindicated authority" (Held 2005: 11). According to Kant, only impartial reasoning could foster a productive dialogue and mutual understanding. Human ability to reason bestows on us a *Cosmopolitan right*. This means that an individual has "the capacity to present oneself and be heard within and across political communities ... the right to enter dialogue without artificial constraint and delimitation" (ibid.). Presumably, Kant believed that this open-ended communication would lead to more worldly attitudes and the identity of a world citizen.

John Rawls' *The Law of Peoples* (2001) echoes Kant's argument (Brock and Brighouse 2005). Though the book contributes poorly to the debate and remains woefully out of touch with a rapidly changing world, what remains important, particularly in Rawls' (2001) definition of justice as fairness, is the intimate connection between Cosmopolitanism and Liberalism, specifically the American brand.[2] Charles Jones notes: "Cosmopolitanism is a moral perspective that is impartial, universal, individualist, and egalitarian" (Jones quoted in Sypnowich 2005: 56). Much like Liberalism, Kantian Cosmopolitanism aims to reconcile (and promote) liberal notions of individualism with multiculturalism and respect for value pluralism. Whereas Stoics may have invested local and global identities with a moral scale, many modern Cosmopolitans believe that both identities can be happily reconciled. In Ulrich Beck's recent interpretation, Cosmopolitanism differs from nationalism and globalism/universalism in that "[i]t neither orders differences hierarchically nor dissolves them, but accepts them as such, indeed invests them with a positive value" (Beck and Grande 2007: 13). Cosmopolitanism perceives "others as different *and* at the same time as equal"; it dismisses "either/or" conjunctions and permits a "both/and" principle to operate, embracing the "unity in diversity" outlook of liberal pluralism (ibid. [emphasis added]). Quite simply, nothing in Cosmopolitanism's core tenets or its multiple incarnations conflict with the liberal agenda and its principles.

But, as I argue, this means that Cosmopolitanism suffers from all the same dilemmas and criticisms – and more! – that afflict Liberalism. Indeed, Liberalism's dilemmas now drive a wedge among Cosmopolitans. When the clash between local and global cultures cannot be avoided, Cosmopolitans divide into two separate camps, each privileging one level of association over the other. While Liberalism has tried to negotiate the divergent pulls of individual and group identities, Cosmopolitanism has for the most part abandoned any attempt to understand the nature of identity. Nor are Cosmopolitans able to escape the accusation that a common human culture of individualized and rights-bearing citizens is just another hegemonic attempt to impose the values of a particular culture and society onto the rest of the world. The exaggerated role assigned to Europe, and now its institutional progeny, the European Union (EU), does not advance the impartiality claims of Cosmopolitans. And, like Liberalism, Cosmopolitanism suffers from an under-theorized notion of power, especially through economic interest. Therefore, Cosmopolitanism responds weakly to the rapid integration of global markets and the spread of a corporate, homogenized culture that threatens any notion of diversity.

In short, both Liberalism and Cosmopolitanism ignore structural inequalities and their effect on societies and identities. Consequently, they tend to reinforce rather than challenge the dominant power imbalance in the global order. Any approach to global governance, I argue, must begin by analyzing the relationship between identity and (in)security.

Identity and (in)security

Cosmopolitanism reflects, above all else, a frame of mind. In historic accounts, a Cosmopolitan is often portrayed as a worldly person (usually male) influenced by many cultures and committed to none. He is a child of the modern era of mobility and unlimited choice in everything from what one wears to who one is and what identity one creates. He is a traveler, a global tourist, and a connoisseur of all the diverse experiences that the world has to offer. An essential characteristic of a Cosmopolitan is his open orientation to the rich cultural tapestry of humanity. Along with this liberal attitude comes the sense that he is equally at home anywhere in the world. No place or community claims special and permanent loyalty from him. In this sense, a Cosmopolitan is a figure who is typically associated with "the comfortable culture of middle-class travelers, intellectuals and business people" (Kofman 2007: 239).

Many emphasize the virtues of Cosmopolitanism in a globalizing world order. When borders seem less permanent and technological developments in communications allow millions around the world to connect easily, distance and separation (or even isolation) lose their power to divide and alienate. A resulting physical and virtual mobility means that cultural interactions are more frequent, leading to hybridization, exchange, and understanding. Most students of globalization assume that the growing interconnectivity among different groups of people results in more frequent dialogue, which grants greater access to alternative perspectives. This inter-subjective exchange of meaning figures essentially in the formation of empathy and understanding. They agree with Cosmopolitan authors like Salman Rushdie who "celebrate hybridity, impurity, intermingling, the transformation that comes of new and unexpected combinations of human beings, cultures, ideas, politics, movies, songs"; they "rejoice in mongrelization [*sic*] and fear the absolutism of the Pure. Mélange, hotchpotch, a bit of this and a bit of that is how newness enters the world. It is the greatest possibility that mass migration gives the world" (Rushdie quoted in Appiah 2006: 112). Cosmopolitans believe that mere exposure to other cultures and ways of being is sufficient to nudge one towards a Cosmopolitan identity. A journey has a transformative effect of turning a traveller into a thoughtful and reflexive world citizen.

Nonetheless, identity remains an unsettled topic for most Cosmopolitans. There is little agreement on a moral ordering of different levels of identity. *Thick* Cosmopolitans believe that only global identities are valuable, moral and significant; local ones, as Nussbaum (Nussbaum and Cohen 1996: 11) argues, are nonessential. This, in turn, leads to the claim that local identities cannot and should not take priority over broader human loyalties. Our co-nationals, therefore, do not have any extra-claims on our allegiance, loyalty, or assistance. Local attachments and conflicts suggest a return to barbarism. Hence, to the extent that Cosmopolitans are interested in identity at all, it is to overcome these limits.

Thin Cosmopolitans object to such unflinching impartiality and universalistic identity formation. Some point out that our attachments are parochial and grow outward. In embracing universal affiliation, we risk "[ending] up nowhere – feeling at home neither at home nor in the world" (Barber quoted in Boon and Delanty 2007: 31). Or as Heidegger observed, "the frantic abolition of all distance brings no nearness" (Heidegger quoted in Dobson 2006: 169). Nor is it clear that embracing a conceptually borderless world, where local identities are considered shameful and backwards, will lead to anything other than utter alienation. As many cultural critics have observed, we already lead very individualized lives (Bauman 2011). Expansion of human rights globally has granted many the freedom of a rights-bearing individual; the spread of global markets has further unraveled our connections to various communities, including familial ties. The growth of these global markets certainly has not led towards any common sense of responsibility among free market actors. In fact, some would argue that the marketization of all human spheres has diminished the power of all appeals to a common identity, however broadly imagined. "Intimacy," Martin Jacques (*The Guardian*, September 18, 2004) has argued, "is a function of time and permanence." Deep loyalties cannot simply be engineered and the breaking down of borders that separate us may not generate any positive feelings among us. Intimacy "rests on mutuality and unconditionality. It is rooted in trust. As such, it is the antithesis of the values engendered by the market" (*The Guardian*, September 18, 2004). If Jacques (ibid.) is correct that "[w]e live in an ego-market society," how can we generate the necessary commitment to human flourishing implied in *thick* Cosmopolitanism? Nussbaum and other *thick* Cosmopolitans presume that moral arguments alone can establish a sense of commitment and care for others' well-being that usually exists between members of small communities. But as Jacques points out, although "[o]ur relationships may be more Cosmopolitan … they are increasingly transient and ephemeral" (ibid.).

Cosmopolitans fail to recognize that material considerations and context perforate cultural interactions. Culture is intimately connected to materiality. Here, most Cosmopolitan thinkers are unable or unwilling to reflect critically on their own social status in local, regional, and global contexts. As Sypnowich (2005: 57) recognizes, the Cosmopolitan stance is one of inequality vis-à-vis the rest of the human community: "[T]he Cosmopolitan is typically a privileged person, who has access to foreign travel, some knowledge of art and the means for enjoying it, who possesses sophisticated tastes and a cultivated, open mind." The relatively privileged position of most academics in Western democracies makes them natural allies of and advocates for the Cosmopolitan ethic. It is puzzling that the very people who write about a Cosmopolitan ethic for everyone else are unable to reflect on their own social, economic, and cultural embeddedness and recognize that "those who express mistrust of Cosmopolitanism, however bigoted and pernicious their views, might well be giving expression to a resentment of cultural inequality that is spawned by material inequality" (Sypnowich 2005: 58). Cosmopolitan arguments, in short, lack insight into identity *and* security. A Cosmopolitan identity owes much to the sense of security and permanence provided by the socio-economic and cultural support systems that allow individuals to venture beyond the immediate and the familiar.

Note, for example, America's economic dominance. Not only does it mean that the world's wealth is unevenly distributed but it also normalizes the vulnerability of cultural practices in underdeveloped countries to the behemoth of Western consumerism (Sypnowich 2005). While Appiah (2006) is willing to concede the overwhelming presence of American pop culture in remote corners of the world, without a theory of global economic order, he is unable to link the presence of American goods and the influence of American practices to any clear power inequalities. The most he can concede is that the US benefits from its sheer size and economies of scale and that more open trade is "good."

This limited understanding of structures and actors that wield power in the global order betrays an equally limited notion of power. Cosmopolitanism, like Liberalism, tends to equate power and coercive force with the direct power of the state. Most Cosmopolitan thinkers perceive the state as an embodiment of all that is wrong with the current world order. Yet the focus on the state as the main culprit of the twenty-first century is unfortunate. It tends to link all major problems associated with modern society with the rise of the nation-state. Hence, they find themselves in an uncomfortable situation of having to argue against the only viable actor that can put into effect the very policies dear to the Cosmopolitan cause. Human rights enforcement and universal legal principles such as Responsibility to Protect (R2P) depend entirely on state enforcement.[3] Similar observations can be made about the state's role in social redistribution. Despite the rhetoric in favor of global regimes, states are, at the moment, the only political structures that can mitigate the devastating externalities of the global market. Finally, by directing all their critiques against the nation-state, Cosmopolitans underestimate the structural role played by other forces in shaping the international order. Tara McCormack (2009) underscores that much of the critical agenda has become part of the mainstream with global norms like the R2P enshrined at the highest level of global governance organizations.

Cultural/Critical cosmopolitanism

Quite a few cosmopolitan thinkers see the EU as an embodiment of a critical cosmopolitan project. Not only has the union already achieved most of what cosmopolitan models advocate for fixing the democratic deficit – post-national citizenship, supranational institutions of justice, and unhindered mobility – but it also represents the merging of a plurality of modernities. Boon and Delanty (2007) see Europe, for example, as a dynamic space that cannot be reduced either to European nation-states or equated with some broader global mission. Instead, Europeanization is something much more multi-layered and polycentric. It relates simultaneously to local and global elements, existing *"both within and beyond the boundaries of the nation state"* (Boon and Delanty 2007: 31 [emphasis added]). To them, Europe represents "a newly emerging social reality," criss-crossing discourses and identities and giving rise to various socio-cognitive transformations (Boon and Delanty 2007: 31). Rather than undermining national identities and eroding the foundations of nation states, "Europeanization" involves a cultural logic of self-transformation. This "self-reflexive development of one's social, cultural and political subjectivity" is a learning process that might lead to self-transformation (ibid.). In other words, through the process of Europeanization, Europeans are learning that identities are not stable or fixed but are always changing and adapting and are called into question by the transformation process itself. Indeed, even Europe itself has no substantive cultural or social identity, since its subjectivity too is an ambivalent concept (Boon and Delanty 2007: 32). The new post-national belonging is an empowering development for in recognizing the fluid and open-ended nature of identity and borders, it gives force to those categories disadvantaged by the concept of territorial citizenship: migrants and ethnic minorities (Boon and Delanty 2007: 30).

Lastly, Boon and Delanty (2007: 33) see Europeanization as springing forth from creative tensions between "the inside and the outside of our affiliations." They agree with Beck and Grande (2007) that most dichotomies no longer usefully mark understandings of the fluidity of the current epoch. We must adopt a new frame of analysis: border thinking. "In the context of Europe, border thinking (or the upsurge of polyvocality) amounts to an increasing awareness of the vacillation of borders – of the *vaporization* [emphasis added] of old established certainties." This radical uncertainty leads us to realize that we, too, are borders "in that we are not quite this nor quite that" (Boon and Delanty 2007: 34). According to Boon and Delanty (2007: 25), the loss of certainty is positive for it constitutes a new discursive space, allowing us to embrace a more communicative logic.

Similarly, Chris Rumford (2007) offers a concept of "Critical Cosmopolitanism." To Rumford, Europe presents an excellent counter-hegemonic discourse to globalization. Like Boon and Delanty, Rumford conceives of Europe as a fluid space, a borderland, where different borders are constantly being reconstituted by different actors and increasingly by citizens themselves. Relatedly, Rumford sees this process of Europe's Cosmopolitanization as emancipatory: that is, a release from the narrow constraints of national identity and national belonging.

But, much like its Liberal counterpart, this cultural interpretation lacks any notion of structural power. Emancipation thus does not envision freedom from the constraints of the neo-liberal economic order or those imposed by poverty and inequality. Cultural/Critical Cosmopolitans do not see in migrants economic actors fleeing destitution. For Cultural Cosmopolitans, these represent only challenges to the rigid territoriality and identity resulting from the nation-state system.

In this way, Cultural/Critical Cosmopolitanism fails to engage with the very categories it seeks to undermine with its critical perspective. Culture, identity, belonging, and territoriality (borders) all form the core of cultural arguments, yet none of the writers contributing to the debate offer a clear genealogy of these essential concepts. Boon and Delanty (2007) recognize that Nussbaum's radical critique of local attachments is problematic for our ideas of political mobilization but they proceed, similarly, with a claim that we have no stable identities left. This chronic uncertainty seems not very different in its political implications from Nussbaum's universalism; in fact, it might lead to psychological developments that are more dangerous and destructive of all genuine political life than is remoteness induced by moral Cosmopolitanism. Hence, while cultural Cosmopolitans embrace radical uncertainty and celebrate increasing insecurity, they fail to consider the possibility that these states of being are not compatible with any stable notion of the self. Embrace of insecurity and uncertainty advocated by Critical Cosmopolitans may produce the toxic localism that they seek to overcome. (The rise and some electoral success of right-wing political parties across Europe in the last few years cannot lead us to such a sanguine position on radical uncertainty.)[4] Furthermore, none of these discussions distinguishes between a process of Europeanisation that is freely chosen and one that is so clearly imposed by other forces and actors. Hence, while some might celebrate "hybrid identities," many have no choice in the matter. The latter's experience with European transformation has been and remains highly *dis*empowering. Finally, as an analytic, Cultural/Critical Cosmopolitanism is short on praxis. At times, it appears to be of no immediate import beyond academic musings. The emphasis on dialogical Cosmopolitanism and global discourse communities contributes usefully to a debate on the nature of democracy in a post-national world but a practical import remains missing. As Duncan Kelly (2000: 38) says, while such conversations are crucial, "[p]olitics as endless conversation ... ultimately leads to a neutered discussion." Without a proper accounting of power and the nature of politics, dialogical Cosmopolitanism remains an academic distraction only.

Conclusion

As Gideon Rachman (2010: 208) notes, "[t]he idea that the European Union might represent the culmination of world history is depressing." Certainly, today's debates in Europe, about how to deal with the crisis in Greece, who is responsible for the Euro's poor performance and lack of economic growth, as well as the proper relationship with Europe's internal Others and a continuous influx of refugees, should leave any Cosmopolitan dispirited. All these debates are necessary and significant. But contrary to Beck's assessment, they do not constitute a critically engaged and reflexive public sphere. The proposals that have been adopted for various economic solutions signal a return to pre-crisis austerity measures and an overall neoliberal agenda. This is hardly a hallmark of critical engagement with the problems that caused the crisis in the first place. Inability to address societal fears about the economic situation has certainly contributed to the rise of far-right parties and attitudes that a few decades ago would have existed mostly on the fringes of society. Today, far-right parties are making steady inroads in the core countries of the EU and are forming alliances across state boundaries to solidify their appeal and political muscle. Their electoral successes bluntly remind us of how, under the right conditions, even the crudest forms of xenophobic nationalism can seem a "progressive" alternative to the Liberalism of an integrated EU. Cosmopolitan models for all their variety do not engage with these realities and do not offer a workable answer for the forms of governance that could offer a chance for a different future. Even critical versions of Cosmopolitanism remain stubbornly uninterested in the enormous structural power exercised by the global economy and its agents.

As I have argued throughout, most of the problems faced by Cosmopolitan models of global governance are imported directly from its theoretical foundation in Liberalism. At its core, Cosmopolitanism seeks to identify a common first principle of co-existence upon which to build the institutional framework to resolve thorny issues such as "the criteria of inclusion/exclusion, the nature of the society/community to be governed, and the similarity of interests/principles of the subjects of governance" (Aksu 2008: 7). Like Liberalism, Cosmopolitanism's emphasis on individual agency focuses on the power that constrains individual choice (including the choice of identity), through the coercive power of the state. Most Cosmopolitans, therefore, have a difficult time recognizing the insecurities created by economic and financial globalization. Indeed, free trade and the market are typically listed among the core values to be embraced by Cosmopolitan commitments.

Yet ironically, Cosmopolitans and Liberals overlook human agency. Most people in most societies cannot, in fact, choose among competing visions of reality and future. Despite the platitudes that we get from Cosmopolitan writers, choice has little to do with how globalization is perceived and how it appears in people's lives. What happens to identity communities under the stress of a violent conflict provides a quick glimpse into the nature of the relationship between identity and insecurity. What we see in Darfur, former Yugoslavia, and again in Syria, is an increased preeminence of identity ties as insecurity increases. In Sudan, even prior to the onset of the Darfur crisis, "a half-century of brutal military confrontation has sharpened the place of race and religion in the conflicts" (Jok 2007: 247). As the citizens of Sarajevo found out in 1995, once the bullets start flying and the bodies are piling up, the only rational choice is to retreat to one's identity group even where strong cross-community ties had existed prior to the conflict. The relationship between identity and security provides crucial insight into the nature of societal relations and their breakdown and caution us against an over-emphasis on flexibility and uncertainty in the formation of self-understanding. Indeed, emphasis on the fluid nature of identity can lead to a greater sense of ontological insecurity as a person's stable sense of self erodes. This in turn can lead to a retreat into a more rigid identity.

We cannot reduce politics to a game of catch-up and rubber stamp a "naturalized" economic order. An odd revulsion for all things political plagues much of what passes for vigorous accounts of analytical thinking in today's literature on global governance. Cosmopolitans argue against the very notion of power or interest-based politics. They see the post-modern era as a dawn of a new, more conciliatory, more benign, less violent and less contentious politics based on mutual recognition of universal commonalities and a consensus culture. The emphasis on consensus, however, too often hides the fact that there are clear winners and losers in a globally integrated order. A truly critical approach to the problem of cross-cultural engagement recognizes that we need secure foundations from which to engage with one another as equals.

Notes

1 See, for example: Kantian legal Cosmopolitanism, moral, cultural, civic, rooted, methodological, democratic, realist (or Cosmopolitan realism), populist, actual existing, "cool,"

critical, new, capitalist, thin (or weak), thick (or strong), layered, "dialogic," "distributive," embedded and embodied, impartialist, aesthetic, institutional Cosmopolitanism, "cosmo-lite," and even "Cosmopolitanisation" (Harris 2003; Brock and Brighouse 2005; Held 2005; Dobson 2006; Beck and Grande 2007; Boon and Delanty 2007; Kofman 2007).

2 Many Cosmopolitans tend to view the global market as a natural ally of individualization and value pluralism. This liberal heritage leads Ulrich Beck and Edgar Grande (2007) to list free trade among the core values of a Cosmopolitan outlook. See for example, Nussbaum and Cohen (1996), Buchanan (2005), Pogge (2002) and Appiah (2006).

3 Focus on human rights, human security, and other individual-based normative principles has highlighted the gaps in and put a pressure on existing state institutions that fail to ensure equal and effective protection of rights. R2P puts a particular emphasis on the positive obligation of states towards the citizens as a condition of sovereignty.

4 Perhaps one of the more noxious forms of such parties is the Golden Dawn party in Greece. Golden Dawn is a neo-Nazi party, which received almost 7 percent of the vote in the 2012 national election. It takes a very strong stance on immigration as a national problem and has advocated mining of borders to prevent illegal immigrants from entering Greece (*The Guardian*, September 18, 2004).

References

Aksu, Eşref. (2008) *Early Notions of Global Governance: Selected Eighteenth-Century Proposals for "Perpetual Peace" – with Rousseau, Bentham and Kant Unabridged.* Cardiff: University of Wales Press.

Appiah, Kwame Anthony. (2006) *Cosmopolitanism: Ethics in a World of Strangers.* New York: W.W. Norton & Company.

Bauman, Zygmunt. (2011) "Privacy, Secrecy, Intimacy, Human Bonds – and Other Collateral Casualties of Liquid Modernity." *The Hedgehog Review* (Spring): 20–29.

Beck, Ulrich, and Edgar Grande. (2007) *Cosmopolitan Europe.* Translated by Ciaran Cronin. Cambridge: London: Polity.

Boon, Vivienne and Gerard Delanty. (2007) "Cosmopolitanism and Europe: Considerations and Contemporary Approaches." In Chris Rumford (ed.), *Cosmopolitanism and Europe*, pp. 19–39. Liverpool: Liverpool University Press.

Brock, Gillian and Harry Brighouse. (2005) "Introduction." In Gillian Brock and Harry Brighouse (eds), *The Political Philosophy of Cosmopolitanism*, pp. 1–10. Cambridge: Cambridge University Press.

Buchanan, Allen. (2005) "In the National Interest." In Gillian Brock and Harry Brighouse (eds), *The Political Philosophy of Cosmopolitanism*, pp. 110–127. Cambridge: Cambridge University Press.

Dobson, Andrew. (2006) "Thick Cosmopolitanism." *Political Studies* 54: 165–184.

Guardian, The. (2004) "The Death of Intimacy." (http://www.theguardian.com/uk/2004/sep/18/britishidentity.comment) (Downloaded: November 30, 2013).

Guardian, The. (2012) "Greece's Far Right Golden Dawn Party Maintains Share of the Vote." (http://www.theguardian.com/world/2012/jun/18/greece-far-right-golden-dawn) (Downloaded: November 27, 2013).

Harris, Nigel. (2003) *The Return of Cosmopolitan Capital: Globalisation, the State and War.* London: I.B.Taurus.

Held, David. (2005) "Principles of Cosmopolitan Order." In Gilan Brock and Harry Brighouse (eds), *The Political Philosophy of Cosmopolitanism*, pp. 10–28. Cambridge: Cambridge University Press.

Held, David and Anthony McGrew (eds). (2000) *The Global Transformations Reader: An Introduction to the Globalization Debate.* Cambridge: Polity.

Jok, Jok Madut. (2007) *Sudan: Race, Religion and Violence.* Oxford: Oneworld Publications.
Kelly, Duncan. (2000) "Multicultural Citizenship: The Limitations of Liberal Democracy." *The Political Quarterly* 71(1): 31–41.
Kofman, Eleonore. (2007) "Figures of the Cosmopolitan: Privileged Nationals and National Outsiders." In Chris Rumford (ed.), *Cosmopolitanism and Europe*, pp. 259–270. Liverpool: Liverpool University Press.
McCormack, Tara. (2009) "Critical Security Studies: Are They Really Critical?" *ARENA Journal* 32: 139–153.
McGrew, Anthony. (2000) "Democracy beyond Borders?" In David Held and Anthony McGrew (eds), *The Global Transformation Reader*, pp. 405–419. Cambridge: Polity Press.
Nussbaum, Martha Craven and Joshua Cohen. (1996) "Patriotism and Cosmopolitanism." In Martha Craven Nussbaum and Joshua Cohen (eds), *For Love of Country: Debating the Limits of Cosmopolitanism*, pp. 3–21. Boston, MA: Beacon Press.
Pogge, Thomas. (2002) *World Poverty and Human Rights.* Cambridge: Polity Press.
Rachman, Gideon. (2010) *Zero-Sum World: Politics, Power and Prosperity after the Crash.* London: Atlantic Books.
Rawls, John. (2001) *The Law of Peoples: With "The Idea of Public Reason Revisited."* Cambridge, MA: Harvard University Press.
Rumford, Chris. (2007) "Globalisation: Cosmopolitanism and Europe." In Chris Rumford (ed.), *Cosmopolitanism and Europe*, pp. 1–19. Liverpool: Liverpool University Press.
Rumford, Chris. (2008) *Cosmopolitan Spaces: Europe, Globalization, Theory.* New York: Routledge.
Sholte, J.A. (2000) *Globalization: A Critical Introduction.* Houndmills: Palgrave Macmillan.
Sypnowich, Christine. (2005) "Cosmopolitans, Cosmopolitanism, and Human Flourishing." In Gillian Brock and Harry Brighouse (eds), *The Political Philosophy of Cosmopolitanism*, pp. 55–75. Cambridge: Cambridge University Press.

3

DAMS AND "GREEN GROWTH"?

Development dissonance and the transnational percolations of power

Payal Banerjee

From a superficial view of geopolitics, regions like Sikkim hardly even show-up on the map. They appear remote, too small, highly localized, and inconsequential to the grander stage of the global. Important concepts like "global energy security" or "international relations" seem too big for their boots. But what if such regions of the world, especially those in the rapidly developing BRICS (Brazil, Russia, India, China, and South Africa) countries, are not merely connected, but rather central to the mainstream logic of transnational capitalist development *and* have alternative lessons to impart? This chapter opens that conversation.

In 2002, the Indian Planning Commission estimated that the country's energy demand would increase by at least 350 percent over the next two decades (Government of India (GOI) 2002). Moreover, in view of market expansions, Indian policy-makers and their international counterparts have continued to emphasize the need to meet this demand by harnessing renewable *green* energy (GOI 1998; World Bank 2007). Accordingly, government policy-implementation measures in India have corresponded with this perspective. A series of new state guidelines and commitments have subsequently sanctioned the construction of an unprecedented number of hydroelectric power projects (HEPs) and dams across the country. Moreover, the decades following the post-1991 economic liberalization (broadly, the New Economic Policy) have also witnessed an episodic but extensive privatization of the energy sector. These reforms have created for many private companies a new opportunity to expand their repertoire of operations and enter the hydropower and thermal sectors as power producers (Dharmadhikary 2013). A range of incentives and promotional packages – including key policy changes favoring companies' ability to sell power based on market principles – reversed previous entry barriers and state controls, and welcomed private developers into the hydropower sector as important stakeholders. Given that the arrival of private HEPs represented an extremely lucrative prospect of revenue generation, individual state governments have persuaded the newly emerging power companies to invest in their regions.

India's high economic growth rates, combined with increased energy production since the mid-1990s, have also translated into extensive demand for new infrastructure and raw materials. An unprecedented rate of natural resource exploitation has ensued as a result. Both public sector units and private companies have intensified the extraction of resources from forests, mines, water bodies, and coastal areas. These have contributed to serious ecological problems and conflicts with communities over ownership rights, displacement, and compensation. In an effort to address social inequality, in general, and avoid mega-project induced displacements and environmental problems, in particular, the Indian state has implemented a larger number of protective measures. The consensus from past and present research, however, is that such policies have not successfully served the majority of those affected by development projects (Gadgil and Guha 1995; Banerjee and Sood 2012; Shrivastava and Kothari 2012).

The ongoing privatization of India's energy resources has not only incentivized independent power producers as key stakeholders, but it has also established a specific link between two arenas: energy security and commercial development. This shift in the power sector, has been deeply entrenched in the overarching processes of resource privatization and massive transfers of the "commons" from communities on to private/corporate interests. Indeed, the growing consensus is that these practices have contributed greatly to people's displacement, loss of livelihoods, poverty, and a host of other socio-economic problems, specifically for those who are already marginalized. Based on empirical research in India's northeastern Himalayan state of Sikkim, this chapter takes a closer look at India's HEP policies, their implementation methods, and the socio-economic and ecological concerns that have surfaced in response over the last decade.[1] The urgency of these concerns, specifically given the presence of state-mandated counter-measures to prevent such problems, reveals a deeper crisis in the state's development logic: it upholds privatization of mega-projects as key to achieving energy security even at the cost of personal, communal, and ecological security for its own citizens.

This chapter proposes that development practices and crises in such seemingly localized and small regions, particularly in the BRICS economies, be examined from the lens of transnational political economy, taking into account, to begin with, questions that do not ignore corporate stakeholders' priorities in finance capital and investment, the nature of transfer of resources and revenue distribution, and urgent issues of environmental and social protections. This method has the potential to reveal how recent growth-oriented activities in such seemingly "remote" areas figure in the national and therefore the world economy. But more importantly, an engagement with the points of view of Sikkim's activists from different walks of life carries the possibility of understanding and seeing rivers, mountains, and forests as not mere resources to be capitalized, but as the foundations of culture and history.

Policy framework: HEP projects and dams in India

Indian policy-makers and leaders in the post-1947 independence era had placed immense hope on the capacity of HEP plants and large dams to generate electricity and harness water for irrigation and industry. State leadership viewed investments in such capital-intensive mega-projects as a pathway to development. Large dams increased from 300 in 1947 to over 4,000 in 2000 (the majority being irrigation dams). Although hydroelectricity represented about 50 percent of India's power supply in the 1960s, its contribution began to fall over time. By the early 1970s, the share of hydropower declined to 44 percent and decreased further to 25 percent over successive decades (partly as other power sources got developed). More recent data from the GOI (2010) indicate the following distribution for different sources of electricity in India: hydropower, 25 percent (37,086 MW); thermal power, 65 percent (106,433 MW); nuclear power, 2.9 percent (4,560 MW); and renewable energy sources, about 8 percent (16,429 MW); while the small-scale hydropower stood contributed about 2,820 MW (GOI 2010).

Since its pursuit of economic liberalization in 1991, India's rapid economic growth has provoked widespread concerns about potential energy deficits. In this context, HEPs have acquired a new emphasis. The Policy for Hydro Power Development of 1998 placed hydropower as "the most economic and preferred source of electricity" for the country's development (GOI 1998: 1). A pro-market orientation restructured the power sector, whereby specific "policy instruments" prioritized the role of private investments in hydro-projects. To "accelerate the pace," reform objectives sought a tripartite partnership between the central administration, state governments, and the corporate sector (GOI 1998). The Indian Prime Minister's "50,000 MW Hydroelectric Initiative," launched in May 2003, imparted fresh momentum to hydropower generation. With a sanction from the Ministry of Power, India's Central Electricity Authority (CEA) formulated the initiative and launched the project by commissioning a series of what are called the Preliminary Feasibility Report (PFR) of Hydroelectric Schemes. Seven state-affiliated public sector consultants prepared PFRs, identifying a target 162 HEPs in 16 states nationwide, with an aggregate installed capacity of 50,560 MW, to be executed over the 11th and 12th Five-Year Plans between 2007 and 2017. This project would require an estimated $60 billion during the proposed 10-year timeline. To further expedite India's hydropower potential, the government charted an updated policy framework under the New Hydropower Policy of 2008, which advanced the state's commitments towards the HEPs and invited private sector participation (GOI 2008). The policy states its vision as follows:

> Even though public sector organisations would continue to play an important role in the development of new schemes, this alone would not be adequate to develop the vast remaining hydro potential. Greater private investment through IPPs [independent power producers] and joint ventures would be

encouraged in the coming years and atmosphere conducive for attracting private sector funds would be provided.

(GOI 2008: 26)

Overall, policy measures introduced during the 1990s and early 2000s have gradually privatized and deregulated certain core functions – e.g. power generation, transmission, and distribution – that were previously under the authority and management of the State Electricity Boards (SEBs). The Electricity Act (2003) expedited these processes by permitting "direct commercial relationships between generating companies and consumers/traders," which enabled the entry of corporate stakeholders as independent power producers.

(GOI 2008: 20)

HEP controversy in India's northeast

India's northeast has long suffered from under-representation in mainstream national agendas.[2] Over the last decade, the region has attracted prime attention regarding energy security. Recent estimates suggest that the northeast region, endowed with about 37 percent of India's river-waters, could contribute approximately 42 percent of the country's hydropower. The World Bank (2007) has projected that the region will lead India's hydropower generation over the course of the 13th and 14th Five-Year Plans between 2020 and 2030. Other studies total the northeast's hydroelectric generation capacity at 70 percent of India's total hydropower potential (Dharmadhikary 2008). Currently, the region hosts about 168 HEPs, either in operation or in various phases of construction. These enumerations have earned the northeast a new designation: India's "future powerhouse" (Menon, Vagholikar, Kohli, and Fernandes 2003; Mahanta 2010; Vagholikar and Das 2010). Of the 162 HEP schemes identified in the feasibility reports for the 50,000 MW Hydroelectric Initiative, a large share of the 72 projects have been proposed for the northeast, particularly in the states of Sikkim and Arunachal Pradesh, representing a substantial area in the eastern Himalayan mountain ranges and forests (Dharmadhikary 2008). Furthermore, a review of policy documents and forums on India's energy concerns reveals the articulation of an unmistakable link between the northeast region's hydropower potential and the country's energy security. The Pasighat Proclamation on Power adopted during the North East Council's Sectoral Summit on the Power Sector in 2007 is a notable example in this regard (Vagholikar and Das 2010). Furthermore, the definition of what counts as a mega-project – and therefore qualifies for policy measures and special provisions under this status – has been recalibrated for this region's projects in favorable terms. For the eight northeastern states (and Jammu and Kashmir in the north), HEPs with a capacity of 350 MW or more meet the criteria for mega-project status (compared to a capacity of at least 500 MW elsewhere).

In this region, the state of Sikkim has become one of the hubs of India's HEP development efforts. The Preliminary Feasibility Report (PRF) following the Prime Minister's Hydroelectric Initiative announced in 2003, designated 10 of 162 HEP projects for Sikkim (Central Electric Authority).[3] Prior to these initiatives, Sikkim hosted about a dozen of what the Indian government calls Hydel Schemes[4] during the period between 1966 and 2000 (GOI 2004). In view of substantial revenues from the HEPs, the Sikkim state government has encouraged investments in this sector and awarded project contracts to public sector entities, such as the National Hydroelectric Power Corporation (NHPC), and to many private companies, such as Teesta Urja Limited (TUL) and Gati Infrastructure Limited, among others. The state of Sikkim retains the status of a joint-venture partner in these projects. From the late 1990s, the number of hydropower dams increased following proposals for roughly 29 new HEPs on the Himalayan River Teesta and its tributaries across the state.

The Indian state and its private sector partners have maintained that HEPs are indispensable for development. They generate electricity for industry and consumers in rural and urban India, thereby increasing revenues and creating employment. Nonetheless, civil society nationwide has opposed a large number of the Hydel-dams on the grounds that these projects cause environmental degradation, increase the severity of natural disasters, and violate socio-economic rights. The Sikkim government's HEP initiatives have also encountered similar resistance since 2007 (Bunsha 2008; Banerjee and Sood 2012).[5] Organizations such as the Affected Citizens of Teesta (ACT) and the Sikkim Bhutia Lepcha Apex Committee (SIBLAC) have been at the forefront of the anti-dam movement. These involve activists from Sikkim's various ethnic groups and religious leaders against state officials and hydropower corporations over a variety of socio-economic and environmental concerns. Activists have documented that construction activities – blasting, digging, tunneling, extensive use of concrete and heavy machinery, sound pollution, and deforestation to make space for roads, power houses, and other infrastructure – have resulted in acute ecological problems in the mountains and surrounding forests. The dams have restricted river and tributary flows and dumping of excavated waste materials, along with construction debris, has polluted riverbeds and forests. The HEPs have also severely impacted residents' physical safety and living environment, as many homes were damaged during construction processes. Biophysical transformations associated with shifts in the river system have contributed to people's dislocation. Activists charge that power developers, backed by the state and its development mandates in the HEP sector, have exploited land acquisition laws for the dams. Activists also accuse the companies of reneging on their promise to provide adequate compensation and/or employment to those affected by the HEPs. When offered, jobs were short-lived or mismatched with the skills of the local residents. The Sikkimese activists' critique of development via mega-projects and privatization is paralleled in the findings of a report by International Rivers (2008: 10), which has indicated that one of the key reasons behind the thrust in "hydropower is [that] private companies [are] looking for profits." Over the last few years, about 11 HEPs in Sikkim have been scrapped due to long-standing protests, investigations under Right to Information (RTI) petitions, as well as recent cases of Public Interest Litigation (PILs) filed by the citizen groups. In response, the Sikkim High Court passed orders with injunctions until the release of writ petitions. It is not uncommon, however, for local governments to revive projects previously scrapped in response to protests or sanction new ones elsewhere on the same river.[6]

Energy, equity, environment

Undeniably, the Indian government has taken a proactive role in addressing the intersection of environmental and socio-economic issues. The 11th Five-Year Plan (2007–2012), structured on the vision of "Inclusive Growth," exemplifies this very imperative. Additionally, the state has legislated protections against environmental and socio-economic transgressions. For example: the government's Environment Protection Act (1986), the National Environment Policy (2006), the National Water Policy (2012), the National Forest Policy (1988), and the Environment Impact Assessment (2006) laws, among others, seek to promote conservation measures and establish regulation for the use of natural resources. These policy measures not only provide a detailed survey of India's environmental situation but they also reveal quite unequivocally the respective state ministries' awareness of the country's present environmental crisis and outline strategies to redress these problems. Moreover, some of the mandatory requirements for mega-project development include preparations for and approval of environmental impact assessment studies, often overseen by state agencies. To bolster such measures, the Ministry of Environment and Forests has sought to "pla[n], promot[e], co-ordinat[e] and overs[ee] the implementation of India's environmental and forestry policies and programmes" in a manner that underscores "sustainable development and enhancement of human well-being."[7]

The state government of Sikkim has also undertaken to implement the "Green Mission," a set of multi-dimensional strategies to encourage sustainable development, organic agriculture, bio-diversity conservation, and responsible eco-tourism.[8] Government policies at the national level have also prioritized social equity and inclusive growth, particularly for people whose livelihoods are inextricably linked with land-based resources. The Scheduled Tribes and Other Traditional Forest Dwellers (Recognition of Forest Rights) Act of 2006 (or the Forest Rights Act of 2006), for instance, seeks to protect the rights of communities that need access to forests for livelihood.[9] The National Rehabilitation and Resettlement Policy (2007) provides another example. The recent Right to Fair Compensation and Transparency in Land Acquisition, Rehabilitation and Resettlement Bill of 2013 has established mechanisms to ensure adequate compensation and prevent cases of land-rights violations and displacement witnessed in the past decades. The Right to Information Act of 2005 seeks to promote transparency and mandates timely responses to citizens' requests for government information. Other examples of large-scale social equity and inclusive growth-oriented policies include: the Right to Education Act (2009), the Integrated Child Development Services Scheme

(1975), the National Rural Employment Guarantee Act (2005), measures for food security and the Mid Day Meal Scheme for under-privileged children in schools, to name just a few. And yet, acute violations of state-mandated environmental laws and socio-economic safeguards riddle the HEP development ventures. And the state itself is often a partner and stands for the "public" in public–private partnerships (PPPs).

What do these gaps signify?

One could attribute these violations to implementation inefficiencies due to India's size, population, and socio-political heterogeneity. The partial validity of this constraint notwithstanding, these gaps reveal a much broader systemic crisis. The state's prioritization of a specific growth model – manifested by state-backed commercialization of resources and privatization in the name of energy security – has reached such an intensity that even the state has to bend some of its own environmental regulations and social safeguards or even take recourse to violence against its own people. The following section provides a brief outline of how the emphasis on creating an investment atmosphere amenable to private enterprise in development projects has come at serious social, economic, and environmental costs.

Environment and development

From 2003 to 2008, India's economy grew by an average 8–9 percent per year. Since 1991, industrial production has increased three times and the production of electricity has more than doubled (Shrivastava and Kothari 2012). Demands of high-growth and urbanization, bolstered with economic zones and commercial services hubs, have intensified the use of land and natural resources. In 2006, the mining of major minerals in India generated almost 2 billion tonnes of waste. Between 1993 and 1994 and 2008 and 2009, the rate of mineral extraction increased by 75 percent (Shrivastava and Kothari 2012). Underground water sources and aquifers have been depleting rapidly as a result of water mining at twice the rate of natural replacement. India currently experiences one of the highest levels of underground water overuse in the world and this often occurs at locations where multinational corporations run manufacturing sites (Aiyer 2000). Extensive use of forests for mining and infrastructure development has resulted in the rapid decline in forest cover, land degradation, and the displacement of communities reliant on forests for livelihood. Even a cursory survey of news and academic materials published over the last decade would reveal numerous examples of both legal and quasi-legal means by which resources have been accessed from mines, water bodies, forests, coasts, and agricultural and pastoral lands (Shrivastava and Kothari 2012). Massive tracts of land from *adivasi* or tribal areas and forests nationwide have been leased out for industries, steel plants, mining ventures, and dam construction. The *adivasis*, one of the most marginalized groups in India, have not received much of the share of development and there are growing concerns about the effectiveness of the Forest Rights Act (Balsakh 2011). A conservative estimate of development project affected and physically displaced people stands at 60 million since 1947. The Planning Commission's recent assessments of about 21 million of such displaced persons suggests that more than 40 percent are tribals, when demographically this group constitute only 8 percent of India's population.[10] In Sikkim, some of the proposed HEPs fall near or within the protected land of local ethnic groups, such as the Dzonghu region of the minority Lepcha community. Other HEPs have encroached within the protected zones surrounding national reserved forests. When these violations provoked protests, the state's response ranged from relatively benign actions (negotiations with activists) to more repressive ones (arrests, direct orders to quit hunger strikes), along with other long-term tactics to delegitimize or ostracize leaders (e.g. unwritten policies to blacklist activists and their family members).

There is also growing evidence that the government itself may waive preliminary assessment requirements to incentivize the early monetization of natural resource discoveries. The Ministry of Petroleum and Natural Gas, for example, has permitted companies like Reliance Industries and Cairn India to begin operations for oil and gas production before the approval of field investment reports.[11] In Sikkim's HEP sector, certain projects were granted clearances before environment and social impact assessments were approved, while in other cases the HEP developers' construction activities were in blatant violation of Supreme Court orders, environmental clearance requirements, and forest and wildlife protection policies.[12] The Ministry of Environment and Forests recently admitted that environmental clearances are eventually granted to almost all development projects.[13] These moves gravely undermine the legitimacy of mandating environmental assessment approvals as a precondition for HEP development. Further, there are no meaningful provisions to ensure continued monitoring of companies' environmental compliance once projects are granted clearances.[14]

The hydropower policies do not neglect to explicitly identify social and environmental measures necessary to prevent or minimize human dislocations and ecological hazards. And yet, a review of the HEP development trajectory in the northeastern states, as in other parts of India, suggests that social and environmental mandates have largely been marginal to the mega-projects' implementation methods. State initiatives that facilitate rapid commercialization, as seen in the example of granting preliminary assessment waivers to boost early monetization of energy resources, create the circumstances that exacerbate ecological problems and displacement, while transferring environmental risks to the public. The fundamental rationale, pace and depth of mainstream growth imperatives mobilized on the rationale of large-scale commercialization have severely undercut and contradicted the social-environmental protective measures. As a corollary, one might even propose that the very existence of social and environmental safeguards allows the state to orient and attune its commitments in favor of privatization. The safeguards provide a convenient justification to adopt development measures that ultimately compromise social equity. The energy question has thus become one that is deeply entrenched in processes involving massive transfers of the public commons from communities on to private/corporate ownership. Indeed, the growing consensus is that these practices – particularly those established in the name of energy and national security – have contributed greatly to displacement, loss of livelihoods and escalating poverty, often especially for those who are already marginalized. This makes the question of power generation – particularly the production of the so-called "renewable green and clean" hydropower – inseparable from the other dynamics of Indian national security: namely, social and environmental justice.

The foundations for alternatives

Anti-dam organizations such as the ACT (Affected Citizens of Teesta) and SIBLAC (Sikkim Bhutia Lepcha Apex Committee)[15] in Sikkim have, to begin with, offered a lucid analysis of how existing protective or regulatory policies have done the work of elevating the state as the front-runner of sustainable development and social equity, making it easier for the state to exculpate itself from the many forms of disruptions, whether in the riparian ecosystems or in people's lives or livelihoods. About 11 HEPs in Sikkim have been scrapped in the wake of long-standing protests, investigations under Right to Information (RTI) petitions filed by the citizens, and recent cases of Public Interest Litigations (PILs), which challenged the building of mega-dams, citing damages to wildlife, ecology, and cultural rights. In response, the Sikkim High Court passed orders with injunctions until the release of writ petitions. The controversial Tashiding project is also at the center of a legal battle with Sikkimese Buddhist monks, who have brought charges of religious violations and ecological degradation. Right to Information (RTI) investigations have also revealed that the TingTing and Tashiding HEPs have been constructed within a radius of 10 km from the Khangchendzonga National Park, which goes against established environmental norms. Some HEPs have been temporarily halted pending the completion of writ petitions and/or further environmental clearances following extensive research. Other HEPs are facing construction delays and uncertainties due to financial problems and escalating costs (e.g. projects at Tashiding, Teesta State VI, Bhamsey, Teesta Stage III, and Jorethang Loop). Activists have remarked that local governments, despite having scrapped HEPs in response to public protests, frequently revive and sanction new projects on the same river or site.[16] To offer alternative approaches, Sikkimese activists have not limited themselves to analyses of the political economy of privatization or the scientific indicators of ecological degradation.

In addition to the mobilization of signature campaigns, hunger strikes, interactive public meetings, fact-finding missions, and petitions to address the legislative aspects of the state's endorsement of HEPs,[17] the ACT and other organizations have drawn equally skillfully from the state's civilizational resources to revive an alternative discourse about sustainability and the meaning of our physical surroundings and landscape. The epistemologies of Sikkim's popular legends, which emphasize the importance of rivers Teesta and Rathong Chu along with the state's plural spiritual traditions, which are characterized by notions of a sacred presence in the region's mountains, forests, and rivers, have become integral to the activists' formulation of why the question of energy generation for countries like India cannot supersede concerns around land acquisition/land-grabs, livelihoods and the environment. In this vein, consider the following excerpt from a SIBLAC flyer distributed during the celebration of Guru Padmasambhav at a prominent Buddhist monastery:[18]

> Guru Rinpoche's hidden treasures (*ter*) and religious sacredness of Rathong Chu and surrounding mountains is [*sic*] threatened by the proposed hydroelectric projects. We are [being asked] to sacrifice this sacred river with its treasures and destroy the future of our unique Bhumchu tradition. Given its unparalleled significance, which Guru Rinpoche has revealed and its cultural uniqueness, it will be a sacrilege to allow the multi-national companies to exploit our sacred Rathong-Chu and nearby mountains only to export electricity to various states in India ... We must conserve the treasures and protect them from polluting influences. This is important not only for ourselves, but for the welfare of all the sentient beings.

The characterization of Sikkim's mountains and rivers as the people's treasury of invaluable cultural and civilizational legacy that continue to be relevant in terms of everyday spiritual practices, provides immense possibilities for imagining economic activities that are not reliant on corporatized mega-projects that treat forests and water as mere raw materials.[19] The state's current *Green Mission* might provide, if allowed to manifest some of the core tenets of the state's civilizational resources in meaningful terms, an ideal platform to expand sustainable development projects.

Notes

1 The author conducted research in the eastern Himalayan state of Sikkim in August 2011 and from August 2012 to the present.
2 The Northeastern (NE) region of India consists of the following states: Assam, Arunachal Pradesh, Meghalaya, Mizoram, Manipur, Nagaland, Tripura, and Sikkim.
3 See, Central Electric Authority (n.d.).
4 Development projects across sectors are often referred to as "schemes" by the central or state governments.
5 People's resistance movements against dams and other mega-projects have a long history in India and only intensified over recent years. For more details, the reader may consult Intercultural Resources (2010) or www.icrindia.org.
6 Author's interviews. Also, see Sarma (2013).
7 See, Ministry of Environment and Forests official website <http://envfor.nic.in/about-ministry/about-ministry> last accessed on May 13, 2016.
　　For more details, see Government of India's Ministry of Tribal Affairs at http://tribal.nic.in/index.asp.
8 See, the Sikkim state government's website at < https://www.sikkim.gov.in/portal/portal/StatePortal/Government/SikkimGreenMission> last accessed May 13, 2015.
9 For more details, see the Government of India's Ministry of Tribal Affairs (http://tribal.nic.in/index.asp).
10 Shrivastava and Kothari (2012).
11 The Hindu, "Petroleum Ministry permits cos to produce oil, gas before investment plans are cleared", at http://www.thehindubusinessline.com/economy/petroleum-ministry-

permits-cos-to-produce-oil-gas-before-investment-plans-are-cleared/article5264980.ece [last visited December 2, 2016].
12 Dutta (2013); Mazoomdar (2013).
13 Sreenivas and Sreekumar (2013).
14 Sreenivas and Sreekumar (2013).
15 The SIBLAC has among its supporters many monks from the state's Buddhist monasteries.
16 These insights are based on the author's fieldwork. See also, Dhiraj Kumar Sarma's (2013) cover story "Big Dams, Big Dilemmas?" published in the July 2013 issue of the *Eclectic NorthEast* (26–36).
17 The ACT has also brought charges against the state government for neglecting specific protective laws designed to safeguard people's rights, such as laws and procedures for land acquisition, including the Amending Act 68, 1984 of Land Acquisition Act 1984, Land Acquisition (Companies) Rules of 1963, and the Land Acquisition (Companies) Act of 1963. As a consequence, activists have come to view the state as a facilitator that allows private companies with HEP contracts to acquire land and resources with ease.
18 This annual event takes place in the summer, usually in August (the exact date is based on the local calendar).
19 This observation is based on SIBLAC's anti-dam campaign flyer distributed at one of the major monasteries located in the capital city in 2010.

References

Aiyer, Ananthakrishnan. (2000) "The Allure of the Transnational: Notes on Some Aspects of the Political Economy of Water in India." *Cultural Anthropology* 22(4): 640–658.
Balsakh, Pradeep. (2011) "Is the Forest Rights Act Working?" *India Together*, May 17, at http://www.indiatogether.org [last visited October 19, 2013].
Banerjee, Payal and Atul Sood. (2012) "The Political Economy of Green Growth in India," UNRISD Occasional Paper Number 5, Geneva, United Nations.
Bunsha, Dionne. (2008) "Teesta's Tears." *Frontline* 25(12), at http://hindu.com/fline/fl2512/stories/20080620251209500.htm [last visited September 9, 2011].
Central Electric Authority. (n.d.) Preparation of Preliminary Feasibility Reports: Under 50,000 MW Hydroelectric Initiative, at http://www.cea.nic.in/reports/hydro/feasibility_report_50kmw_he.pdf [last visited April 26, 2013].
Dharmadhikary, Shripad. (2008) "Massive Dam Plans for Arunachal." *India Together*, February 17, at http://www.indiatogether.org [last visited October 19, 2011].
Dharmadhikary, Shripad. (2013) "Corporate Interests Rise above All." *India Together*, May 6, at http://www.indiatogether.org/2013/may/eco-power.htm [last visited June 20, 2013].
Dutta, Soumik. (2013) "Hydro Power Projects Violating SC Order in Sikkim: NBWL Report." October 3, at http://gulail.com/hydro-power-projects-violating-sc-order-insikkim-nbwl-report/2/ [last visited November 9, 2013].
Gadgil, Madhav and Ramchandra Guha. (1995) *The Use and Abuse of Nature in Contemporary India*. London and New York: Routledge.
Government of India. (1998) Policy for Hydro Power Development, 1998, at http://www.nhpcindia.com [last visited June 23, 2013].
Government of India (GOI). (2002) The Planning Commission. Report of the Committee on India: Vision 2020, at http://www.teindia.nic.in/Files/Reports/CCR/pl_vsn2020.pdf [last visited November 14, 2013].
Government of India (GOI). (2004) Ministry of Power Central Electricity Authority. Preparation of Preliminary Feasibility Reports: Under 50,000 MW Hydroelectric Initiative, at

http://www.cea.nic.in/reports/hydro/feasibility_report_50kmw_he.pdf [last visited April 26, 2013].
Government of India (GOI). (2008) The Ministry of Power. The New Hydropower Policy 2008, p. 20, at http://www.ielrc.org/content/e0820.pdf [last visited October 31, 2013].
Government of India (GOI). (2010) Ministry of Power. Data for 2010, at www.powermin.nic.in [last visited June 23, 2013].
Hindu, The. (2013) "Petroleum Ministry permits cos to produce oil, gas before investment plans are cleared", at http://www.thehindubusinessline.com/economy/petroleum-ministry-permits-cos-to-produce-oil-gas-before-investment-plans-are-cleared/article5264980.ece [last visited December 2, 2016]; Date of publication: October 23, 2013.
Intercultural Resources. (2010) "A Calendar of Resistance: A Resource Book." New Delhi, India, at www.icrindia.org/. [last visited 23 July 2013]
International Rivers. (2008). "Mountains of Concrete: Dam Building in the Himalayas," at www.internationalrivers.org [last accessed on June 20, 2012].
Mahanta, Chandan. (2010) "India's North East and Hydropower Development: Future Security Challenges." *South Asian Survey* 17(1): 131–146.
Mazoomdar, Jay (2013). "Sikkim Constructing Hydel Projects in Violation of SC Order." *Tehelka Magazine* 10(42) (19 October).
Menon, Manju, Neeraj Vagholikar, Kanchi Kohli and Ashish Fernandes. (2003) "Large Dams in the Northeast: A Bright Future?" *The Ecologist Asia* 11(1) (January–March): 3–8.
Ministry of Environment and Forests. (n.d.) http://envfor.nic.in/about-ministry/about-ministry. Government of India, Ministry of Environment, Forests and Climate Change, official website, 'About the Ministry' at http://envfor.nic.in/about-ministry/about-ministry [last visited 13 May 2016].
Sarma, Dhiraj Kumar. (2013) "Big Dams, Big Dilemmas?" *Eclectic North East* (July): 26–36.
Shrivastava, Aseem and Ashish Kothari. (2012) *Churning the Earth: The Making of Global India.* New Delhi: Viking/Penguin.
Sreenivas, Ashok and N. Sreekumar. (2013) "Private Investment Not a Panacea for All Ills." India Together, October 4, at http://www.indiatogether.org [last visited October 19, 2013].
State Government of Sikkim. StatePortal/Government/SikkimGreenMission (https://www.sikkim.gov.in/portal/portal) (Downloaded: 13 May 2015).
Vagholikar, Neeraj and Partha J. Das. (2010) *Damming the Northeast.* Pune/Guwahati/New Delhi. Kalpavriksh, Aaranyak and ActionAid India.
World Bank. (2007) *Development and Growth in Northeast India: The Natural Resources, Water, and Environment Nexus.* Washington, DC: World Bank.

4

LATITUDES OF ANXIETIES

The Bengali-speaking Muslims and the postcolonial state in Assam[1]

Rafiul Ahmed

Haunting fear and pervasive anxieties seem to endure genocidal impulses against minorities across the globe. Contemporary Assam – one of the major states in India's north-east region – seems to be under the constant grip of anxieties. Identity and population politics based on ethnic, religious, and linguistic markers have mobilized specific equations of belonging leading to widespread violence. Looking beyond the brutality of such spectacular moments, a matrix composed of the border fence, census numbers, and a new category of "D" (Doubtful) voters now imposes the most "routine" violence[2] on certain citizens in contemporary Assam. At the center of this political storm is the Bengali-speaking Muslim community, a minority whose long history in Assam is part of the larger story of migration and settlement from neighboring Bengali-speaking regions dating back to the plantation economies and labor practices of the British Raj.[3] This clash had previously proceeded along ethnic and linguistic markers involving Assamese and Bengali-speaking people. The state today, however, has increasingly deployed a religious rhetoric of Hindu–Muslim communalism to characterize such tensions.

Widespread rage against Bengali-speaking Muslims in Assam affects this community's dominant image. It conjures an "enemy alien" that poses an existential threat to Assamese people, land, and security (Upadhyaya 2013). The slogan "Bangladeshi go back" has re-appeared in the popular media after the tumultuous days of the Assam Movement in the 1980s. Such reports have represented Bengali-speaking Muslims as "foreigners" and "illegal" immigrants. Anxiety and fear have reached such an extent that not a day passes without national dailies reporting of demands for a barbed-wire fence along the Assam–Bangladesh border.

Advocates hypnotized with the clarity of their metric precision use spurious statistics to construct "invasion" narratives – the Bengali-speaking Muslims turning Assam into a "mini-Bangladesh." It frames migration as Assam's "most fatal malady," a "plague," and a "ticking bomb." Imigrants are referred to as "infiltrators," "encroachers," and "invaders" (Glebova 2011). This representation of Bangladeshi immigrants as a horde unlawfully occupying scarce cultivable land in Assam casts them as a threat to the cultural identity, economic wellbeing, and national security of the *Axamiyā* community. Such characterization of Assam has drawn widespread attention to the rest of India, creating the impression that the state is hovering on the edge of perpetual insecurity.

Reminding us about the rising violence and exclusion in this "high-globalization" period, Appadurai (2006) raises a fundamental question: *why do minorities across the globe appear so threatening despite the fact that they are so few in numbers?* One has to ask the same question in the context of Assam, where the much-vilified Bengali-speaking Muslims largely constitute a peasant community underrepresented in government jobs, higher bureaucracy, the army, and politics in general. To be precise then, it becomes important to ask: *how are the multiple layers of fear and anxiety of the majority manufactured and reproduced to construct the perceived threat?* To explore this question, this chapter uses postcolonial theory to examine the nature of modern states and their practices. In this regard, Sankaran Krishna's (1997, 1999) formulation of the postcolonial state's "cartographic anxiety" in relation to its body politics is most useful. Krishna uses the term "cartography" to encompass representational practices – not only a line on a map but also all kinds of coercive and bloody practices that produce moments of suspension in postcolonial societies. For Krishna such state of suspension is a facet of a larger postcolonial anxiety and sources of both epistemic and physical violence.

Locating Krishna's "state of suspension" in the context of postcolonial Assam will entail one to map the latitudes of growing anxieties that sustains violence against the Bengali-speaking Muslim minorities in Assam. Towards this, the chapter attempts to examine how the tripartite matrix of the border, the census, and citizenship pushes the boundaries of violence into a routine one in postcolonial Assam. Further, it also elaborates upon the implications of these anxieties for Indo-Bangladeshi relations. Although Assam figures prominently as a prime border state and a place that is integral to the region's borderlands as a whole, it is yet to become a prime reference point for the Indo-Bangladesh foreign policy framework except for its exclusive claustrophobic focus on "security" issues.

Fencing and fantasy

Every time Nazir Rahman Bhuiyan, a villager in Bangladesh, walks from one part of his house to another, he crosses an international border, a recently fenced boundary between India and Bangladesh. According to a spokesman for the Indian Ministry of External Affairs, the rationale for this fence is comparable to what compelled the US and Israel, respectively, to build fences against Mexico and the West Bank. That is, fences prevent illegal immigration and terrorist infiltration (Schendel 2005 cited in Shamshad 2008: 1). This "fencing" rhetoric has not only preoccupied official discourses about borders at the national level, but it has also become deeply entrenched in regional politics. Geographically speaking, Assam is located in a geopolitically volatile zone. It shares a number of contested international boundaries with China, Burma, and Bangladesh. Accessible only through the narrow, "chicken's neck"[4] area via the neighboring state of West Bengal, the Bangladesh borderlands in India's north-east span territorially to form a triangular corner in Assam down along the slopes of the Jaintia Hills and Garo Hills in the state of Meghalaya and further down through an elongated strip in the state of Tripura.

The Brahmaptura River cuts through the Assam–Bangladesh border.[5] Flowing along the Dhubri district, the Brahmaptura has myriad *chars* that puncture the landscape. These are the riverine islands formed by the Brahmaputra and its myriad tributaries. When the river dries up during the winter months, it creates a perforated land bridge. The majority of Bengali-speaking Muslims in the region live in *chars*, outside the purview of the urban areas of Assam. The *chars* form the mobile ecologies of the Brahmaputra; they appear and disappear with the rhythm of the seasons. This rhythm is instrumental in shaping the mobile lifestyle of the *char* dwellers. It has made a permanent imprint on the economic, social, and cultural practices of the Bengali-speaking Muslims. The very nature of this border thus defies the cookie-cutter image of a closely bounded national geography. Nonetheless, "imaginative geographies" often "seal off" the landscape, seeking to physically preserve the sanctity of the border. Advocates typically see shadowy, "foreign hands" infiltrating and destabilizing the region and, by extension, the nation.

The India–Bangladesh border, however, owed little to modern concepts of spatial rationality. Political pressures played no small part in partitioning the eastern territories, in haste and in ignorance, along the Radcliffe Line. Chatterji (1999) traces the partition politics through a historical lens. She asserts that the border was not drawn dispassionately, with mere clinical precision and attention to detail, as was at the time imagined in popular politics, which used surgical metaphors to signify the dismemberment. Rather it was a hastily and ignorantly drawn line, in whose drafting political pressures played no small part. In no sense, moreover, did this border-drawing operation end in August 1947.[6] The process by which the border between India and East Pakistan was established was thus far more protracted – taking place over almost two decades – than the establishment of the border between India and West Pakistan. Even physical demarcation took years to accomplish, while the acquisition of citizenship in the two states (and later Bangladesh) remains incomplete even today (Roy 2012).

The porous and discrete nature of the Assam's border along the erstwhile East Pakistan haunted the Assamese elites for a long time. The demand for a barbed fence in the Assam–Bangladesh border became intense since the 1950s. Chief Minister Bimala Prasad Chaliha of the former Congress-led Assam government, for instance, launched a campaign to deport immigrants who had settled in the state since January 1951. Along with his party, he advocated extensive operations to "clear up" the border area of immigrants to deal with what was then described as Pakistani infiltration.[7] New Delhi would not take action against immigration from East Pakistan but Assamese politicians managed to acquire 180 additional police watch posts and permission to erect a barbed-wire fence in selected places along the Assam–East Pakistani border.

Fencing the border as rhetoric resurfaced with new vigor in the late 1970s. The All Assam Students Union (AASU) spearheaded a state-wide anti-foreigner agitation; it mobilized an *Axamiyā* identity against "Others." Initially, they targeted *Bohiragotos* (outsiders), including people from other parts of India and, in the later stage, the movement came to brand all outsiders as *Bidexi* (foreigners), specifically, Muslim minorities of East Bengal origin. The AASU and later their representative political party, Assam Gana Parishad (AGP), played a pivotal role in giving rise to a *casus belli* – a fervent cry to save the homeland on behalf of the sons of the soil. Recovering Mother Assam's (*Axami Ai*) lost sanctity by deporting all "illegal" immigrants to the other side of the border came to define the movement.

The AASU found resolution in the Assam Accord[8] of 1983, signed between the movement leaders and Rajiv Gandhi, then Prime Minister of India. To address the infiltration of the so-called "illegal" Bangladeshis, movement leaders demanded the complete sealing off the Assam–Bangladeshi border with a fence. The Indian government approved of an Indo-Bangladesh Border Road and Fence project in 1986; subsequently, it started a two-phase project to build a fence. In this way, the fence became a vital symbol and barometer of Assamese nationalism. For instance, the Congress government (2001-May 2016) in Assam published a *White Paper on Foreigners' Issue* (Government of Assam 2012) that included updates on the fence project. Consider, for example, a brief passage from this document: "a total of 228.118 km of new fencing was sanctioned under Phase-I&II, out of which, based on field conditions, the actual required length was 224.694 km. Against this 218.170 km of fencing (97.1 percent) has been completed" (Government of Assam 2012: 29–31). The detailed description of the project, its various units, proportions, and projections underscore the state's investment in establishing own, local identity.

Certain speeches and gestures by politicians accentuate this fear and anxiety of the border. Parties in government build constituencies by paying visits to the border area and commenting on the progress of the fence. These visits embody a stocktaking exercise: it updates and reassures the state's anxious majority of the status of the fence. Its completion rate thus indicates the efficiency and seriousness of the state's concerns with the border. In fact, the release of the *White Paper on the Foreigners' Issue* was followed by an official visit by former Union Home Minister Sushil Kumar Shinde. He visited the Dhubri sector of the Assam–Bangladesh border to inspect border guarding measures (*The Hindu* 2012b).

The bureaucratic and political pilgrimage of the border fence has become a part and parcel of the realpolitik in engaging Assam. Recently, the present State Home Minister, Kiren Rijiju, expressed concern about the 783 porous stretches in the Indo-Bangladesh border and urged to tighten the surveillance by intensifying patrolling "nakas" (border ambushes) and deploying more observation posts (*ZEE News* 2014). Quite amazingly the present Union Home Minister, Rajnath Singh while visiting the Indo-Bangladesh border declared, "there can be no non-lethal strategy on borders" (*The Hindu* 2015). The Bharatiya Janta Party's (BJP's) election campaign for the 2016 Assam Assembly election lost no opportunity in grinding the axe. While releasing its vision document for the Assam polls, the BJP promised that, if elected, it would accomplish the complete sealing of the India–Bangladesh border (Hebbar 2016).

While the issue of fencing has become the Holy Grail for politicians at the regional and national levels, the Indo-Bangladeshi border has turned into South Asia's killing field. Increasing militarization and securitization of the borderlands – a densely populated area interspersed with paddy fields and grazing areas along with forested lands – have contributed to untold miseries for poor Muslim peasants who live on either side of the fence. Human Rights Watch (2010) describes the Indian Border Security Force (BSF) as "trigger happy" for the unit's involvement in indiscriminate killings and torture of unarmed immigrants trying to cross the border. The report estimates that well over 1,000 people have been killed over the last decade. A journalist from *The Guardian* commented that while a single casualty by US law enforcement authorities along the Mexican border makes headlines, the deaths of hundreds of villagers at the hands of Indian forces have been ignored and no officials prosecuted so far (Adams 2011).

Authorities in postcolonial Assam continue to view Muslim minorities with cross-border family ties and lineages as an existential threat to national security. This territorial phantom pain, emerging out of the porous and fluid Assam–Bangladeshi borderlands, reminds the majority population to guard and seal the border with metals and guns. In a similar context, Samaddar (1999: 19) rightly points out that *borders born out of a partition produce even more partition(s)*. He succinctly argues that the border not only fixes the illegality of immigration, it plays a crucial part in determining state responses – the "practices of the statecraft" (ibid.: 20–21).

To sum up, the renewed interest in a fence at the Assam–Bangladesh border in recent years reinvigorated the colonial romance of drawing boundary lines – as a way to mediate the familiar *here* and the unfamiliar *there*. While the political rhetoric of border played an instrumental role in securitizing it, without a subsequent discourse of immigrant subjectivity such rhetoric becomes defunct, empty, and toothless. I now turn to explain the production of immigrant subjectivity in the public discourses in Assam through a discussion on politics of numbers and issues of citizenship and belongingness.

Seduction of numbers

The urgency with which Bengali-speaking Muslims have come under official scrutiny has no parallel in the history of Assam. Everyone in Assam seems to be counting the "Bangladeshis" – the census, special tribunals, the local intelligentsia and, of course, the media. Quite recently there has been an avalanche of numbers concerning the proportion of Bangladeshis in Assam. Indeed, various figures of unaccounted Bangladeshis have been put forward, both from official and unofficial sources. Political leaders, bureaucrats, public intellectuals and media personalities pay routine homage to these figures, quoting them according to their arguments, and making them a permanent feature in Assam's political discourse. Wildly fluctuating and suspiciously rounded figures (10 million in 1997 by Communist Party of India's Indrajit Gupta, 20 million by BJP's L.K. Advani in 2003, 12 million by Congress's Sriprakash Jaiswal in 2004) of alleged illegal Bangladeshi immigrants, based on nothing in particular or attributed vaguely to "intelligence reports," have dominated the discourse on the ethnic strife in Assam (cited in Sengupta 2012).

So unbridled was the euphoria of counting Bangladeshis that even the supposedly neutral office of the governor was implicated. The former governor Lt Gen (retired) S.K. Sinha became popular for the "new" count of "Bangladeshis," which he stated in a report addressed to the President of India. In 1997, Sinha (1998) concluded in the report, with great anxiety and urgency, that Assam was on the verge of a "silent and demographic invasion." The report estimated that 4 million Bangladeshi immigrants were in Assam, with another 5.4 million in West Bengal, 0.8 million in Tripura, 0.5 million in Bihar, 0.5 million in Maharashtra, 0.5 million in Rajasthan and 0.3 million in Delhi. The report claimed that this pattern of unabated illegal immigration from East Pakistan/Bangladesh was irreversibly altering the demographic complexion of Assam and thus posed a grave threat to Assamese identity and national security. The report came to be widely cited, even by academics and the judiciary.

In fact in recent years, scholars have devoted considerable effort to devising a quantitative analysis of data from various sources, including the Indian census. Noted political scientist Myron Weiner (1993) wondered whether there exists a numerical threshold of "overforeignization" that triggers reactions from the natives. Meanwhile, several Assamese scholars were busy with the task of estimating the number of so-called "illegal" Bangladeshi immigrants in state. Nath *et al.* (2012), using the Leslie Matrix method, estimated the number of undocumented or illegal immigrants in Assam to 830,757 illegal immigrants between 1971 and 1991 and 534,819 between 1991 and 2001, which brought the total to 1,365,574 over 30 years from 1971 to 2001. Goswami *et al.* (2003) used the Survival Method to study the 40-year period between 1951 and 1991 and came up with a figure of 2.9 million immigrants in Assam, and concluded that out of this sum, 31 percent were interstate migrants and 69 percent being international immigrants. Of this latter group, 24 percent were legal and 45 percent illegal immigrants.

Some favoring "dispassionate analysis" attempted to come up with more refined methodology to enumerate accurate figures using religion-wise immigration data (Borooah 2013). Innumerable other studies conclude with numerical evidence to show how the Muslim community has grown, and how this growth negatively affects Assam (Nath 2010). A Malthusian fever seems to grip the state. Such rationalization and naturalization of statistics render so-called facts sacrosanct. Moreover, the Indian census has become a tool for perpetuating a relentless campaign to cleanse Assam of so-called Bangladeshis. In recent years the announcement of census figures for Assam has become a tongue-waging affair. Media reporters, blog enthusiasts, and digital activists seem to reap the harvest out of their chauvinist hatred without lifting a gun. All they have to do is to juggle religious data to come up with spurious sensational analysis. "2011 Census Figures Rings Alarm Bell in Assam,"[9] "Demographic Jitters,"[10] "2011 Census May Create Political Storm"[11] – thus read some of the headlines that have appeared in the media recently. Historically speaking, however, census has not been an unlikely bureaucratic weapon. Note the example of C.S. Mullan. Posted to the region as superintendent of census operations during the time of the British Raj, Mullan led the Census of Assam in 1931. It used the term "invasion"[12] in the Assamese context for the first time. He instigated what has evolved since the 1930s into a "hate campaign" in the state. To provoke the Assamese against Bengalis, Mullan (1931: 50) wrote:

> Wheresoever the carcase, there will the vultures be gathered together – Where there is waste land thither flock the Mymensinghias.[13] In fact the way in which they have seized upon the vacant areas in Assam valley seems almost uncanny. Without fuss, without tumult, without undue trouble to district revenue staffs, a population which amount to over half a million has transplanted itself from Bengal to the Assam Valley during the last twenty five years. It looks like a marvel of administrative on the part of the Government but it is nothing of the sort: the only thing I can compare it to is the mass movement of a large body of ants [sic].

He added: "it is sad but by no means improbable that in another thirty years Sibsagar district will be the only part of Assam in which an Assamese will find himself at home" (ibid.: 52). Noted historian Amalendu Guha (1977) described Mullan as an irresponsible European civil servant who, in an effort to predict the future, "mischievously" used the word "invasion" to describe the immigration of people from East Bengal's Mymensingh district at a time when no national boundary existed. Mullan's verdict on the Bengali invasion makes it possible for those who seek to historicize and authenticate the threat of a Muslim invasion back to the days of the British Raj.[14]

Britain's colonial administration played no small role in poisoning relations between Bengalis and Assamese elites (Hussain 1994).[15] The British typically employed Bengalis in the lower tier of administrative jobs, especially in the plantations and railways, yet denied the same to Assamese as a matter of policy. In fact, the British kept the opening for Assamese middle class deliberately narrow. They did little to develop areas of opportunities for higher education in Assam. Besides, it utterly lacked any kind of professional institutions for skill development and remained exclusively dependent on the Calcutta gentry for trade and commerce. The region was merely a site for extractive industry and a supplier of raw materials. This unique colonial political economy of Assam produced a more stunted and narrow Assamese middle class than its Bengali counterparts (Gohain 1973). Such differential treatment of the Bengalis and Assamese middle classes facilitated the sustenance of colonial hegemony – pitting each against the other.

In post-independence India, hegemonies of language and ethnicity added to this mutual mistrust. Assam witnessed extensive violence under the rubric of the *Bongal*

Kheda[16] – an organized campaign of ethnic cleansing of the Bengalis of the north-east and sought to evict Bengali settlers in the 1950s, 1960s and 1970s. The 1980s Assam Movement significantly hastened these processes wherein organizations like the AASU further fueled these issues leading to indiscriminate violence and loss of life. In Nellie, a small town not far from the state capital, around 3,000 Bengali Muslims, mostly women and children, were massacred. The Indian government, eager to resolve the problems associated with this agitation, dropped all charges against those who were accused of committing the atrocities in the Nellie riot. As a result, those who had instigated or participated in the riots were never tried for their crimes (Mander 2008).

Deployment of a communal line – the Hindu–Muslim binary – to deal with the Bangladeshi migrant issue has allowed politicians to stretch India's current border insecurities. The rise of right-wing elements in north-east's regional politics, led by the Bharatiya Janata Party (BJP), however, have singled out religion, specifically Islam, to underscore questions of population movements across Bangladesh border regions. The BJP is well known for popularizing the idea of "competitive breeding." It argues that Muslims will soon outnumber Hindus in India.[17] Along with its Hindutva-oriented collaborators like the Rashtriya Swayam Sevak Sangh (RSS), Vishva Hindu Parishad (VHP) and Shiv Sena, the BJP has criticized erstwhile official policies towards Bangladeshi migrants as being overly lenient and accommodating. After successfully politicizing the religious dispute in Ayodhya (1992), the BJP unleashed nation-wide propaganda against Bengali-speaking Muslim migrants. The party's ideologues published populist articles and full-length books on the issue and organized systematic campaigns to mobilize people against migrants. Captions for leading BJP essays, such as "Demographic Aggression against India: Muslim Avalanche from Bangladesh" and "Is India Going Islamic?," stoked people's fear of Bengali Muslim infiltration (Rai cited in Upadhyaya 2013: 1–97). These polemical writings and speeches clearly distinguished between a Hindu "refugee" and a Muslim "infiltrator." Publications in this vein also inflamed the public that more than 15 million Bangladeshi Muslims have settled in various parts of India; they warned Indians against the "grim consequences of the exodus of Muslims from the Islamic and densely populated country called Bangladesh" (ibid.: 11).

The routine production of a quantitative rationality as discussed above has made the numbers of immigrants a "sacrosanct" fact in the everyday life of common people in Assam. The repeated exercise involving various iterations of counting and classifying minority Muslims on the basis of census data reflect both an enduring anxiety and efforts to somehow name and categorize the problem in order to bring it under control. The collective amnesia of the majority in Assam has transformed these acts it into a "normal" one. To count the so-called Bangladeshis is to assess the gravity of a demographic threat. To ask "how many Bangladeshis in Assam?" is acting normally. It is everywhere – in the daily discussions of state Assembly, red-corridors of government offices, teashops, newspapers and television channels. Meanwhile, the state's role in upholding an image of a homogenous and pure Assamese nationhood goes unexamined.

Specter of citizenship

Rastam Ali, from Borpayek in Nellie, Assam, is 45 years old and a small trader by profession. His father, Kalam Shah Ahmed, was a cultivator and an inhabitant of the same village. Rastam had been qualified to vote in India and had exercised this right twice. Suddenly in 1996, Rastam became a "D-voter" and lost the right to vote. Like Rastam Ali, a large number of Bengali-speaking Muslims in Assam recently have come under a new category of citizens, the "D-voters." The letter "D" stands for doubtful or disputed citizenship status. Paradoxically, his brothers and other family members were somehow not marked as D-voters (Begum 2011). The number of "D-voters" has swelled over the years. According to the Government of Assam's *White Paper on Foreigners' Issue* (2012) the letter "D" was attached to a total of 2,31,657 people who could not prove their citizenship.

The category of "D-voters" is a new classification. The letter "D" is marked for those who could not demonstrate their Indian citizenship status to officers especially appointed for this verification purpose and henceforth their voting rights are to be scrapped. This very category is a by-product of recent revisions made to the National Register for Citizenship (NRC) in Assam. The NRC contains the names of Indian citizens. Historically speaking, it was compiled only for Assam in 1951. Census enumerators prepared it from census slips of 1951. However, it entailed serious implications for reasons that a) any accidental omission meant losing one's citizenship; and b) being a "secret administrative document", there was no way that one could have access to verify it (Roychoudhury 1981). Given the complexities[18] involved with the preparation of NRC 1951, it is not hard to gauge that it was discriminatory towards the Bengali-speaking Muslims.

The AASU, despite the 1951 NRC's dubious character, during the Assam Movement in the 1980s tried to make it a template to detect the so-called "foreign-nationals." Finally, it was made as a part of the Assam Accord.[19] The then Congress government at the center yielding to its demands, started exploring modalities to go ahead as it decided to publish the final electoral roll for Assam on August 27, 1985. In fact, much ahead of the finalization of Assam Accord, the Election Commission of India (EC) mooted its plan to accommodate the rising demands of the AASU boys under the directives of the Home Ministry. Working under the "directives" and injunctions of the Home Ministry, the Commission was almost transformed into an agency of it, losing its independent credibility as an institution. Enacting a series of circulars during the process of preparation of the electoral rolls, it put the Bengali-speaking Muslims at the disposal of the Electoral Officers (EOs). There were official instructions as well as unofficial ones by which the EOs were given powers to act as per "their own conscience" to strike out names in the electoral rolls (Choudhury 1985).[20]

The assertion for updating the NRC reached its pinnacle in the aftermath of violence in the Bodoland Territorial Area District (BTAD)[21] of lower Assam in 2012 and 2014. The violence involved group clashes between ethnic *Bodos* and Bengali-speaking Muslims. A former Election Commissioner of India belonging to the *Bodo* community advocated prompt revisions of the NRC to expedite deportation of those found to be "illegal migrants" (Brahma 2012). AASU left no opportunity to react to such a charged scenario. Sammujal Bhattacharya, a prominent AASU adviser, commented in the aftermath of the BTAD 2012 violence (Bhattacharya quoted in Choudhury 2013b: 22):

> We want speedy identification and deportation of illegal migrants. The demography of Assam is under threat, indigenous communities are turned into minority all because both the Centre and the state have used them as vote banks and tried to legalise the illegal migrants. The fallout has been violence.[22]

Meanwhile, the Supreme Court of India sharply intervened. It instructed the Congress government to settle the matter immediately by preparing a fresh NRC as per the Assam Accord. Through a series of discussions between the Assam government, central government and AASU a new change in citizenship rules was proposed. Under increasing pressure, the Assam government pushed back the cut-off year by 20 years and agreed to define the "indigenous" people of Assam as those whose names figured in the NRC in 1951. Now this list is to be tallied with the 1971 voter list to ascertain their descendants. Under the sub-section 3 of section 4-A of the Citizenship Act the enumeration is to be done through invitation of claims rather than a door-to-door enumeration, which is the usual case in other parts of India. In this new scenario all the applicants are required to fill up the NRC dossier with a desired list of documents to be verified by designated officers.[23]

Moreover, the increasing communalization of politics with each passing election became a matter of additional anxiety for the Bengali-speaking Muslims. The BJP right from its initial entry in Assam was harping on to make the issue of deportation a central component of the party's election campaign. A part of its aggressive advocacy has been the ploy to grant citizenship to the Bengali-speaking Hindu immigrants from Bangladesh on a humanitarian basis (Vyas 2011; *The Sentinel* 2013). In its recently released vision document prior to the 2016 Assembly election, stretching upon the continuity of common elements of Hinduism both in the Hindi heartland and Assam, it clearly signaled who are welcome and who are not (Hebbar 2016). The Congress also didn't step back in wooing voters on communal lines. The Chief Minister of Assam from the Congress party spoke about giving refugee status to Bengali-speaking Hindus to wrest support from Bengali-speaking Hindu-dominated areas. So, cornered in such circumstances, it started playing the Hindutva card to thwart the challenge of the growing influence of BJP in Assam (Choudhury 2013a).

While the political battles are fought over ballot boxes, simultaneously the contestation of citizenship is played on a different turf – the judiciary. A number of Public Interest Litigations (PILs)[24] have been lodged by Assamese middle-class dominated organizations like AASU and APW and civil society organizations representing the Bengali-speaking Muslim minorities in Assam. The Supreme Court of India has been consistently cynical about the so-called "infiltration" issue. It endorsed the view that the illegal immigrants had reduced the people of Assam to a minority in their own state, and represented a threat of "external aggression" and internal disturbance. Perhaps the larger impact of judicial activism is to be seen in the amendment of the Citizenship Act of 1955 from a more inclusive *jus solis* to a more restrictive *jus sanguinis* in response to the perceived increase in the number of illegal immigrants from Bangladesh (cited in Jayal 2013: 52).

The above political developments in Assam have reinvigorated questions about how the state determines *who* is a citizen. An upsurge in "autochthony" is increasingly becoming an unexpected corollary of democratization. What is acutely troubling is the widespread usage of the prefix "illegal," both in official and private discourses, to distinguish between native ethnic Assamese and immigrants.[25] Perhaps no other label than "illegal" adequately defines the social position of Bengali-speaking Muslims in Assam's public discourse. Not only common people in day-to-day life use the term, but it is also used frequently by government and the media (Choudhury 2013b). More importantly, tribunals, fast-track courts and detention camps frequently use the term. Yasmin Saikia (2012), a prominent Assamese expert on South Asian history, holds that even the British fell short of applying the term "illegal" to those outside the purview of their rule. They might have used *badmash* or thug, but not "illegal." Indeed, the very term "illegal" denies the essence of being a human. Saikia raises a pertinent question, asking *how, exactly, people become "illegal"?* The term's prominent usage in Assam's public discourse displays its utility as a political technology – a social quarantine hostile to Bengali-speaking Muslims that produces a classifying effect (Ahmed 2014).

Like numbers, the discourse of D-voters has dragged the Bengali-speaking Muslims under the official microscope. The Bengali-speaking Muslims are now increasingly – in official documents, journalism and common conversation – simply Muslims, and all of them are suspect as open or closet Bangladeshis. Under such changed circumstances, "doubt" has become a permanent feature of Assam's everyday public discourse. Everything about Bengali-speaking Muslims has become a source of doubt – their mobility, land use, attire and, of course, their beards (ibid.). The everydayness of such discourse in Assam has transformed them as bearded, *lungi*-clad, parasitic strangers. D-voters are made into a recalcitrant element – a hint of another vision – the irrecoverability of a pristine past on the part of the majority in Assam.

Re-imagining Indo-Bangladesh relations

The "majority" thus performs the "minority" through this juxtaposition of border, census, and citizenship. Appadurai (2006) argues that predatory identities emerge in the tensions between majority identities and nationalist identities. Using this insight in the case of postcolonial Assam, this chapter shows that Assamese identity has attained a predatory status wherein the majority strive to close all gaps between themselves and what is marked as the purity of the national whole. This group has successfully mobilized the "incompleteness of anxiety" to merge and align national purity with Assamese identity. Assam's regional politics thus plays out Krishna's conceptualization of the postcolonial state's cartographic anxieties. Fantasies of a sealed border, desire for quantifiable precision in population census, and efforts to define citizenship to conclusively separate legitimate citizens from the "illegal and deportable" have become indispensable requirements of today's democratic politics.

Needless to say, the above expressions of democratic politics are also responsible for unaccountable violence. This has put a heavy premium on the lives of those who seem to be, in one way or another, untraceable and uncountable. This postcolonial Assam's celebrated aporia has made Muslims' minorities an eyesore in its quest for modern nation building. To take a cue from Pandey (2006: 186), the postcolonial state's attitude towards the Muslim minorities in Assam appears to be a revisit of the colonial archive on the one hand. On the other, it reflects the neoliberal character of the postcolonial state in Assam and its anomalies in the course of a fading "development state." The postcolonial state in Assam seems to be deeply aware of the fact that the Bengali-speaking Muslims' lack in resources, education, and initiative and to the extent unworthy of the privileges accorded to proper citizens. However, there is no escape from this population, unwelcome and sometimes illegal or barely legal immigrants. All the postcolonial state can do is to discipline them. "Routine violence," thus, forms the essential elements of its disciplinary gaze.

It is also important to note Assam's significance in Indo-Bangladeshi diplomatic relations. India and Bangladesh have not arrived at any consensus regarding the vital issues that concern both parties, such as regulating cross-border migration, reviving older ties of commerce with Assam through border trade, and sharing the water of the mighty Brahmaputra River. Although the Indian state persistently pushes the "Look East Policy" to develop the north-east as a growth corridor with South East Asian countries, it neglects to meaningfully engage in this regard with its nearest neighbor, Bangladesh. Although, globalization tendencies have facilitated the modernization process to negate grounds for identity-based politics, it has failed to address the root cause of the existing cartographic anxieties (Guhathakurta 2010).

Quite ironically, Bhupen Hazarika, Assam's foremost cultural icon, spent his lifetime writing and advocating the significance of the *Xomonnoy* (confluence) of the rivers Brahmaputra along with Ganga and Padda (Bangladesh) in contributing to a shared cultural history in the region over centuries. In a poll conducted in Bangladesh, Hazarika's song "*Manush Manusher Jonno*" ("Humans are for Humanity") was chosen as the second most favorite song after the Bangladesh national anthem (*The Daily Star* 2011). And yet neither Hazarika's vision nor his reference to shared civilizational resources has found any place in current diplomacy.

Postcolonial cartographic anxieties continue to proscribe recognition of common civilizational resources between India and Bangladesh. Breaking this impasse involves undoing the remaining shell of the Westphalian nation-state framework. We need to look for historical and cultural "relationalities." Perhaps it would entail what Krishna (1999) vouches in favor of a "countermemorial" reading to unsettle the monological imaginations of South Asia that forever seeks to align territory with identity. However, such efforts cannot be another drive for "pure origin" or a romance of the syncretic civilization. Rather, it needs to uncover the "shared" and "lived" registers like the nested rhythms of waves does in Hazarika's songs – which tells the tales of common men's joy, folly, and sorrow on both sides of the border, to eventually return to a fluvial calm in search of a higher pedestal of selfhood – the "confluence." Only in the creative possibility of such a "deterritorial" moment can Assam find an opportunity to play the role of a bridge between India and Bangladesh.

Notes

1 This is an expanded version of the article earlier published in *Perceptions*, 2014, 21(1): 55–70.
2 Pandey (2006) has used the term "routine violence" to articulate violence as a social fact – that comfortably sits in the everydayness of our life in the most disguised forms.
3 They are referred to as the *Na Axamiyā* (New Assamese) who migrated during the colonial period from the erstwhile East Bengal and settled in the Brahmaptura valley. They pioneered wet paddy cultivation and jute plantation in Assam valley. It was coined by Assam's cultural icon Jyotiprasad Agarwala to symbolize the evolution of the Assamese community through a rich history of assimilation. The term "Bengali-speaking Muslim" itself is an oxymoron since the majority of them while settling down in the Brahmaputra valley adopted Assamese as their mother tongue. To contextualize from Chatterji's (1996) discussion on the term "Bengali Muslims", it reflects *Assameseness*, *Bengaliness* and *Muslimness* coexisting uneasily on the opposite sites of a deep fundamental divide. See Chatterji (1996) for a detailed discussion on the issue of Islam, Bengal and the concomitant process of identity formation.
4 This is a narrow strip of land located in the Indian state of West Bengal. It connects India's north-eastern states to the rest of India. It borders Nepal, Bangladesh, and Bhutan.
5 As per a report maintained by the Ministry of Home Affairs' web-portal, Government of India (2014); India shares 4,096.7 km of its land border with Bangladesh. Among other states of the north-east it quotes a figure of 263 km being shared by Assam. While the *White Paper on Assam's Foreigners Issue* prepared by the Home and Political Department, Government of Assam in 2012 quotes a slightly different figure of 267 km. It states that out of this 223.068 km is the land border and 44.232 km are river stretches and other non-feasible gaps across the river border. Within 44.232 km, the Brahmaputra River has a stretch of 32.750 km in Dhubri District (Government of Assam 2012: 29).
6 The Redcliff Line was announced by Sir Cyril Redcliffe on August 17, 1947. He was entrusted with the task to demarcate India and Pakistan. The task required equitably dividing 175,000 square miles (450,000 km^2) of territory with approximately 88 million people.
7 Following such instances, the Immigrants Act, 1950 (Expulsion from Assam) was passed by the Indian parliament in February 13. Popularly known among the immigrants as the *Mian Kheda Ayen* (the law that drives away migrant Muslims!) it was part of a concerted move to drive immigrant Muslims in several districts of Assam that led to a mass exodus from Assam to East Bengal. According to official sources they consist of 52,600 families or about 1 lakh (cited in Roychoudhury 1981: 267).
8 The Assam Accord (1985) was a Memorandum of Settlement (MoS) signed between representatives of the Government of India and the leaders of the Assam Movement in New Delhi on August 15, 1985. The accord brought an end to the Assam Agitation and paved the way for the leaders of the agitation to form a political party (the Asom Gana Parishad) and form a government in the state of Assam soon after.
9 *The Sentinel* (2014).
10 Hussain (2004).
11 *The Assam Tribune* (2015).
12 In fact, Mullan (1931: 49) dramatically compares the migration of Bengali-speaking Muslims to the Burmese invasion of Assam in 1820. The Burmese attack of Assam

during the *Ahom* rule (early thirteenth century to 1826) is deeply etched in the psyche of Assamese people. Locally articulated as the *Manor Akromon* in the *Buranjis* (chronicle of history maintained by the *Ahom* kings), the attack is represented as the most ruthless. Mullan (ibid.) saw the new migration as an invasion of the whole "structure of Assamese culture" and "civilization."

13 This blanket term is used by Mullan to represent the Bengali-speaking peasants as a homogeneous community hailing from Mymensingh – an old district that was constituted by the British East India Company in 1787. However, significant socio-cultural differences exist between them.

14 Somewhat ironically, Mullan has achieved something of a cult status. The repeated reproduction of the quote from his 1931 census in writings by Assamese middle-class intellectuals has turned it into an emblem of feat accuracy – being able to measure what was uncountable. Sinha (1998: 11) in his report paid due homage to him, stating the importance of Mullan's work and the importance of the 1931 Census for national security!

15 On the other hand, to segregate the East Bengal migrants of Bengali-speaking Muslims from the Assamese, it enacted the "Line System" in the 1920s. Under this, an imaginary line was drawn to segregate the immigrants from the "indigenous" tribes.

16 The term literally means to "drive the Bengalis out." Chakravarti (1960) notes that during the 1960s the campaign term *Bongal-* was used in a wider sense that did not refer merely to Bengalis alone but all outsiders living in Assam. An offshoot of a larger linguistic drive of Assamese nationalists to claim Assamese as the official state language, the campaign targeted non-Assamese leading to widespread violence and loss of lives in the Brahmaputra valley.

17 The discourse of competitive breeding thrives on pernicious myths about the Muslim community by Hindu fundamentalist groups of all shades. Some recent critical writings have touched upon various dimensions of it. For more nuanced discussions see Rao (2010), Bhagat (2001) and Bhagat and Prahraj (2005).

18 It is worth mentioning here that any accurate census enumeration in Assam could have been a daunting task considering the politically volatile situation pertaining during the emergence of East Pakistan in 1947 and subsequently Bangladesh in 1971. These events led to an exodus of millions of people, both Bengali Muslims and Hindus, seeking refuge on both sides of the border. For instance, although promised a safe passage for return under the Nehru–Liaquat Pact of 1950 – a bilateral treaty signed by India and Pakistan agreeing to guarantee rights of minorities – those who returned to Assam much later than March 1951 in all probability could not have been included as the census enumeration was over by then.

19 It determined the midnight of March 24, 1971 as a "cut-off" date (midnight) to determine the "foreigners" from the citizens: a) all those who had migrated before 1966 would be treated as citizens; b) those who had migrated between 1966 and 1971 could stay provided they put themselves through an official process of registration as foreigners; and c) all those who migrated thereafter were simply illegal immigrants.

20 Again, the complexities involving the task were hardly realized – or else were deliberately overlooked – let alone the solutions. For instance, many of the constituencies did not have full electoral rolls. Only in 77 constituencies of the total 126 could the government itself procure full copies of the 1971 electoral rolls (cited in Choudhury 1985). In addition, many of the boundaries of the electoral constituencies also changed by the mid-1980s.

21 *Bodos* represents an ethnic and linguistic community in Assam and is spread over both valley and hill areas mostly in lower Assam. The BTAD is an outcome of a part settlement with the government in 2003 after the cessation of the Bodo Movement for a separate homeland. It was carved out of areas of both *Bodo* concentration and the mixed population of lower Assam.

22 Besides AASU, Assamese middle-class-dominated civil society organizations like Assam Public Work (APW) reacted sharply during the course of violence. The APW in a petition to the Supreme Court of India suggested the deletion of supposedly 40 lakh Bengali-speaking Muslims from the voters list of 2006 alleging that they got their names entered into the electoral roles illegally and they should forthwith be deported (*The Hindu* 2012a).

23 As a part of verification the applicants are required to produce an enormous number of documents prior to March 24, 1971 like land or tenancy records, citizenship certificates or permanent residential certificates or passport or court records or refugee registration certificates. The fear of failure to collect such documents has led to instances of suicide. Taking advantage of this, a section of middlemen have made the NRC update process a profitable business. They are everywhere, but more active in *char* areas, tea gardens and remote villages where people are poorer and less literate. They offer the whole package – from collecting legacy data, filling in forms, collecting documents and even arranging the specially required photograph with a white background, but all for an exorbitant amount (Guha and Habib 2015).
24 In the Indian law, PIL means the litigation for the protection of public interest. Article 32 of the Indian constitution contains a tool that directly joins the public with judiciary. A PIL may be introduced in a court of law by the court itself (*suo motu*), rather than the aggrieved party or another third party. For the exercise of the court's jurisdiction, it is not necessary for the victim of the violation of his or her rights to personally approach the court. In a PIL, the right to file suit is given to a member of the public by the courts through judicial activism. The member of the public may be a non-governmental organization (NGO), an institution, or an individual.
25 The tag has become more popular and widespread especially after the political scenario that followed the 1980s Assam Movement.

References

Adams, Brad. (2011). "India's Shoot-to-Kill Policy at the Bangladesh Border." *The Guardian*, January 23. (http://www.theguardian.com/commentisfree/libertycentral/2011/jan/23/india-bangladesh-border-shoot-to-kill-policy) (Dowloaded: March 30, 2013).

Ahmed, Rafiul. (2014). "Assam's D-voters." *Himal*, May 26. (http://himalmag.com/assams-d-voters/) (Downloaded: 1 June 2014).

Appadurai, Arjun. (2006). *Fear of Small Numbers: An Essay on the Geography of Anger*. Durham, NC: Duke University Press.

Begum, Anjuman Ara. (2011). "Narratives of D-voters in Assam." January 3. (http://twocircles.net/2011jan03/narratives_dvoters_assam.html) (Downloaded: March 10, 2013).

Bhagat, R.B. (2001). "Census and the Construction of Communalism in India." *Economic and Political Weekly* 36(46/47): 4352–4356.

Bhagat, R.B. and Prahraj, Purohit. (2005). "Hindu–Muslim Fertility Differentials." *Economic and Political Weekly* 40(5): 411–418.

Borooah, Vani Kant. (2013). "The Killing Fields of Assam: Myths and Realities of Its Muslim Migration." *Economic and Political Weekly* 48(4): 43–52.

Brahma, H.S. (2012). "How to Share Assam." *The Indian Express*, Oped, July 12.

Chakravarti, K.C. (1960). "Bongal Kheda Again." *Economic and Political Weekly* 12(31): 1193–1195.

Chatterji, Joya. (1996). "The Bengali Muslim: A Contradiction in Terms? An Overview of the Debate on Bengali Muslim Identity." *Comparative Studies of South Asia, Africa and the Middle East* 16(2): 16–24.

Chatterji, Joya. (1999). "The Fashioning of a Frontier: The Radcliffe Line and Bengal's Border Landscape, 1947–52." *Modern Asian Studies* 33 (1): 185–242.

Choudhury, Ratnadip. (2013a). "Congress' Hindutva Hand." *Tahelka*, October 12. (http://www.tehelka.com/2013/10/the-congress-hindutva-hand/) (Downloaded: March 12, 2014).

Choudhury, Ratnadip. (2013b). "The Agony of Being Labeled a 'Bangladeshi' in Assam." *Tahelka* 10(42), October 19. (http://www.tehelka.com/2013/10/the-agony-of-being-labelled-a-bangladeshi-in-assam/2/) (Downloaded: November 20) (Downloaded: 1 June 2014).

Choudhury, Sujit. (1985). "Election Commission and the Assam Accord." *Economic and Political Weekly* 20(49): 2146–2147.
Glebova, Ksenia. (2011). "Most Fatal Malady: Media, Migration and Identity in Assam." *Mahanirban Calcutta Research Group Publication*, December. (http://www.mcrg.ac.in/rw percent20files/RW38/2.Ksenia.pdf) (Downloaded: March 12, 2013).
Gohain, Hiren. (1973). "Origins of the Assamese Middle Class." *Social Scientist* 2(1): 11–26.
Goswami, A., A. Saikia and H. Goswami. (2003). *Population Growth in Assam 1951–1991 with a Focus on Migration*. New Delhi: Akansha Publishing House.
Government of Assam. (2012). *White Paper on Foreigners' Issue*, Home and Political Department, October 20. (http://online.assam.gov.in/web/homepol/whitepaper) (Downloaded: October 22, 2013).
Government of India. (n.d.). *Management of Indo-Bangladesh Border*, Ministry of Home Affairs. (http://mha.nic.in/sites/upload_files/mha/files/BM_MAN-IN-BANG-270813.pdf) (Downloaded: May 2, 2014).
Guha, Amalendu. (1977). *Plantes-Raj to Swaraj: Freedom Struggle and Electoral Politics in Assam 1826–1947*. New Delhi: Indian Council of Historical Research.
Guha, Nabarun and Nasreen Habib. (2015). "Will I Be Counted?" *Eclectic Northeast*, August, pp. 26–33.
Guhathakurta, Meghna. (2010). "Cartographic Anxieties, Identity Politics, and the Imperatives of Bangladesh Foreign Policy." *South Asian Journal of Peacebuilding* 3(2): 1–10.
Hebbar, Nistula. (2016). "We Will Seal Bangla Border Says BJP." *The Hindu*, March 26. (http://www.thehindu.com/todays-paper/tp-national/we-will-seal-bangla-border-says-bjp/article8397879.ece) (Downloaded: March 28, 2016).
Human Rights Watch. (2010). "'Trigger Happy': Excessive Use of Force by Indian Troops at the Bangladeshi Border." December. New York: Human Rights Watch.
Hussain, Monirul. (1994). *The Assam Movement: Class, Ideology and Identity*. New Delhi: Manak Publications Private Limited.
Hussain, Wasbir. (2004). "Demographic Jitters." *The Outlook*, September 20. (http://www.out lookindia.com/website/story/demographic-jitters/225190) (Downloaded: May 12, 2014).
Jayal, Nirha Gopal. (2013). *Citizenship and Its Discontents: An Indian History*. Cambridge, MA: Harvard University Press.
Krishna, Sankaran. (1997). "Cartographic Anxiety: Mapping the Body Politic in India." In John Agnew (ed.), *Political Geography: A Reader*, 81–92. New York: Arnold.
Krishna, Sankaran (1999). *Postcolonial Insecurities: India, Sri Lanka and the Question of Nationhood*. Minneapolis: University of Minnesota Press.
Mander, Harsh. (2008). "Nellie: India's Forgotten Massacre." *The Hindu*, December 14. (http://www.thehindu.com/thehindu/mag/2008/12/14/stories/2008121450100300.htm) (Downloaded: March 30, 2013).
Mullan, C.S. (1931). *Census of India, 1931, Volume III, Assam Part I – Report*. Calcutta: Assam Govt. Press.
Nath, B.K., D.C. Nath and B. Bhattachaya. (2012). "Undocumented Migration in the State of Assam in North East India: Estimates since 1971 to 2001." *Asian Journal of Applied Sciences* 5: 164–173.
Nath, H.K. (2010). "Illegal Migration to Assam: Magnitude, Causes, and Economic Consequences." *SHSU Economics and International Business Working Paper* No.1006, December.
Pandey, Gyanendra. (2006). *Routine Violence: Nations, Fragments, Histories*. Stanford: Stanford University Press.
Rao, Mohan. (2010). "On Saffron Demography." *Economic and Political Weekly* 45(41): 27–29.
Roy, Haimanti. (2012). *Partitioned Lives: Migrants, Refugees, Citizens in India and Pakistan, 1947–65*. New Delhi: Oxford University Press.

Roychoudhury, Anil. (1981). "National Register of Citizens, 1951." *Economic and Political Weekly* 16(8): 287–288.

Saikia, Yasmin. (2012). "In the Beginning Was a Loaded Word: How Can Human Being be 'Illegal'? How the Language of Dehumanisation is Fuelling the Assam Crisis." *The Outlook*, September 17. (http://www.outlookindia.com/magazine/story/in-the-beginning-was-the-loaded-word/282211) (Downloaded: October 12, 2013).

Samaddar, Ranabir. (1999). *The Marginal Nation: Transborder Migration from Bangladesh to West Bengal*. New Delhi: Sage.

Sengupta, Uttam. (2012). "Census Figures Nix Illegal Migration Theory." *The Outlook*, August 27. (http://www.outlookindia.com/magazine/story/census-figures-nix-illegal-migration-theory/282004) (Downloaded: March 14, 2014).

Shamshad, Rizwana. (2008). "Politics and Origin of the India–Bangladesh Border Fence." Paper presented at the 17th Biennial Conference of the Asian Studies Association of Australia in Melbourne, July 1–3, 2008. (http://artsonline.monash.edu.au/mai/files/2012/07/rizwanashamshad.pdf) (Downloaded: May 4, 2013).

Sinha, S.K. (1998). "Report on Illegal Migration into Assam." South Asia Portal for Terrorism, November 8. (http://www.satp.org/satporgtp/countries/india/states/assam/documents/papers/illegal_migration_in_assam.htm) (Downloaded: March 11, 2012).

The Assam Tribune. (2015). "2011 Census Data May Create Political Storm." August 26. (http://www.assamtribune.com/aug2715/at050.txt) (Downloaded: August 28, 2015).

The Daily Star. (2011). "Manush Manusher Jonne." November 11. (http://archive.thedailystar.net/newDesign/news-details.php?nid=209592) (Downloaded: November 10, 2013).

The Hindu. (2012a). "Deleting Assam Voters on Religious Basis Not Possible: Centre Tells SC." August 10. (http://www.thehindu.com/news/national/deleting-assam-voters-on-religion) (Downloaded: March 10, 2014).

The Hindu. (2012b). "Shinde Reviews Border Guarding Measures." October 21. (http://www.thehindu.com/news/national/shinde-reviews-border-guarding) (Downloaded: June 15, 2013).

The Hindu. (2015). "No Non-Lethal Strategy on Borders." April 2 (http://m.thehindu.com/news/national/rajnath-visits-bangladesh-border/article7058004.ece/) (Downloaded: April 3, 2015).

The Sentinel. (2013). "Hindu Refugees from B'desh will be Given Citizenship." December 3. (http://www.sentinelassam.com/mainnews/story.php?sec=1&subsec=0&id=177049&dtP=2013-12-03&ppr=1#177049) (Downloaded: December 2, 2014).

The Sentinel (2014). "2011 Census Figures for Assam Ring Alarm Bells for the Indigenous People." September 11. (http://www.sentinelassam.com/editorial/story.php?sec=3&subsec=0&id=160099&dtP=2013-05-26&ppr=1) (Downloaded: September 12, 2014).

Upadhyaya, Priyankar. (2013). "Securitization Matrix in South Asia: Bangladeshi Migrants as Enemy Alien." Consortium of Non-Traditional Security Studies in India. (http://www.rsis-ntsasia.org/resources/publications/research-papers/migration/Priyankar%20Upadhyaya.pdf) (Downloaded: June 22, 2013).

Vyas, Neena. (2011). "Enrol Bangladeshi Hindus as voters: BJP." *The Hindu*, January 4. (http://www.thehindu.com/news/enrol-bangladeshi-hindus-as-voters-bjp/article1030359.ece) (Downloaded: June 24, 2013).

Weiner, Myron. (1993). "Political Demography of Assam's Anti Immigrant Movement." *Population and Development Review* 9(2): 279–292.

Zee News. (2014). "783 Porous Stretches, 149 Gaps Along International Borders: Govt." December 12. (http://zeenews.india.com/news/india/783-porous-stretches-149-gaps-along-international-borders-govt_1512561.html) (Downloaded: December 15, 2014).

PART II
History

5

THE NATION-STATE PROBLEMATIC

South Asia's experience

Binoda K. Mishra

Historically, political systems in South Asia have been territorial states but without nationalities or nationalism. The concepts of nation and nationalism arrived only recently in the region, and like every other imported concept, they are heavily loaded with modern/Western characteristics. In the absence of a suitable socio-economic base, these concepts have created conflicts that seem unending even now.

Nation-building in South Asia is a story of adaptation to alien values by prudent political elites. In the name of modernization, they have asked South Asians to relinquish traditional values in favor of Western ones that were projected as rational and the only way to a better socio-political future. Post-independence elites felt they had little choice. For the sake of political expediency, colonial masters had previously dissected the region's societies into compartments, thereby debasing a composite nationhood that was endogenous to the Indian subcontinent.[1]

Colonial dissection began as early as 1822 through divide and rule. In a systematic manner, the British demarcated nationalist feelings into religious lines. Landmarks of this endeavor included the partition of Bengal in 1905, the introduction of communal suffrage in 1909, the introduction of separate electorates in 1919, and the final act of partition of the subcontinent along religious lines in 1947. Still, these acts of partition failed to create viable homogeneous nation-states, and produced, instead, permanent fissures that had the potential to split the subcontinent apart.

The notion of a modern nation-state in the subcontinent did receive resistance. It came from within the region's two major religious communities: Hindus and Muslims. Rabindranath Tagore and Muhammad Iqbal, two leading poets and philosophers of late-colonial India, criticized the notion of a modern nation-state. To them, it served as the root cause for conflict on the subcontinent. Homogenous nationalism, they rightly felt, did not suit the socio-political consciousness of the people of South Asia. Having seen the perilous effects of nationalism in other parts of the world, Tagore denounced nationalism as a destructive force, one that could destroy Indian civilization. In turn, Iqbal blamed the Western notion of nationalism for creating a modern conflict on the subcontinent. Not only did nationalism make religion relative rather than universal but it also tied religion to territory. None of these characteristics suited the historical and cultural temperament of the region.

However, religion ultimately divided South Asia. Two infant nations set out to build viable, modern states but irreconcilable problems threatened then – and threaten still today – the viability of the state and the unity of the nation. India's national leadership hoped to capitalize on the nationalist fever that swept the country during the independence movement. Pakistan's leadership sought religious nationalism as the basis for a strong and united statehood. But both nations struggled to build their desired nation-states. A primary threat came from the question of "ethnicity": that is, a multiplicity of nationalities, their overlapping geographical boundaries, and the failure to articulate a common identity.

Let us look at each in turn.

Multiplicity of nationalities

Many had hoped that the process of nation-building would be smooth, with both India and Pakistan adopting representative forms of government. The independence movement in India was called the "nationality" movement to underscore the national unity of the Indian state. Similar terminology was used in Pakistan for creating an Islamic nation. But as soon as the partition took effect, social fissures started widening and a web of nationalities appeared, not only in multi-cultural, multi-lingual, and multi-ethnic India but also in Pakistan's so-called homogeneous state. Within 25 years of its being founded, Pakistan proved to be a non-viable nation as much as a non-viable state.

Linguistic nationalism challenged Pakistan's religious nationalism. The Bengali-speaking majority of East Pakistan asserted their right to "Bengali" linguistic nationalism. Interestingly, this linguistic nationalism shared borders with the Islamic community but did not accept the Bengali-speaking Hindu population of either India or Eastern Pakistan. Bangladesh (meaning "Bengali-speaking people") emerged to set a precedence of secession by nations from nation-states; it showed no interest in taking within its fold the country's numerous Indian Bengalis. In a theoretical sense, one can call Bangladesh an assertion of sub-nationality within the larger nationality of South Asian Islamic nationhood.

India also saw the rise of linguistic nationalism. India's leadership was alarmed at the prospect of linguistic nationalism escalating into crisis proportions that could threaten the Indian union. But the problem stopped short of crisis proportions when individual states reorganized along linguistic lines in 1956. They had learned an essential lesson: communities in India needed to create their own linguistic nationalities *within* Indian statehood. Put differently, India's peoples could not come to terms with an overarching Indian national identity.

Even now, geographical, ethnic, and religious identities pose a fierce challenge. Linguistically organized states, ethnically composed north-eastern states, not to mention occasional Sikh nationalism, constantly raise the appeal of secession. These challenges expose a lack of congruity between political and national identities, not that the region's ethnic identities are always well-articulated. But the mere fact that local communities often present themselves in binary opposition to the national state demonstrates other, more primordial identities that prefer to be recognized outside of India's national polity.

These ethno(primordial)-nationalist movements are not unique to India. Rather, these feature in all South Asian countries. Some identities cross state boundaries, accounting for inter-state conflicts. India and Pakistan fighting over Kashmir and Bangladesh serve as cases in point. Elsewhere, ethnic conflicts internal to the political systems of South Asian states include the Mohajir movement; the Sindh, Pukhtun, and Baloch problems in Pakistan; the Chakma problem in Bangladesh; and violent Tamil separatism in Sri Lanka. They may differ in objectives but share in one fundamental principle: challenge the sovereignty of their *national* political systems. In India, for example, the Northeast alone is home to 36 major or minor ethnic nationalist movements. The rise of Hindu nationalism further weakens India's political nationalism. Bhutan, a kingdom in the sub-continent, suffers similar pressures from an exclusive ethno-nationalism. The Drupka community aims to turn Bhutan into a "mono-ethnic polity" (Chatterjee 2005: 83). Nepal has not seen ethnic conflict as such but ethnic representation in the constituent assembly points towards a sensitivity between local, ethnic identities and a national, Nepalese one. Most groups in Nepal, including the Newars, Tamangs, Magars, Gurung, Sherpa, Limbu, Rai and Tharu, do not accept the label of "ethnic groups" or "minorities." They prefer to be called nations and believe they fulfill all the relevant criteria: language, religion, culture, territory, and a history of independent statehood – which they would achieve (again) if granted the right to secede.

The nation-state model cannot accommodate South Asia's growing number and intensity of ethno-nationalist assertions and conflicts. The problem persists not only because multiple nationalities exist in South Asia but also due to an incongruity between the social and geographical markers of these identities.

Overlapping boundaries

There is no consensus on the definition of an ethnic group or ethnic community. But a working definition helps to provide a basis for identifying ethno-nationalism. An ethnic group is defined as:

> Either a large or small group of people, in either backward or advanced societies, who are united by a common inherited culture (including language, music, food, dress and customs and practices), racial similarity, common religion, and the belief in common history and ancestry and who exhibit a strong psychological sentiment of belonging to the group.
>
> *(Ganguly and Taras 1998: 9)*

This definition categorizes ethnic communities into one of two types: *homeland societies* and *diaspora communities* (Phanis and Ganguly 2001). Given the long history of inland migration within South Asia, none of the above-mentioned criteria could remain in a geographically compact area. Most ethnic groups or communities are dispersed within the region. Exceptions to this general rule are the Maldives, to some extent Sri Lanka's Tamils, and north-eastern India's ethnic communities who share a fairly compact geographical location. Such amalgamations of various identities make it difficult to pinpoint nationalities and their potential to threaten the state's politically constructed national identity. One can argue that had there been congruous geographies to each of these ethnic identities, the present political system would have failed long ago or would not have been created in the first place. From this perspective, this amalgamation seems conducive to the evolution of a nation as defined by Ernst Barker. He stated in 1927:

> A nation is a body of men, inhabiting a definite territory, who normally are drawn from different races, but possess a common stock of thoughts and feelings acquired and transmitted during the course of a common history; who on the whole and in the main, thought more in the past than in the present, include in that common stock a common religious belief; who generally and as a rule use a common language as the vehicle of their thoughts and feelings; and who, besides common thoughts and feelings, also cherish a common will, and accordingly form or tend to form, a separate state for the expression and realisation of that will.
>
> *(Barker quoted in Phanis and Ganguly 2001: 19–20)*

Given that minorities in excess of 5 percent of their total population occupy 90 percent of states in the world, every state can be considered multi-ethnic. Yet not all of these states experience national assertions within their political boundaries. Some plausible explanations for the harmonious coexistence of multiple ethnicities in multi-ethnic states are the inland diasporic nature of the nationalities, the overwhelming presence of the majority ethnic community, and the proper assimilation of ethnic communities into the constructed national identity of the political system.[2] Problems of ethno-nationalities challenging political nationalities seem to appear primarily in societies where the political system – the state – has failed to articulate a national identity that either accommodates the various nationalities or makes it preferable for the population vis-à-vis their local, exclusivist identities.

Failure of articulations

Since most nation-states are artificial creations, the political system must constantly re-constitute itself. Methods adopted by nation-states to invigorate the spirit of nationalism vary with the state's social geography, the nature of local communities, and the nature of the government in charge. According to O'Leary (2001), regimes generally adopt one of two approaches – negative and positive – to eliminate and/or manage differences among local nationalities. Genocide and ethnic expulsion can eliminate differences, as seen in the case of Nazi Germany. Alternatively, ruling elites could apply forms of secession, decolonization, or partition. Other tactics include arbitration and federalism (O'Leary 2001). Irrespective of method, the ruling regime aims to subsume all local, primordial identities into an overarching national identity.

In South Asia, all the methods mentioned above have been adopted to some degree at some point in the process of nation-building. The partition of the Indian subcontinent and the further partition of Pakistan, the systematic assault on the Chakmas in Bangladesh, the federal features in the Indian constitution, the attempts of imposing Sinhalese ethnic hegemony in Sri Lanka, the recent resolve to turn Nepal into a federation, and the expulsion of Nepalese from Bhutan all exemplify attempts at creating a homogeneous (mono-ethnic) nation-state out of multi-ethnic states. Needless to say, all of these methods have failed or backfired. Ethnic cleansing is neither practical nor morally acceptable in most South Asian countries given their democratic structures and long tradition of "inter-communal"[3] comity. But due to the multiplicity in identity and their geographical overlaps, federalism on the basis of "natural nationalities" is also not workable, either. Moreover, identity formation keeps changing in South Asia. The question of nationality thus remains fluid for regimes, causing difficulties in effectively controlling potentially threatening nationalities. Neither does secession offer an answer. Where it has taken place, secession still cannot redress the absence of congruity between natural nationalities and territorial borders.

South Asia's amalgamated natural nationalities and tradition of inter-communal comity *should* present ruling regimes with the best opportunity to construct a national political identity. But, on the contrary, South Asian states periodically suffer from assertions of natural nationalities. The question is why political systems have failed to articulate an inclusive national identity to which all citizens could willingly accept instead of their natural nationalities? Many blame the subcontinent's former colonial masters. But this is inadequate.

We need to examine the nature of the state. How has it tried to articulate a national political identity? How has the state sought to include local nationalities into an overarching, national identity? Two approaches − structural and distributive − have marked the state's response to these questions in South Asia (Phanis and Ganguly 2001). The structural approach does not address the ethnic question specifically; whereas, the distributive approach aims to complement the structural approach by integrating natural nationalities into the national political identity.

In India, the distributive approach has included strategies such as improving secularism and protecting minority rights. The classical concept of secularism that implies a division of jurisprudence between the temporal and spiritual spheres was modified to allow the regime in charge to create provisions for the minor religious nationalities. The objective was to reassure religious minorities that their nationalities are guaranteed within the larger polity. For example, the Indian political system has sought to consolidate a national political identity by providing extra resources for education for minority groups, economic preferences for "backward" social categories, and political representation for the same.

Pakistan, for its part, had a relatively easy task: its nation was created on the basis of a Muslim identity. But cultural diversity required reformulating this national identity. In the initial period after independence, Pakistan debated two strategies: 1) to create an Islamic nation based on Islam that would accommodate other nationalities according to provisions prescribed by the Quran and Shariat; and 2) to promote a Pakistani nationality that would subsume all nationalities. However, Pakistan has not been able to create a consensus around the nature of Islamization and this strategy has often evoked violent reactions. Pakistan has turned to federalism to manage the issue of cultural diversity. But the country's periodic lapses into dictatorship have turned federalism into an unacceptable form of power concentration among a few elites, thereby causing more (sub)nationals to assert themselves.

Bangladesh has also used Islam as a tool of national identity formation, though stopping short of Pakistan's approach; nevertheless Bangladesh's shift from the Indian model of secularism towards a religious nationalism has certainly created more problems than its positive effect of uniting the nation. For instance, Islamization alienates the non-Muslim population of Bangladesh, the Hindus and the Buddhist Chakmas. The Hindus have adopted constitutional and political methods to redress their grievances but the Chakmas have turned to violence. This problem remains ongoing for Bangladesh.

Sri Lanka conceals its majoritarian domination. The regime in charge has adopted constitutional methods to ensure minority representation but distributive mechanisms ensure its marginalization. The Sri Lankan regime has also adopted some positive strategies like secularism and ethnic electoral federalism. But such strategies have been trumped by other discriminatory distributive strategies and the dynamics of competitive electoral politics to ensure Sinhalese dominance over Tamils.

Nepal's ruling regime has included most of its natural nationalities under Hinduism. Those left out of this identity were allowed to practice their own identities under a national Nepali identity. A single language, Khas (Nepali), was adopted as the official language to project a concrete image of Nepali unity. Nonetheless, Nepal has felt the pressure of local nationalities resisting an overarching Nepali nationality, even though no major ethnic fissures have yet to emerge. The new Republic of Nepal has attempted to make fresh attempts at developing a national identity. Provisions for ethnic representation and plans for creating a federation are steps in that regard.

Bhutan seems to have managed the problem of nationalities better than most South Asian states. Two primary ethnic groups populate Bhutan: Bhutanese and Nepalis. Some worry that Nepalis are trying to replace Bhutanese in positions of majority and power. The kingdom has squelched such concerns by imposing restrictions on the movement of Nepalis. At the same time, Bhutan's government has embarked on a strategy of inclusion by adopting a method of proportional representation. In this way, official positions would absorb Nepalis, thereby encouraging social alliances between the two communities.

The nearly homogeneous Maldives has had no problem of nationality but regionalism is emerging as a problem. After the withdrawal of the British from the Addu atoll, a problem of geographical nationalism seemed to arise. But the regime in charge has adopted a strategy of development to lure the population of the Addu atoll into the national mainstream.

Conclusion

The process of nation-building in South Asia is still ongoing. Both optimistic and pessimistic conclusions can be drawn. According to analysts like Gellner (1983: 50–52), South Asia's nationalistic assertions resemble what the industrialized West went through when it transitioned from the "low cultures" of agro-literate societies to the "high cultures" of modernization through industrialization. But one essential feature differentiates the two processes: the West's transformation consolidated nation-states, whereas, in South Asia, this transition has led to social and political instability. Primordial, "low cultures" not only perpetually fight against the "high culture" of the state but they also fight among themselves. Even in the West, nationalism alone cannot arouse feelings of a national community. It rests, rather, on demonstrating success as a collective unit. Reinforced by a territorial sovereignty, these feelings can create a successful nation-state.

A most important question arises: is the concept of a nation-state inappropriate for South Asia? Or to put it differently, is modernity with nationalism (with its emphasis on homogeneity) preventing an articulation of national identity that is congruent with the aspirations of local populations within the national polity? By any analysis, nationalism evolved in the West. Its development in South Asia, in contrast, came through emulation more than evolution. The leaders of the freedom movements in South Asia had a notion of nationalism that was firmly grounded on the territorial connotation of the nation-state and the statist ideals inherited form their colonial masters in the West (Smith 1998). The political units of South Asia qualify as nations only if we take Anthony Giddens' definition of a nation. He defines a nation as a "collectivity existing within a clearly defined territory, which is subject to a unitary administration, reflexively monitored both by the internal state apparatus and those of other states" (Giddens 1985: 116). He further suggests that nationalism is a psychological phenomenon, which is evident from "the affiliation of individuals to a set of symbols and beliefs emphasizing commonality among the members of a political order" (ibid.).

South Asia as a socio-political space did not and does not have the requisite socio-economic infrastructure to build on and hold the West's definition of a political superstructure. Does that make South Asia an ancient or traditional state? There is no simple answer to this question. A probable alternative could be the creation of an accommodative political structure that would give space to traditional institutions as agents of modernization.

One can argue that South Asia's post-colonial nation-states have survived for more than half a century (with one secession only), thus providing sufficient evidence of a functioning civic nationalism. Mere survival, however, does not a nation-state make. The essential measure of a modern nation-state lies in its ability to fulfill its basic functions as a representative government or democracy.

Under colonialism, the people of South Asia had only one basis to unite and that was the "will" to belong to one nation. This "will" prevailed over all the other criteria of group formation. Since independence, however, has this will been lost? Or have the people decided to revert to more primordial nationalities?

South Asia's experience with nation-building exposes the weaknesses in the concept of nationalism. This raises another key question: is nationalism an essential feature that every state must possess? To address this question, however, requires another project – for which I will have to leave to another occasion.

Notes

1 See Chatterjee (1994) on the various components of nationhood under the construct of "fragment," though his categorization is not exhaustive. Many more components can be identified to constitute a nation in the subcontinent. Nation in this context certainly transcends the identity of such components and fragments.
2 In most cases, particularly in Asia and Africa, state-building preceded nation-building, making the state's national identity not as natural as its ethnic nationalities.
3 The term "communal" here is used to refer to groupings that could be formed along various identities.

References

Chatterjee, Partha. (1994) *The Nation and its Fragments: Colonial and Postcolonial Histories*. New Delhi: Oxford University Press.
Chatterjee, Shibashis. (2005) "Ethnic Conflicts in South Asia: A Constructivist Reading" *South Asian Survey* 12(1): 75–88.
Ganguly, Rajat and Ray Taras. (1998) *Understanding Ethnic Conflict: The International Dimension*. New York: Addison Wesley Longman.
Gellner, Ernest. (1983) *Nations and Nationalism*. Oxford: Basil Blackwell.
Giddens, Anthony. (1985) *The Nation-State and Violence*. Cambridge: Polity Press.
O'Leary, Brendan. (2001) "Introduction" and "The Elements of Right-Sizing and Right Peopling of State" In Brendan O'Leary, I. S. Lustick and T. Callaghy (eds), *Right-Sizing the State: The Politics of Moving Borders*, pp. 1–14, 15–73. Oxford: Oxford University Press.
Phanis, Urmila and Rajat Ganguly. (2001) *Ethnicity and Nation-Building in South Asia* (revised edition). New Delhi: Sage Publications.
Smith, Anthony D. (1998) *Nationalism and Modernism*. London: Routledge.

6

THE DIAOYUTAI/SENKAKU ISLANDS DISPUTE

An ethos of appropriateness and China's "Loss" of Ryukyu[1]

Ching-Chang Chen

Why are China and Japan in war-like hostilities over a clutch of eight tiny, uninhabited islets in the Western Pacific?[2] They have little to no strategic and/or economic value.[3] Yet these islets, named the Senkaku Islands in Japanese and the Diaoyu Islands in Chinese, have embroiled the region like no other.[4] In September 2012, the Japanese government purchased the islets outright from their private landlord. This move, in turn, triggered a series of large-scale anti-Japanese demonstrations in major Chinese cities, a slump in Japanese exports to China and in Chinese tourists to Japan, and frequent appearances of Chinese petrol vessels and aircraft in surrounding waters and airspace.[5] In April 2013, China's Ministry of Foreign Affairs referred to the Diaoyus for the first time as part of China's "core interests," a term normally associated with "rogue" territories like Xinjiang, Tibet, and Taiwan.[6]

To understand this puzzle, I submit, we need to turn to Sino-Japanese relations *before* Westphalia. It sets the context for the current Senkaku/Diaoyutai Islands dispute. Close inquiry reveals that an *ethos of appropriateness* guided ruling elites in the region.[7] It accounts for the Qing Dynasty's apparent passivity when, in the 1870s, Meiji Japan annexed the Ryukyu Kingdom, which later became Okinawa Prefecture and ruled over the Senkaku/Diaoyutai Islands. This ethos of appropriateness considered whether state actions were legitimate given the nature of international society in East Asia at the time: that is, the tribute system. It formalized a relational hierarchy with China at the center and highest while all subordinate states descended in rank order according to familiarity with Confucian norms and practices. Relative power (including territorial possessions) did not figure in this ethos. Rather, the hierarchy's legitimacy required a credible commitment on the part of the dominant state not to exploit subordinate ones (Kang 2010). To coerce Japan to give up Ryukyu or divide up the kingdom would have violated this key aspect of status in East Asia's international hierarchy. It would have entailed, in other words, a far greater cost: loss of China's moral authority as the center of the Confucian world order.

This chapter proceeds in three sections. To understand identities and interests in the region, the first section examines the constitutional structures and institutions of East Asian international society before the arrival of Western powers. In the second section, I draw on primary Chinese sources to trace how Qing officials debated various options regarding the Ryukyu crisis. Here, Li Hongzhang's (1823–1901) rationale prevailed: China should not, he argued, "take advantage of a just cause for one's own benefit" (*yishi lizhong*). The concluding section discusses the implications of this study for understanding international society, in general, and contemporary Sino-Japanese territorial disputes, in particular.

International society outside Europe: The case of East Asia

I begin by disputing Martin Wight's (1979) famous categorization of the Sinocentric world order as the product of a "suzerain system" rather than an international society. For this reason, I use the term "East Asian international society" deliberately. Given that only two major wars broke out in this part of the world from the founding of the Ming dynasty (1368) to the Opium War (1839–42), mere "chance" cannot explain how East Asian countries could maintain their "long peace" nor that this impressive stability only reflected a power asymmetry between China and its neighbors (Buzan and Little 2000).

As Shogo Suzuki (2009) has shown, the constitutional structures of East Asian international society involved three normative dimensions: (1) the "moral purpose of the state" (reasons for establishing a political entity to serve the common good), (2) the "organizing principle of sovereignty" (which legitimizes the entity's possession of sovereignty), and (3) the "norm of procedural justice" (implementation of the above principles must follow certain procedures). The "moral purpose of the state" sought to promote social *and* cosmic harmony:[8] it ensued when member states would conform to their "proper" positions within this hierarchical society. The principle of sovereign hierarchy meant that states (both suzerains and vassals) had to perform appropriate Confucian rituals to acknowledge their relative positions (i.e., ritual justice) to gain legitimacy. A tribute system emerged, consequently, as a fundamental institution. Paying tribute to the suzerain, then, was more than an attempt to "buy" security. Tributary relations shaped the identity (and hence interests) of participating members.

Three interrelated points follow. First, in principle, foreign peoples (*yi* or "barbarians") could become a member of this East Asian international society or even part of the "middle kingdom," if they participated in the totality of Confucian civilization. This included all facets beyond tributary protocol such as food, dress, language, rituals, and so on. Second, while member states competed for the highest possible positions in this international society, a state could run the risk of "demotion" or even lose its membership should it fail to perform the necessary rituals pertinent to its proper place in the hierarchical order. Third, although China normally assumed the role of the "middle kingdom" at the apex of this order, it was also possible for other states to assert their "superior" moral status and demonstrate their ability to promote social harmony by constructing their own alternative, non-Sinocentric tribute system (Hamashita 1997; Suzuki 2009).

"Civilization" grounded this East Asian international society.[9] According to D.R. Howland (1996), Chinese conceptions of civilization (*wenming*) consisted of three elements. First, *wenming* literally meant a desired state of human society made luminous (*ming*) through writing or "patterning" (*wen*). The world was *wenming* when all was in harmony and there was no need to resort to military subjugation (*wugong*). The emperor, as the "Son of Heaven," embodied this ideal stage of virtuous leadership. Second, any individual (but usually a man) was *wenming* or "civilizing" when patterning his behavior in accordance with Confucian expectations. This meant submitting to his rightful lord (*jun*), whether through a father–son or master–servant relationship. Civilization, in short, signified a "spatially expansive and ideologically infinite" process of Chinese imperial lordship (Howland 1996: 14).[10] Third, individuals approximate moral behavior in proportion to their physical and/or spiritual proximity to the emperor. His benevolence would bring the people closer and cherish them. With the emperor at the center of this concentric and hierarchical world order, various regional bureaucratic offices instantiated it with imperial envoys traveling to and from the capital. "Outside" peoples, moreover, would respond to the realm's imperial virtue by sending tribute missions to the court. Tributary relations thus represented an act of reciprocity through which outsiders accepted the *nominal* lordship of the Son of Heaven and his calendar; in turn, Chinese investiture legitimized the foreign ruler and his domain.

These norms and institutions account for China's response to Japan's incorporation of Ryukyu during the 1870s. As Hamashita (1997: 8–9) has noted, one cannot assume that East Asian international society collapsed *completely* after the intrusion of Western powers:

> Considering the fact that the history of East Asian international relations was founded upon the principle of a tributary relationship sustainable for over a thousand years, it is difficult to assume that its demise could be brought about by a single event, such as the Opium War … Rather, it is conceivably more acceptable to view it as a demise that was caused by internal change within the tribute system itself.

In this regard, the Ryukyu Kingdom's demise signaled a first step towards change in the Confucian world order. It prepared the ground for a region-wide adoption of norms and institutions originated in European international society. The next section will illustrate this change: it led to rising Sino-Japanese rivalry in the following decades.

Extinguishment of the Ryukyu Kingdom and China's response

In the nineteenth century, Japan sought to become a member of Europe's international society in order to survive it. East Asia's tributary states system with its ritualistic, hierarchical Confucian norms became increasingly hard to tolerate in the eyes of Meiji leaders and intellectuals alike. Now the West's legal procedural norms would replace the East's ritualistic procedural norms. This places tributary states in a dilemma: either turn into a sovereign independent state or be absorbed by one.

The Ryukyu Kingdom's ambiguous status as a part of Japan *and* China's tributary state system not only embarrassed the Meiji government but also posed a threat.

> The Ryukyu Kingdom's participation in the Tribute System could potentially highlight Japan's inability to conform [to] international law, and consequently its lack of commitment to fully join the international order as defined by European International Society. This would, in turn, jeopardize Japan's quest to attain the status of a "civilized" power as defined by the members of European International Society.
>
> *(Suzuki 2009: 155)*

Japan's subsequent move to abolish the kingdom accomplished two goals. It underscored a realist act of securing its southern periphery and it demonstrated the Meiji government's commitment to attaining membership in the European society of states. The move was an incremental one. In 1872, Japan's foreign ministry recognized the Ryukyu king Sho Tai as "lord of the Ryukyu fief" and took over the kingdom's treaty and diplomatic matters. This was followed by Japan's success in getting China to admit that the former's 1874 expedition to punish "Taiwanese savages" was a "just act" to redress the murder of *Japanese citizens*.[11] In 1875, Japan's home ministry abolished the kingdom's trading mission in Fuzhou and prohibited the kingdom from sending tributary envoys to, and receiving investiture from, China.

This move escalated into a Sino-Japanese diplomatic crisis in 1877. When Chinese officials received secret petitions from Ryukyuan envoys to protest their domination by Japan, they sent memorials to the court. From these documents, we learn that Chinese officials were fully aware of the geopolitical/geostrategic implications of this tributary state's demise and the Qing court's lack of satisfactory policy options. Viceroy of Fujian-Zhejiang and Fuzhou General He Jing, for instance, did not consider Ryukyu in itself crucial to China. But he was keenly aware of the consequences of failing to protect the islands from foreign intrusions. He suggested that the Qing court should take advantage of the Satsuma Rebellion current in Japan at the time, and apply diplomatic pressure on the Meiji government to deal with the dispute in accordance with international law (Qing Grand Council 1963, vol. 1: 21). Diplomat Huang Zunxian warned in an essay, "On the Liuqiu [Ryukyu] Affair" (*Lun liu shi shu*), that tolerating Japan's actions would amount to "feeding a tiger which China can no longer rein in":

> [G]iven Liuqiu's proximity to Taiwan, it would not be possible to maintain even one peaceful night in Taiwan and Penghu should Japan establish

exclusive control over Liuqiu, turn it into a prefecture, train its soldiers and arm them to harass China's periphery.

(quoted in Wu 1980, vol. 8: 3–4)

The Chinese Minister to Japan He Ruzhang predicted that the Japanese would not only prevent Ryukyu from sending tribute but also seek to eliminate the kingdom. After that, they would turn to Korea. To pre-empt Japan's expansion, He presented three options to the court: his first and best solution was to dispatch warships (*bing chuan*) to demand Ryukyu's resumption of tribute missions while negotiating with Japan. The second was that, when persuasion failed, China could support Ryukyu's armed resistance with auxiliary troops should Japan use force against the Ryukyuans. The third resorted to international law, inviting Western diplomats to condemn the Japanese government (Liang 1986: 116). He Ruzhang admitted that China was not in good shape to use force, but he still recommended the first two options. His rationale: "Japan's recent situation [the Satsuma Rebellion of 1877] was even worse than ours" (quoted in Liang 1986: 117).

China's foreign ministry, *Zongli yamen*, decided not to engage in coercive diplomacy against Japan. China's concurrent dispute with Russia in Xinjiang was a factor, but that could not motivate the all-powerful Viceroy of Zhili and Minister of Beiyang, Li Hongzhang, to embattle the troubled Meiji government. His purpose was not simply to appease Tokyo or to prevent Japan from leaning towards Russia. Despite the Qing officials' increasing realization that Meiji leaders would yield only to (European) international law or superior military might (a necessary instrument of any "civilized" state in the age of imperialism), Li appeared to believe in what "ought to be done" for China – and that was to pursue harmonious intercourse with Japan (*jiaoji zhong yinyozhiyi*) (Wu 1980, vol. 7: 3–4). Li even offered 100,000 rifle bullets from the Tianjin Arsenal to the troubled Meiji government as a gesture of goodwill.

Prince Gong, head of the *Zongli yamen*, sent a letter in 1879 to Shishido Tamaki, then Japanese Minister to China. The letter used the language of Western international law yet continued to embrace the constitutional structures of East Asian international society. Prince Gong emphasized the significance of Sino-Ryukyuan tributary relations and Chinese investiture while acknowledging the Ryukyu Kingdom's status as a "double tributary state" (Japanese Ministry of Foreign Affairs 1949: 178–179). He repeatedly stressed that Ryukyu was part of China *and* recognized as an independent state by all countries (*Liuqiu jiwei Zhongguo bin geguo renqi ziwei yiguo*); accordingly, the kingdom's abolition breached Article 1 of the Sino-Japanese Friendship Treaty (which stipulated that their respective territories should be "treated with propriety") and international law (Japanese Ministry of Foreign Affairs 1949). Moreover, Prince Gong lamented, Japan should have protected, not subsumed, a "weak and small" state like the Ryukyu Kingdom. Here, Prince Gong implied that Japan had violated the "moral purpose of the state," which was to promote cosmic harmony in East Asia's international society.

Shishido countered in Westphalian terms. It was not possible, he stated in response, for the Ryukyuans to be subjects of Japan and China at the same time.

The islands could be an independent state *or* part of one; the two possibilities were mutually exclusive. Shishido effectively refuted the relevance of Chinese investiture by declaring the Ryukyu "fief" to be a domestic matter only. In this way, Meiji Japan rejected the Confucian world order's ritual justice in favor of the Westphalian world order's legislative justice.

A turning point in this dialogue of the deaf came when former US President Ulysses S. Grant visited China and Japan in mid-1879. Grant agreed to mediate the dispute at the request of Li Hongzhang and Prince Gong, and offered the services of American diplomats in Japan. They proposed dividing the Ryukyu Islands into three parts: the central part would belong to the residual Ryukyu Kingdom protected by both Chinese and Japanese consuls; the southern part, since close to Taiwan, would belong to China; and the northern part, close to Satsuma (Kagoshima), would belong to Japan (Wang 1963: 21).

The Japanese government agreed to negotiate. But Meiji officials demanded that China recognize that the Okinawa main island and above belonged to Japan – even though the Miyako and Yaeyama Islands would belong to China, as proposed by Grant – and the 1871 Treaty of Trade and Friendship would be revised to allow Japan to enjoy the same privileges granted to Western powers in China, especially inland trade. The *Zongli yamen* agreed in October 1880: this compromise could help preserve the Ryukyu Kingdom while discouraging Japan from turning to the Russians.

However, Li Hongzhang objected at the last minute. The two parties never ratified the agreement and it was forfeited in January 1881. What happened? Speculations abound. Some Chinese historians suggest that the Qing's concurrent negotiations with Russia on Xinjiang convinced Li not to make such a big concession to Japan over the Ryukyu question (Shi 2006). Others suspect that "inter-agency rivalry" played a part, for Li was in charge of signing the 1871 treaty but not involved in its revision (Liang 1986). But let us look at Li's reasoning in his own words.

In his memorial to the emperor, Li made two main points to "postpone" (*yandang*) the Ryukyu question: (1) the Ryukyuan elite would not agree to reducing their kingdom to Miyako and Yaeyama, which were relatively impoverished (and historically peripheral), and it would be too expensive for China to station troops there; and (2) granting inland rights to Japan would counter China's interests (Qing Grand Council 1963, vol. 2: 15–17). Superficially, Li seemed to have based his case on the costs and benefits of not ratifying the agreement. Under scrutiny, however, we see that pure material interest did not drive his decision-making. In fact, the article that gave Japan preferential treatment was *not* the same as that signed in China's unequal treaties with Western powers in the nineteenth century; it required Japan to give China *equivalent* treatment as well (Qing Grand Council 1963, vol. 2: 9–10). Like He Jing and Huang Zunxian, Li was also keenly aware that abandoning those "impoverished" islands to Japan or the West would lead to control of China's Pacific choke points (*e wo taipingyang yanhou, yifei Zhongguo zhili*). The consequences of doing nothing clearly outweighed the costs of administering these islands. Furthermore, Li recognized Japan's fait accompli ever since He Ruzhang called for coercive diplomacy. A wise statesman would have reaped what was left on the negotiating table.

Rather, opposing *yishi lizhong* (starting with a just cause and ending up with satisfying self-interest) accounts for Li's puzzling (in)action. Put differently, Li acted like a traditional Confucian, not a Westphalian politician. His reluctance to allow Japan to enjoy the same benefits as Western powers (*liyi junzhan*) was not because he was worried about Japanese economic penetration into China's inland but because treating Japan like a Western country would not reflect its "proper" place in East Asian international society. Doing so would have disrupted the society's organizing principle. As Howland has noted, the Treaty of Trade and Friendship itself revealed how Japan was placed in an ambivalent position in the eyes of Chinese leaders during the 1870s. Japan was "neither as distant and different as the Westerners, nor as close and commensurate as China's dependencies" (Howland 1996: 35).

An analogy might be useful here. Imagine China as the father in the East Asian family. It prized Ryukyu, like Korea, for resembling the father and its subsequent filial behavior. Japan, a "rogue" member, had forced Ryukyu to pay a "protection fee." With its newly developed muscles trained in Europe, Japan broke into Ryukyu's house and threatened to take Ryukyu's property and life. Astonished, China tried to stop Japan but found that there was little it could do, not necessarily because China could not fight Japan but more because the use of force would expose China's failure to keep the family in harmony. China had almost agreed with its American neighbor's suggestion of dividing up Ryukyu with Japan in order to keep Ryukyu alive. But, in the end, China chose to accept Ryukyu's death rather than undermine its moral authority as the Father.

Later on, Qing officials learned from the Ryukyu fiasco that the normative restraints that had sustained East Asia's international society could no longer apply to a "treacherous" Japan, now an *outsider*. Note diplomat Yao Wendong's assignment to compile a study of Japan's geography upon the arrival of the second Chinese Minister in 1882. Despite his popularity among the major poetry societies in Tokyo and his ability to communicate with his hosts in Japanese, Yao never referred to Japan as a country that shared a common civilization with China (*tong wen zhi guo*). He completed *The Military Essentials of Japanese Geography* (*Riben dili bingyao*) with the express purpose of helping China's military "in case of some unexpected emergency" (Howland 1996: 233). In this sense, the path leading to the Sino-Japanese War (1894–95) over Korea was paved when China "lost" Ryukyu as a member of East Asia's international society.

Conclusion

Westphalian scholars typically cite three reasons for the Qing's apparent inaction regarding the Ryukyu crisis: (1) a declining Qing could not compel a modernizing Japan with military force (Schelling 1966; Christensen 2011) due to (2) China's material inferiority (Johnston 1995; Wang 2011) complicated by (3) the corruption and incompetence of late Qing leaders who could not comprehend China's perils in an age of imperialism (Guo 1996).

Close analysis of Qing reasoning at the time, however, shows a very different ethos at work. It did not sanction China, as the center of the Confucian world order, to lose moral authority by acknowledging Ryukyu's loss to Japan. Furthermore, the Confucian ethos of appropriateness disparaged exploitations of a peripheral member, Japan, at a time when it was weakened by an internal rebellion (Satsuma Rebellion). Indeed, top Chinese officials such as Li Hongzhang were keenly aware of the consequences of their loss. Nonetheless, they feared far more the loss of moral authority as prescribed by East Asia's international society.

The theoretical and policy implications of this analysis are fourfold. First of all, it shows that the failure to "get China right" often has to do with the taken-for-granted assumptions that concepts and theories derived from the European states system and Western experiences are valid across time and space. This chapter's inquiry into the "loss" of Ryukyu indicates that China's strategic behavior was constrained as much by its limited military capabilities as by a normative self-expectation as the paternal figure of the concentric East Asian "family." The Father could not abuse those in the lower ranks of the Cosmic Family. Furthermore, criticizing Qing leaders for failing to defend China's "national interest" as seen through a modern, nationalist lens is both anachronistic and complicit. It justifies the "expansion" of European international society (Bull and Watson 1984) that subjected millions of people to colonialism and imperialism in Asia.

Second, this study challenges IR's myth that international society started with the Peace of Westphalia (1648). Considering that East Asian states had maintained largely peaceful relations within the region for centuries until they were forced to enter into European international society, intellectual production in IR needs to re-imagine the notion of international society (Bilgin 2008; Agathangelou and Ling 2009; Chen 2011; Ling 2014). This should not lead us to a nativist intervention boasting that East Asian international society was superior to Europe's. After all, power relations still prevailed. Rather, the point is that it is imperative for Asians and other non-Western peoples to reclaim their role as co-inventors of international society.

Third, Westphalia complicated the tribute system, not replacing it altogether (Hamashita 1997). Hence, we need to explore how residual rules and norms have shaped today's Westphalian states in East Asia.[12] Finally, since a different worldview underpinned East Asia's international society, calculations of a "power transition" as described in the realist literature cannot account for everything and everyone, across time and space. Indeed, we need to account for differences in knowledge production.

The current IR literature on Sino-Japanese relations tends to focus on either "power" or "interest." This chapter has illustrated, however, how the Ryukyu debacle paved the way for transforming Chinese perceptions of Japan or, to put it differently, how the borders of a once-shared civilization were shifted and reified.

In the early twenty-first-century, it is no easy task to conceive of an alternative, more inclusive bordering practice. Nevertheless, it seems fair to conclude that the Diaoyutai/Senkaku issue is not a uniquely Chinese or Japanese problem. Rather, it is time to reconsider Asian territorial disputes. No victory can emerge without considering the multi-layered nature of contemporary international society.

Notes

1 This chapter first appeared in Chen (2014). Special thanks go to Hitomi Koyama, L.H.M. Ling, and Ming Wan for their valuable comments on this earlier draft. I gratefully acknowledge financial support from the Japan Society for the Promotion of Science, Grant-in-Aid Scientific Research (A) (15H01855) and Young Scientist (B) (16k21495).
2 Hostilities reignited in September 2010 when a Chinese trawler collided with a Japanese Coast Guard patrol boat in waters near the contested islands. For an alternative interpretation of the incident, see Hagström (2012).
3 Any of the islets would be easy to invade and virtually impossible to defend in war. Moreover, possession of the Diaoyus/Senkakus offers no control of the East China Sea. They are too small to affect Sino-Japanese maritime delimitations under international law, even though the islets could serve as legitimate baselines.
4 Taiwan also claims the Diaoyu Islands but has refused to form a united front with the PRC against Japan; its approach to the island dispute has been much less confrontational. See Boyu Chen's chapter in this volume.
5 In January 2013, Chinese warships in the East China Sea allegedly pointed their fire-control radar at a Japanese helicopter and destroyer in close proximity (*Economist*, January 19, 2013).
6 The Chinese Foreign Ministry later modified this reference, broadly defining China's "core interests" as anything concerning state sovereignty, national security, and territorial integrity, and that "the Diaoyu issue is related to Chinese sovereignty" (Shimada 2013, April 26, 2013). Beijing proceeded to include the islands into its self-declared "East Sea Air Defence Identification Zone" in November 2013 (*Xinhuanet* 2015).
7 An "ethos of appropriateness" differs from constructivism's "logic of appropriateness." For the latter, social actors are concerned with the legitimacy (not cost-effectiveness) of their action (Barnett 2014: 159), whereas the "ethos of appropriateness" here refers to the characteristic spirit of a civilization or community as manifested in its beliefs and aspirations shared by its members. I thank L.H.M. Ling for coining this term.
8 European international society, in contrast, expected a state to enable its citizens to pursue individual happiness to the fullest potential possible. The state's internal affairs, then, would remain free of foreign intervention so long as it commanded popular support. Legislation (i.e., legislative justice) safeguarded the principle of sovereign equality, underpinning institutions such as positive international law and diplomacy.
9 Recall Wight's (1977) argument that all known states-systems emerged among peoples who considered themselves belonging to the same civilization, which, in turn, differentiated them from other less "advanced" peoples.
10 This echoes the Eliasian theme that civilization is a process rather than a condition. See Linklater (2012).
11 In 1871, a native tribe (*Mudanshe* in Chinese or *Botansha* in Japanese) murdered 54 Ryukyuans following the latter's shipwreck on southern Taiwan. Local Chinese officials rescued the survivors and escorted them to the Ryukyuan trading mission in Fuzhou in 1872. From the perspective of international law, it was a misstep indeed for China to admit that the Ryukyuans were Japanese citizens; nevertheless, admitting Japan's effective governance over Ryukyu did not necessarily imply that China henceforth had lost Ryukyu as a vassal as far as tributary relations were concerned (Suzuki 2009: 158–159).
12 Even conventional constructivists would agree that if states look alike it does not necessarily mean that they act alike. See Barnett (2014).

References

Agathangelou, Anna M., and L.H.M. Ling. 2009. *Transforming World Politics: From Empire to Multiple Worlds*. London: Routledge.
Barnett, Michael. 2014. "Social Constructivism." In *The Globalization of World Politics*, edited by John Baylis, Steve Smith, and Patricia Owens, 155–168. Oxford: Oxford University Press.
Bilgin, Pinar. 2008. "Thinking Past 'Western' IR?" *Third World Quarterly* 29(1): 5–23.
Bull, Hedley, and Adam Watson, eds. 1984. *The Expansion of International Society*. Oxford: Clarendon.
Buzan, Barry, and Richard Little. 2000. *International Systems in World History: Remaking the Study of International Relations*. Oxford: Oxford University Press.
Chen, Ching-Chang. 2011. "The Absence of Non-Western IR Theory in Asia Reconsidered." *International Relations of the Asia-Pacific* 11(1): 1–23.
Chen, Ching-Chang. 2014. "What Does the Demise of Ryukyu Mean for the Sino-Japanese Diaoyu/Senkaku Islands Dispute?" *Perceptions* 19(1): 87–105.
Christensen, Thomas J. 2011. *Worse than a Monolith: Alliance Politics and Problems of Coercive Diplomacy in Asia*. Princeton: Princeton University Press.
Economist, The. 2013. "Dangerous Shoals". http://www.economist.com/news/leaders/21569740-risks-clash-between-china-and-japan-are-risingand-consequences-could-be
Guo, Qifu, ed. 1996. *Wuwang guochi: Zaichuang huihaung* (Never Forget National Humiliation: Recreating the Glory). Wuhan: Wuhan University Press, 1996.
Hagström, Linus. 2012. "'Power Shift' in East Asia? A Critical Reappraisal of Narratives on the Diaoyu/Senkaku Islands Incident in 2010." *Chinese Journal of International Politics* 5(3): 267–297.
Hamashita, Takeshi. 1997. *Choko sisutemu to kindai Ajia* (The Tribute System and Modern Asia). Tokyo: Iwanami Shoten.
Howland, D.R. 1996. *Borders of Chinese Civilization: Geography and History at Empire's End*. Durham, NC: Duke University Press.
Japanese Ministry of Foreign Affairs, ed. 1949. *Nippon gaiko bunsho* (Documents on Japanese Foreign Policy), vol. 12. Tokyo: Ministry of Foreign Affairs.
Johnston, Alastair Iain. 1995. *Cultural Realism: Strategic Culture and Grand Strategy in Chinese History*. Princeton: Princeton University Press.
Kang, David C. 2010. *East Asia before the West: Five Centuries of Trade and Tribute*. New York: Columbia University Press, 2010.
Liang, Chia-bin. 1986. "*Liuqiu wangguo zhongri zhengchi kaoshi* (An Inquiry of the Sino-Japanese Dispute over the Extinguishment of the Ryukyu Kingdom)." In *Zhongguo jindai xiandaishi lunji*, vol. 15, edited by Executive Committee for the Promotion of Chinese Culture Renaissance, 75–192. Taipei: Taiwan shangwu yinshuguan.
Ling, L.H.M. 2014. *The Dao of World Politics: Towards a Post-Westphalian, Worldist International Relations*. London: Routledge.
Linklater, Andrew. 2012. "Violence and Civilisation in the Western States-Systems." Paper presented at the symposium on "The English School Today: Order, Justice, and Multiculturalism", Ritsumeikan University, Kyoto, March 26.
Qing Grand Council (Junjichu), ed. 1963. *Qing guangxuchao zhongri jiaoshe shiliao* (Sino-Japanese Diplomatic History during Emperor Quangxu's Reign), vols. 1 and 2. Taipei: Wenhai.
Schelling, Thomas. 1966. *Arms and Influence*. New Haven: Yale University Press.
Shi, Yuanhua, ed. 2006. *Jindai Zhongguo zhoubian waijiao shilun* (China and Its Neighboring Countries: A Diplomatic History). Shanghai: Shanghai cishu chubanshe.

Shimada, Manabu. (2013) "Chūgoku, Senkaku wa 'kakushin-teki rieki' to hajimete meigen" [China Declares the Senkakus as Its Core Interests for the First Time]. *Nihon Keizai Shimbun*, April 26.

Suzuki, Shogo. 2009. *Civilization and Empire: China and Japan's Encounter with European International Society*. London: Routledge.

Wang, Yen-wei. 1963. *Qingji waijiao shiliao* (Diplomatic History of the Qing Dynasty), vol. 16. Taipei: Wenhai.

Wang, Yuan-kang. 2011. *Harmony and War: Confucian Culture and Chinese Power Politics*. New York: Columbia University Press.

Wight, Martin. 1977. *Systems of States*. Leicester: Leicester University Press.

Wight, Martin. 1979. *Power Politics*, 2nd edn. Harmondsworth: Royal Institute of International Affairs.

Wu, Ru-lun, ed. 1980. *Li Wenzhong gong (Hongzhang) quan ji, yishu hangao* (Li Hongzhang Collection, Letters with Translation Bureau), vols. 7 and 8. Taipei: Wenhai.

Xinhuanet. (2013) "Background: Air Defense Identification Zones." HYPERLINK "http://english.news.cn/" \t "_blank" English.news.cn, November 24. http://news.xinhuanet.com/english/video/2013-11/24/c_132912942.htm Accessed November 30, 2016.

7

SOVEREIGNTY OR IDENTITY?

Significance of the Diaoyutai/Senkaku Islands dispute for Taiwan

Boyu Chen

Where does Taiwan fit in the Diaoyutai/Senkaku Islands dispute? Officially, Taiwan's government could make claims on the islands. But historically, Taiwan has had and continues to have intimate relations with both China and Japan. Former Ming Dynasty officials and scholars escaped to Taiwan in the seventeenth century to seek refuge from the newly installed, Manchu-run Qing Dynasty. After the Second World War, the Nationalist government under Chiang Kai-shek fostered an anti-Communist ideology and Chinese identity, reinforced by US dominance militarily, politically, economically, and culturally. At the same time, Taiwan also shares an intimate history with Japan. Colonized by the latter between 1895 and 1945, Taiwan's elderly still wax nostalgically about Japan while the younger generation swarms to Japanese *manga* and *anime*. Indeed, Taiwan turned out to be Japan's top donor after the 2011 earthquake. Taiwan also enjoys a variety of bilateral relationships with Japan (Chang 2013). Nonetheless, Taiwanese do not disregard Japan's invasion and colonial rule of China from the 1930s to the 1940s. Some Taiwanese have called for a "brotherhood" between China and Taiwan against what they see as an imperialistic Japan (Lin and Shi 2013; Pan 2012); others suggest that Taiwan join the US–Japanese alliance against China to prevent the latter from invading Taiwan after taking over the disputed islands (Tsai 2012).

This chapter explores the ambiguity of sovereignty in East Asia. Even though international relations (IR) proceeds from sovereignty as a premise for all inter-state relations, it remains elusive in this region due precisely to Westphalian power politics, exercised most blatantly during the colonial/imperialist era of the nineteenth and twentieth centuries, followed by US hegemony after the Second World War. Taiwan exemplifies a state that has experienced all of the above; consequently, it displays a multi-layered response to territorial disputes in the region. This chapter draws on academic and journalistic work on Taiwan's responses to the Diaoyutai/Senkaku Islands dispute. I also turn to the Internet to examine popular sentiments in the region by examining netizens' discourses on the islands from Taiwan's largest bulletin board system (BBS), Station-PTT. This survey finds that the sovereignty dispute surfaces issues of national identity previously not considered. Let's see how.

National identity and the islands dispute

Debates over the islands' sovereignty highlight the role of history on national identity. This historical legacy necessarily frames contemporary inter-state politics. For some Taiwanese, for instance, only Taiwan, as the Republic of China (ROC), has the legitimacy to claim sovereignty over the islands, not China (cf. Chen 2012). Even though international society recognizes it as the legitimate government of the Chinese people, the People's Republic of China (PRC) remains an "outlaw" government, according to this perspective. In contrast, some declare that the islands belong to Japan: in the Treaty of Peace (1951) signed with China to return Taiwan, Japan did not relinquish its rights over the islands. Furthermore, many argue, the islands have nothing to do with China or Taiwan (Peng, Qiu and Zhang 2008).

State actions reflect these ambiguities of history and culture. In response to Japan's claim over the islands, Taiwan's government proposed "The East China Sea Peace Initiative" (Ministry of Foreign Affairs 2012). It proclaims Taiwan's sovereignty over the islands based on three points: (1) the islands were discovered, named, and used by Ming China (1368–1644) and later became a territory of Qing China (1644–1912); (2) although the islands were annexed by Meiji Japan during the Sino-Japanese War, coupled with Taiwan's cession to Japan in 1895, the postwar arrangement "restored the islands to their pre-1895 legal status"; and (3) US transfer of administration rights over the islands in 1971 does not "constitute a transfer of sovereignty."

Some groups in Taiwan, however, are perplexed. The government's references to the Ming and Qing Dynasties seem to echo a "one China policy," suggesting no differentiation between the ROC and the PRC and thereby subordinating Taiwan to China (*Liberty Times* 2010). Those who propose Taiwan's independence and rectification from "Republic of China" to "Taiwan" argue that the Treaty of Peace never claimed sovereignty over the islands; therefore, it is untenable for Taiwan to claim the islands as auxiliary territory. This argument reflects the position of some that Chiang Kai-shek's Kuomintang (KMT) party on Taiwan was an alien and oppressive regime. Others argue outrightly that the islands belong to Japan, stating that it was the first application of international law in East Asia based on the doctrine of *terra nullius* under international law (Lai 2012).

The complexity of Taiwan's national identity reflects contentions regarding "legitimacy." Some Taiwanese regard Japan as their genuine place of origin: it represents a civilized and modern society. Even before the island dispute erupted, one observer noted that "[s]ome Taiwanese intellectuals believed Taiwan should denounce China for its backwardness and betrayal and welcome Japanese rule as an opportunity for the island to be modernized by administrators from Asia's most advanced country" (Roy 2002: 45). In contrast, others insist on Taiwan's Chinese origins, citing the historical and cultural ties across the Strait. They identify themselves as Chinese even though some of them deny the legitimacy of a Communist China (Wu 2011).

National identity issues surface most prominently where national security strategies are concerned. Those who call for a sense of "brotherhood" between Taiwan and mainland China against an imperial Japan usually reflect a strong "Chinese" identity (Lin and Shi 2013; Pan 2012). Those who suggest Taiwan join the US–Japanese alliance against Taiwan's enemy, China, are more inclined to support a Taiwanese, if not Japanese, identity. In short, those who identify themselves as Taiwanese tend to have a positive perception of Japan relative to China, while those who identify themselves as Chinese are more prone to have a negative attitude towards Japan (Chuang and Li 2003). We hear two different voices, accordingly, within the same national polity. In contrast, the people of Japan and China seem united in their stance regarding the islands dispute. The background to these two different voices reflects deep-seated identity issues in Taiwan.

Chinese identity and anti-Japanese sentiment

"Long divided, the world will unite; long united, it will fall apart." Taiwan's President Ma Ying-jeou quoted this famous opening line from the fourteenth-century epic, *The Romance of the Three Kingdoms*, to call on the people of Taiwan and China to create a new history through peaceful resolution to cross-Strait relations (Ma 2011). This quote aimed deliberately to remind both Taiwan and China of their common cultural heritage.

The KMT has long emphasized this Chinese identity, but as a contrast to Communist China. Nonetheless, the KMT's own half-century rule on Taiwan has defined politics as one-party rule only. Democratization did not begin until the late 1980s-early 1990s. Before then, the Taiwanese independence movement was strictly banned. "Taiwanese" was never an option as a national identity; any sign of insurrection or rebellion was directly and brutally suppressed.[1] Since the lifting of martial law in 1987, Taiwanese as a national identity has emerged, and interaction among Taiwan's different ethnic groups has become more prominent.

Indeed, ethnic, political, and cultural meanings infuse "Taiwanese" or "Chinese" as an ethnic label in Taiwan. Public opinion polls usually fail to elucidate these connections.[2] Ethnically speaking, the term "Taiwanese" refers to the descendants of immigrants from China's Fujian Province in the eighteenth and nineteenth centuries. They regard themselves as natives to the island and distinct from the "mainlanders" who escaped from the Chinese Communists in 1949. Politically speaking, however, those who identify themselves as "Chinese" are not necessarily those who came to Taiwan with the KMT forces or who are now their descendants. Rather, they contend that the Taiwanese government, not the Communist regime in Beijing, represents the "true" China. The ROC still retains "China" in its title, they reason. Although the ROC's actual control only extends over Taiwan and the smaller islands of Penghu, Kinmen, and Matsu, along with some even smaller islands, Taiwan's constitution still claims sovereignty over the entire territory of China.

Those who identify themselves strongly as Chinese emphasize their Chinese roots in history, culture, and blood. The history of Japanese imperialism in the last century, they believe, should not be forgotten, even though they themselves had never engaged in any kind of anti-Japanese resistance or experienced Japanese colonial rule directly. Here, we see a continuing legacy of the Chiang Kai-shek regime. It propagated anti-Japanese education and forbade the use of Japanese language in broadcast media as well as imports of Japanese audiovisual entertainment products (Lee 2003).

Nonetheless, many in Taiwan embrace Japan. They often remember nostalgically their times under Japanese occupation. With the restriction on Japanese products lifted in 1992, Japan-mania in Taiwan has fully flourished and spread nationwide, leading to a minority of Taiwan's younger generation to identify themselves as Japanese.

Japanese-ness and anti-Greater China sentiment

Japan remains popular in Taiwan. In 2011, the Japanese Exchange Association commissioned Gallup to poll popular impressions of Japan in Taiwan (Japanese Exchange Association 2012). The poll found that 75 percent of Taiwanese people have amicable feelings towards Japan, higher than the 62 percent that had the same feelings in 2009. And younger people were even more pronounced in their positive impressions of Japan.

According to Li and Chen (1998), Japanese-ness has become a part of daily life in Taiwan, not just a political injunction. Leo Ching (2001) points out that while early anti-Japanese sentiments embraced China as the ancestral homeland (*zu guo*), this was based on desperation and fantasy, not on political or cultural identification. Under colonial rule, Taiwan's elite class formed a relationship of reciprocal dependency with the ruling government. Of particular note were the "Chinese native landowner class" and the "emerging literati." By the end of the 1920s, people in Taiwan began to perceive Japanese culture as their own (Ching 2001). The KMT government sought to alter this situation after relocating to Taiwan in 1949. But it served only to temporarily suppress Japanese culture in Taiwan, not extinguish it altogether.

Taiwan's younger generation underscores this affinity for Japan. Unlike the elderly who were indoctrinated by Japanese education under colonial rule, Taiwan's young people flock to Japanese culture due to commercialism and consumerism. Sony, Wacoal, Shiseido, Family Mart, Toyota, Yamaha, SOGO department, and so on, pervade Taiwanese daily life. Young and old in Taiwan also regard the Japanese lifestyle, as depicted in Japanese TV dramas, as ideal. Japanese TV programs started in Taiwan in 1992 and became an instant hit with Taiwan's youth. Audience ratings for Japanese programs have exceeded those from Hong Kong. In 1996, Tokyo Broadcasting System Television sold the rights for over 1,000 hours of Japanese TV programs to Taiwan (Lee 2003). Many streets and popular shopping districts in Taiwan exhibit a pseudo-Japanese sense of style. Shop signboards are full of Japanese names like "*Yamanote* Line Black Bubble Tea,"[3] or "*Harajuku* Plaza,"[4] and numerous shops display Japanese "*kawaii*" (cute) style goods. Taiwanese tourism reflects this Japanese mania as well: Japan remains the site for Taiwanese tourists to visit. In 2012, almost 2 million Taiwanese visited Japan, second only to Koreans (Japan National Tourism Organization 2012).[5] Today, many in Taiwan and Japan regard the two countries as a "Community of Common Destiny" (Nakamura 1997; Chang 2014). The relationship between Japan and Taiwan, Lam and Chong (2004: 249) note, is "underpinned by a shared history, common values, economic ties, strategic alignment, and social networks between their political and business elite. It is also buttressed by mutual warmth, admiration, at the societal level."

Still, heated debates about Taiwanese identity continue. Public polls, however, fall short of demonstrating the complexity of this issue. Most of these treat "national identity" as an independent variable in explaining national identity's influence on political attitudes, behavior, and other phenomena (Cheng 2009; Shyu 1996; Wu 2001). Data from the Internet provides an alternative way to understand national identity in Taiwan.

Cyber discourse on the islands

As Castells (2001) points out, online discourse takes place in a medium that allows, for the first time, communication among many to many in a chosen time and on a global scale. Cyber discourse serves as a major example. BBSes originally started as bulletin boards to be used not only as an information source but also an interactive forum for public discussions and debates on a broad range of topics. BBSes enable participants to keep pace with current events and news in real time. Giese (2004: 28) points out, "Offline events and major discussions [on BBSes] are picked up at roughly the same time." Accordingly, BBS discussions and debates are highly interactive. Owing to the absence of temporal and spatial limitations, writers on BBSes from all over the world are able to post their ideas onto this open space. Users on social media like Facebook and Twitter have been increasing in the past decade in both China and Taiwan, but BBSes play a significant role in the daily discourse for netizens in the region.

According to Lu (2008), 3 billion users were registered on BBSes in China at the time of his survey. But this number may be deceptive since one netizen is allowed to register at multiple BBSes simultaneously. Lu notes, also, that PTT is the most popular BBS in Taiwan. The number of registered users reached 1.5 million in 2014 (Wang 2014).

The PTT BBS is a terminal-based system in Taiwan. Students from the Department of Information Engineering at National Taiwan University founded this BBS in 1995. The Electronic BBS Research Society now maintains it. PTT now claims to be the largest BBS in the world. Some users on PTT are from

China. PTT has over 20,000 boards with a multitude of topics, and more than 40,000 posts are created daily (PTT 2013).

In December 2012, I collected articles on the islands dispute posted from December 2009 to September 2012 on the cross-Strait board. I found that netizens posted most of their articles during two specific periods: the first, in September 2010, with 32 posts when a Japanese coastguard vessel collided with a Chinese fishing boat and the Chinese captain was arrested on September 7, 2010. The second period of greatest activity occurred in 2012, with 104 posts when the Japanese government declared its nationalization of the islands. For this chapter, I selected texts by netizens who posted more than 10 times during these two periods.

Sovereignty, legitimacy and Taiwan's national identity

On September 29, 2012, *Chronodl* posted: "Diaoyutai Belongs to Japan." *Chronodl* forwarded an article referring to historical records dating back to 1896 that confirmed Japan's occupation/ownership of the islands. *Chronodl* added: "Those who assert Chinese or Taiwanese sovereignty over the Diaoyutai Islands are provoking nationalism, thus obscuring the point of focus, and ignoring the history of the Japanese contribution to the Diaoyu Islands ... The Diaoyu Islands are Japan's territory, named Senkaku." *Highlander* (2012) quickly responded with: "Diaoyutai Belongs to Taiwan": "Diaoyutai never belonged to Japan. A defeated country should not talk such nonsense." *Chronodl* immediately retorted: "It is not important who won or lost. Is this the only thing China can boast of?"

The debate continued but ended eventually with *Highlander* referring to Japan's constant violation of international law by invading neighboring countries. Japan, to *Highlander*, is a deceitful country. "Before 1971," *Highlander* wrote:

> [T]he Japanese government recognized the legitimacy of the ROC, but then denied it afterwards. The property of the ROC, which was legally registered in Japan, was adamantly retained by Japan after diplomatic ties were cut off. Apparently, they dare to flout anything deemed to be legal. I cannot see any justifications for what they are now cheekily bringing up.

TERRIST and *ilyj2012* raised the issue of Taiwan's national identity. That is, should Taiwan unify with China or stay independent? In a post titled "Senkaku and Okinawa," *TERRIST* (2012a) cited a statement by China's government in 1953 that the Diaoyutai belongs to Japan. *TERRIST* denounced the Chinese government's persistent absurdities:

> There is no so-called "indivisible territory of China."[6] Everything except the PRC and Communist control is changeable. Why do Chinese nationalists and people supporting unification with China in Taiwan still expect the Chinese government to take back the Senkaku Islands? Isn't it ridiculous?!

A mainland Chinese, *ilyj2012* (2012a), responded:

> Taiwan should strengthen its power, especially military power, if it desires China to forfeit unification ... The author [referring to *TERRIST*] is supposed to be pro-independence. Try harder! Still a long, long way to go for you!

TERRIST (2012b) chided *ilyj2012* for being such a mainlander:

> Taiwan has been independent. China has not ruled Taiwan for one day ... The only way for China to give up unification of Taiwan is to accept the fact ... Otherwise, please fight for unification like a man! Try harder! Still a long, long way to go for you!

ilyj2012 (2012b) taunted back: "Really? Taiwan has been independent? Could you show me your Republic of *Taiwan ID please*?" *ilyj2012* continued: "*Your* [Taiwan's] constitution even rejects the acknowledgement of Taiwan as an independent country. What should *we* [China] do?" Ultimately, ilyj2012 disapproved of Taiwan's affinity for Japan:

> I feel some attitudes from the Taiwanese extremely odd. When the Japanese occupied Taiwan's Diaoyutai Islands, most Taiwanese stated Diaoyutai was Japan's originally. But when it came to the anti-Japanese demonstrations in China, the Taiwanese expressed strong hatred toward those protesters and called for their comeuppance through grinding teeth. The protest seemed radical, but at least they took a position against Japan. You Taiwanese provide commentary on nothing yet antagonize those who stand for something. Honestly, I don't even know if you are Japanese or Taiwanese. It's really confusing.

In contrast, one netizen from Taiwan, *OceanTaiwan* (2012), suggested a Taiwanese-Japanese-US coalition against China:

> I have little Chinese-ness in my mind. I am a Taiwanese but Japanese to the core. I am also very fond of using good quality products made in Japan and wish for a good allegiance between Taiwan and Japan. The thing is, Taiwan lacks might. The best strategy is to formulate a federal Far-East alliance under the Treaty of Mutual Cooperation and Security between the United States and Japan.

This quote echoes those commentators in the mainstream mass media who advocate joint defense cooperation with Japan to fight against China. What distinguishes those commentators with netizens is that the latter clearly articulate the issue with their own national identity.

Those in Taiwan who identified with Japan scoffed at the Chinese government's "cowardly" attitude towards Japan. Note this post from *Dachiou*:

> Japan's coast guard has successfully kept Taiwanese and Chinese fishing vessels at a distance to 12 nautical miles, while the police hold the Diaoyutai Islands. Taiwan and China, however, react in a cowardly manner without chasing the Japanese fishing vessels away. It is obvious, no matter how Taiwan and China may rally against Japan, Diaoyutai is now undeniably under the holy reign of the grand Japanese empire. China was so beaten flat by Japan that the Chinese fizzle while bristling. They just let people sabotage their own properties. All barks but no bites and with gangs swanking propaganda around – now that is what we call a Grand Country, China.

Usage of language like "under the holy reign of the grand Japanese empire" strongly indicates the author's Japanese identity. In other posts, *Dachiou* clearly demonstrated his dislike of China by saying that Taiwan is not going to get along with China and rather be a traitor of the Han people than ever be a traitor to the Taiwanese people. Here, Taiwanese identity mixed well with Japanese identity (cf. *Dachiou* 2014).

Conclusion

Narratives on the Diaoyutai/Senkaku Islands dispute expose the spectrum of Taiwan's national identity. While Taiwan has long been struggling to legitimize its claim of representing China or to become an independent state, the Taiwanese people still welcome their former colonial master, Japan. These Taiwanese would rather discard their Chinese identity than suffer from what they perceive as an illegitimate, tyrannical regime in Beijing.

Shih (1999, 2006) points out the invented nature of national identity. A state needs to constantly search for an object upon which it can exercise sovereignty to construct or reinforce its national identity. The state needs an external enemy, along with "internal shamings" (i.e., traumatic experiences caused by past defeat), so citizens would be willing to sacrifice for the state. Taiwan's inability to agree on its own name reveals this problem of national identity. Accordingly, the people of Taiwan cannot reach a consensus on whether China or Japan is the enemy in the Diaoyutai/Senkaku Islands dispute, and what each means to Taiwan.

Notes

1 There are four ethnic groups mentioned in Taiwan's official discourse today: the Hoklo, the Hakka, the Mainlanders, and the Aboriginal peoples. Most of the more than 20 million inhabitants of Taiwan are descendants of earlier immigrants from Fujian and Guangdong provinces in South China. The Hoklo are Fukienese descendants of peasants from Fujian. They emigrated to Taiwan in the eighteenth and nineteenth centuries, while the Hakka are descendants of refugees and exiles from Guangdong who came to Taiwan before the nineteenth century (Wang 1998; Shih 2007).

2 When various public opinion polls in Taiwan raise the question of "national identity," these usually present three choices only: "Taiwanese," "Chinese," or "Both." The survey does not include "Do not know" or "Refuse to answer." In 1992, 26 percent of the respondents identified themselves as Chinese; by 2011, this number dropped to 4 percent. In comparison, the percentage of respondents identifying as Taiwanese increased steadily from 18 percent to as high as 54 percent during the same period. The percentage of respondents answering "Both" was about 40 percent over the long term (Election Study Center 2013).
3 Yamanote Line is a railway loop line in Tokyo city.
4 Harajuku is an area between Shinjuku and Shibuya in Tokyo; it is renowned for its high street fashion.
5 Taiwan's nostalgia for Japan contrasts sharply with how Koreans feel about their colonial experience under the Japanese (1910–1945). See Usumiki (1997).
6 For the Chinese government, Taiwan is part of China's "indivisible territory."

References

Castells, M. (2001) *The Internet Galaxy: Reflections on the Internet, Business, and Society*. New York: Oxford University Press.

Chang, M.S. (2013) *"Ri Zhengjing Xuejie Lianshhou Tuidong Ritai Guanxi"* (Japanese Scholars Promote Political and Economic Relationship between Japan and Taiwan). *Liberty Times Daily*, August 29 (http://www.libertytimes.com.tw/2013/new/aug/29/today-p7.htm. (Downloaded June 1, 2013).

Chang, M.S. (2014) *"Lidenghui: Ritai shi Mingyun Gongtongti"* (Lee Teng hui: Japan-Taiwan is Community of Common Destiny). *Liberty Times*, September 21 (http://news.ltn.com.tw/news/focus/paper/815082 (Downloaded: September 21, 2014).

Chen, H.Y. (2012) *"Ma Zhuzhang Diaodaoan Song Guojifayuan Celue Zhongyao"* (It is Important for Ma to Submit the Diaoyutai Case to the International Court of Justice). *China Review News*, August 24 (http://hk.crntt.com/doc/1022/0/9/5/102209534_3.html?coluid=93&kindid=8010&docid=102209534&mdate=0824003714) (Downloaded: June 1, 2013).

Cheng, S.F. (2009) *"Zuqun Rentong yu Zongtong Xuanju Toupiao Jueze"* (Ethnicity, Identity, and Vote Choice in Taiwan). *Xuanju Yanjiu* (Journal of Electoral Studies) 16(2): 23–49.

Ching, L. (2001) *Becoming "Japanese": Colonial Taiwan and the Politics of Identity Formation*. Berkeley: University of California Press.

Chronodl. (2012) *"FW: Diaoyutai shi Zhiben de"* (Diaoyu/Senkaku Islands belong to Japan) September 29 (telnet://ptt.cc) (Downloaded: June 1, 2013).

Chuang, J.Y. and M.C. Li. (2003) "Ethnic Identification and Attitudes towards the Japanese in Taiwan." *Journal of Indigenous Psychological Research* 20: 105–135.

Dachiou. (2014) *"Taiwan Jiushi Buxihuan Zhongguo zai Yiqi"* (Taiwan is Not Going to Go Hand in Hand with China). November 16 (telnet://ptt.cc) (Downloaded: July 10, 2015).

Election Study Center, National Cheng-Chi University. (2013) "Taiwanese/Chinese Identity Distribution Trend." (http://esc.nccu.edu.tw/course/news.php?Sn=166), Aug. 24, 2013. (Downloaded: June 1, 2013).

Giese, K. (2004) "Speaker's Corner on Virtual Panopticon: Discursive Construction of Chinese." In F. Mengin (ed.), *Cyber China: Reshaping National Identities in the Age of Information*, pp. 19–36. London: Palgrave Macmillan.

Highlander. (2012) *"FW: Diaoyutai shi Taiwan de"* (Diaoyutai belongs to Taiwan). September 30 (telnet://ptt.cc) (Downloaded: June 1, 2013).

ilyj2012. (2012a) *"Re: Baoying"* (Retribution). August 22 (telnet://ptt.cc) (Downloaded: June 1, 2013).

ilyj2012. (2012b) *"Re: Jiange yu Chongsheng"* (Senkaku and Okinawa). August 21 (telnet://ptt.cc) (Downloaded: June 1, 2013).

Japan National Tourism Organization. (2012) "Statistical Information" (http://www.jnto.go.jp/eng/ttp/sta/) (Downloaded: June 1, 2013).

Japanese Exchange Association. (2012) *"2011 Niandu Taiwan Minzhong Dui Riben Guangan zhi Yan jiu"* (A Survey on the Taiwanese People's Feelings toward Japan in 2011) (http://www.koryu.or.jp/taipei/ez3_contents.nsf/04/88088B2377C5DDB749257A220034271A/$FILE/2011tainichi-yoroncyousa1zhongwen.pdf). March 2012. (Downloaded: June 1, 2013).

Lai, F.S. (2012). *"Lidenghui, Mayingjiu, Sheidui?"* (Lee Teng-hui, Ma Ying-Jeou, Who is Right?). *Liberty Times*. September 24 (http://talk.ltn.com.tw/article/paper/617475) (Downloaded: June 1, 2013).

Lam, P.E. and J.I. Chong. (2004) "Japan–Taiwan Relations: Between Affinity and Reality." *Asian Affairs* 30(4): 249–267.

Lee, M.T. (2003) "Imagine Here/Practice There: The Japanese TV Drama Tour and the Cross-cultural Identities of Taiwanese Youths." In S.W. Chiou (ed.), *Envisage*, pp. 42–73. Taipei: Yuanliu.

Li, D.T. and Z.Y. Chen. (1998) "Satellite TV and National Imaginary: Japanese Melodrama on Star TV as an Example." *Mass Communication Research* 56: 9–34.

Liberty Times. (2010) *"Zailun Mazhengfu dui Diaoyutai Lichang Lunshu de Huangmiuxing"* (Reiterating the Absurdity of Ma Government's Discourse on Diaoyutai Islands). October 7 (http://www.libertytimes.com.tw/2010/new/oct/7/today-s1.htm) (Downloaded: June 1, 2013).

Lin, J.Y. and J.Y. Shi. (2013) *"Diaoyutai shi Taiwan de, Ranhou ne?"* (Daiyutai belongs to Taiwan, and Then?). *China Times Daily*, January 10 (http://news.chinatimes.com/forum/11051401/112013011000521.html) (Downloaded: June 1, 2013).

Lu, G. (2008) "Old School BBS: The Chinese Social Networking Phenomenon." January 16 (http://readwrite.com/2008/01/16/bbs_china_social_networking) (Downloaded: June 1, 2013).

Ma, Y.J. (2011) *"Zhongguo de Lishi Zongshi 'Hejiubifen, Fenjiubihe'"* (Chinese History Tells Us that "Long Divided, the World will Unite; Long United, It will Fall Apart"). *Huanqiu*, June 28 (http://taiwan.huanqiu.com/news/2011-06/1786149.html) (Downloaded: June 1, 2013).

Ministry of Foreign Affairs, Republic of China (Taiwan). (2012) "The Republic of China (Taiwan) Proposes: The East China Sea Peace Initiative." (http://www.mofa.gov.tw/EnOfficial/Topics/TopicsArticleDetail/2c73470c-4336-42b9-acb4-a814251b5747) (Downloaded: June 1, 2013).

Nakamura, K. (ed.) (1997) *Unmei Kyodotai toshiteno Nihon to Taiwan* (Japan and Taiwan as a Community of Common Destiny). Tokyo: Tentensha.

OceanTaiwan. (2012) *"Re: Diaoyutai Guancha"* (Observation on Diaoyutai Islands). August 26 (telnet://ptt.cc) (Downloaded: June 1, 2013).

Pan, C.Y. (2012) *"Taiwan wu Lianhe Meiri fan Zhong"* (Taiwan Should Not Unite the US and Japan against China). August 18 (http://www.cdnews.com.tw) (Downloaded: February 1, 2013).

Peng, X.J., Y.L. Qiu and M.S. Zhang (2008) *"Lidenghui: Diaoyutai shi Riben de"* (Lee Teng-hui: Diaoyutai belongs to Japan). *Liberty Times*, September 25 (http://news.ltn.com.tw/news/politics/paper/245589) (Downloaded: June 1, 2013).

PTT. (2013) PTT official website (http://www.ptt.cc/index.html).

Roy, D. (2002) *Taiwan: A Political History*. Ithaca: Cornell University Press.

Shih, C.F. (2007) *"Taiwan Minzhuhua Guocheng zhong de Zuqun Zhengzhi"* (Ethnic Politics in Taiwan since Democratization). *Taiwan Journal of Democracy* 4(4): 1–26.

Shih, C.Y. (1999) *Zhengzhi Xinlixue (Political Psychology)*. Taipei: Wunan.
Shih, C.Y. (2006) *Shenfen Zhengzhi: Ouranxing, Nengdongzhe yu Qingjing* (Identity Politics: Contingency, Agency and Situation). Kaohsiung: National Sun Yat-sen University Press.
Shyu, H.Y. (1996) "*Taiwan Xuanmin de Guojia rentong yu Dangpai Toupiao Xingwei: 1991–1993 Nianjian de Shizheng Yanjiu Chengguo*" (National Identity and Partisan Vote Choices in Taiwan: Evidence from Survey Data between 1991 and 1993). *Taiwan zhengzhi xuekan* (Taiwanese Political Science Review) 1(1): 85–127.
TERRIST. (2012a) "*Jiange yu Chongsheng*" (Senkaku and Okinawa). August 21 (telnet://ptt.cc) (Downloaded: June 1, 2013).
TERRIST. (2012b) "*Re: Jiange yu Chongsheng*" (Senkaku and Okinawa). August 21 (telnet://ptt.cc) (Downloaded: June 1, 2013).
Tsai, T.R. (2012) "*Ruguo Diaoyutai Kaizhan Taiwan de Sange Xuanze*" (Taiwan Has Three Options Once the War Launches on Diaoyutai). *Liberty Times Daily*. September 9 (http://www.libertytimes.com.tw/2012/new/sep/9/today-o9.htm) (Downloaded: June 1, 2013).
Usumiki, H. (1997) *Hannichi to Shinichi no Hazama: Kankoku-Taiwan kara Mita Nihon* (Between Anti-Japan and Pro-Japan: Japan Perceived from Korea and Taiwan). Tokyo: Tokyo Keisei Shinhosha.
Wang, F.C. (1998) "*Guangfu hou Taiwan Zuqun Yishi de Xingcheng*" (The Formation of Ethnic Consciousness in Taiwan after 1945). *Historical Monthly* 131: 30–40.
Wang, H.R. (2014) "*Juebu Ganshe! Dibenqiao Yuanjuan PTT Zhuji he Pinkuan*" (Never Intervene! Dibenqiao is Willing to Donate PTT Host and Bandwidth). *iThome*, March 27, 2014 (http://www.ithome.com.tw/news/86249) (Downloaded: July 10, 2015).
Wu, Y.S. (2001) "*Lianggang Guanxi Zhong de Zhongguo Yishi yu Taiwan Yishi*" (The Chinese/Taiwanese Identity in Cross-Straits Relations). *Zhongguo Shiwu Jikan* (China Affairs Quarterly) 4: 71–89.
Wu, Y.S. (2011) "The Evolution of the KMT's Stance on the One China Principal: National Identity in Flux." In G. Schubert and J. Dam (eds), *Taiwanese Identity in the Twenty-first Century: Domestic, Regional and Global Perspectives*, pp. 51–71. London: Routledge.

8

STORIES OF IR

Turkey and the Cold War

Zeynep Gulsah Capan

International Relations (IR) is increasingly concerned with its Western-centrism, using various strategies to deconstruct and overcome it (Jones 2006; Acharya and Buzan 2010; Shilliam 2010; Hobson 2012). Nonetheless, this chapter argues, the literature has not paid sufficient attention to how these critiques of Western-centrism *reproduce* Western-centrism – particularly by and in the non-West. A deeper, underlying Western-centric hierarchy thus remains. Discussed exclusively as the creation of the West, IR is then deconstructed and criticized exclusively by the West. The non-Western actor does not play a role either in constructing or critiquing this Western-centrism. As a result, "failing to acknowledge that the 'East' has the agency to – and responsibility for – constructing IR into what and how it is, the tale of Eurocentric IR becomes another narrative of victimization" (Ling 2014: 457). I apply this critique to narratives of the Cold War for two reasons. First, it is one of the central periods within the stories of IR whereby distinctions follow through the "Cold War/post-Cold War" binary. Second, it informs the basis upon which many of the conceptualizations and theories of IR are premised. It is through a specific understanding of the Cold War that concepts such as "balance of power," "security dilemma," and "anarchy" are explained. More pointedly, I examine how these constructions also frame understandings of Turkey's foreign policy to demonstrate how conceptualizations of the Cold War are reproduced in non-Western settings.

I begin with history: how to conceptualize it and, in particular, its relationship to the "past." How history is conceptualized constitutes one of the main cornerstones of the Western-centric conceptualization of IR. I extend this analysis to the Cold War and its historiography. Specifically, I show how mainstream IR reproduces a particular narrative about the Cold War both in the "center" and in the "periphery." This is important because the literature focuses on deconstructing Western-centric con-ceptualizations in the "center" and most often overlooks how these conceptualizations are also constructed and need deconstructing in the "periphery."

Writing histories

The question of "what is history" often begs a deeper, more profound query: "*why retell the past?*"[1] Paraphrasing Robert Cox (1981) on theory, Jenkins (2003: 21) contends that "history is never for itself, it is always for someone." As such, a historian's questions about the past – and not necessarily the actual events themselves – guide the way in which a historical narrative unfolds. Put differently, history often constructs a past framed by questions about the present. Tales of the Cold War provide a classic example.

Tales of the Cold War

A typical story about the Cold War would place its precipitating events from 1945 to 1950 according to the following chronological order:[2]

- February 1945: Yalta Conference
- April 1945: Death of President Franklin Roosevelt
- May 1945: End of the Second World War in Europe
- September 1945: Ho Chi Minh proclaimed Vietnam an independent republic
- February 1946: George F. Kennan writes the Long Telegram
- March 1946: Churchill's "Iron Curtain" Speech
- April 1946: North Atlantic Treaty Organization (NATO) Treaty is signed
- July 1946: Philippines gains independence from the United States
- March 1947: Speech by President Truman announcing the "Truman Doctrine"
- June 1947: Secretary of State George Marshall's announcement of an economic aid plan
- July 1947: Congress passes the National Security Act
- September 1947: Establishment of the Communist Information Bureau (Cominform)
- February 1948: Communist takeover in Czechoslovakia
- June 1948: West Germany is formed
- June 1948: Berlin Blockade
- August 1949: USSR detonates first atomic bomb
- October 1949: Communist Mao Zedong takes control of China and establishes the People's Republic of China
- June 1950: Korean War

A historian faces many choices when approaching past events and facts. The central subject of these events can be the Cold War or US foreign policy or US–Soviet rivalry; the geographical center can shift based on which events are included/excluded from the story (Europe, South-East Asia, or the Middle East); and, a proper beginning in time could be 1917, with the Russian Revolution; May 1945, with the end of the Second World War in Europe; or February 1946, with the writing of George Kennan's Long Telegram.

Each choice bears different implications for analysis and understanding. The events might remain the same but a different emphasis evokes a different narrative about them. For example:

Narrative 1: End of Second World War, Marshall Plan, Truman Doctrine, Korean War.

Narrative 2: End of Second World War, Marshall Plan, Truman Doctrine, *Korean War.*

Narrative 3: *End of the Second World War*, Marshall Plan, Truman Doctrine, Korean War.

Narrative 4: End of the Second World War, *Marshall Plan*, Truman Doctrine, Korean War.

The italics denote a "turning point" that alters the moral of the tale. If, for example, the narrative focuses on the death of Franklin Roosevelt as the turning point, then it suggests Harry Truman's culpability in starting tensions with the Soviet Union. Had Roosevelt lived, the story implies, this turn of events could have been avoided. If the Marshall Plan is taken as the starting point of tensions between the US and the Soviet Union, then the US is designated as responsible for the rise in tensions; additionally, the Marshall Plan's opening up of markets also becomes an important factor in the story about the Cold War.

In brief, history creates the past by narrating it. Select interpretations perform the past, making the past, as it were, stay in the "past." In this way, historiography replays the "events," stages the "concepts," and peoples them with predetermined "actors." Note these narratives below:

Narrative 5: End of Second World War, Long Telegram, NATO Treaty, National Security Act.

Narrative 6: End of World War II, establishment of Cominform, communist takeover in Czechoslovakia, Berlin Blockade, USSR detonates first atomic bomb.

Narrative 7: Yalta Conference, Ho Chi Minh proclaimed Vietnam as independent republic, Philippines gains independence from the United States, Korean War.

These events all happened. Empirical evidence exists but these events are selectively included or excluded depending on the story being told. Narrative 5 highlights US foreign policy. Including the National Security Act casts the US as the main protagonist of the story and the establishment of the national security state as an important factor in the development of the Cold War. In contrast, Narrative 6 establishes the Soviet Union as the main protagonist. It focuses on the expansion of communism as the main factor in the Cold War. In further contrast, Narrative 7 brings in "Third World" events not included in Narratives 5 and 6.

History in this sense not only narrates but, in narrating, also creates. As such, the past as it were stays in the "past" and history is performatively enacted by interpretations of the "past." Historiography performs the "events" and "concepts" that it is discussing within a stage that is already set and actors that are already predetermined. Such historiographical operations produce objects but are also limited by them, taking place within already set parameters. As such:

> [A] particular study will be defined by the relations that it upholds with others that are contemporaneous with it, with a "state of the question," with the problematic issues exploited by the group and the strategic points that they constitute, and with the outputs and divergences thus determined or given pertinence in relation to a work in progress.
>
> (De Certeau 1988: 64)

Historiography's dual functions manifest in discussions of the Cold War. Not only are there many Cold War(s) but these also operate within the same "Cold War." The terrain itself (i.e., the Cold War) does not alter but different possible routes can be taken to arrive at many possible stories about the Cold War. Thus, despite all the different ways in which an "event" might be narrated and differences "in the degree of detail with which they treat particular episodes and in the particular links they establish between them," writes Rigney (1990: 37), "each one is structured around these canonical events, these areas of common historical account." Different itineraries may exist but the main sites to be visited are already inscribed into the very concept of the Cold War. For instance: one stops by Yalta, Potsdam, Poland, events in Eastern Europe in general; then, Turkey, the Marshall Plan, and the Truman Doctrine. But the time one spends at each stop differs according to the narrative configured by the storyteller.

How so? The next section explains.

Reproducing IR stories

Two Western-centric moves underpin the mainstream story about the Cold War. First, the story centers on Great Britain or US foreign policy; second, a specific reading of the international system places its origins in Euro-American history. Constant themes of this narrative involve the Euro-American balance of power in the world and its security dilemma(s).

As prime examples, I draw on four schools of thought: traditionalist, revisionist, "pericentric," and structuralist. These offer the main stories in IR about the Cold War.

Traditionalists

Traditionalists focus on Europe for origins of the Cold War. "Since the end of the eighteenth century," writes Halle (1967: 2), the world has experienced four great wars and the fourth one was the Cold War. All sought to maintain a balance of power on the European continent. This narrative puts the Cold War in direct lineage from the Napoleonic Wars to the Concert of Europe, from the unification of Germany to the First World War, and from the inter-war period to the Second World War. Maintaining a balance of power in Europe – and its subsequent security dilemmas – thus becomes the central story of world politics.

Traditionalists place Turkey within this context, beginning with pre-war times. Hale (2000: 19–20) writes, for instance, that "Ottoman statesmen either had to avoid both conflicts and form alliances ... relying on the workings of the balance of power to pressure the status quo [or they] could try to negotiate a reasonably stable alliance with one or more of the European powers" (Hale 2000: 20). The Ottoman Empire and contemporary Turkey, in this narrative, can only *respond* to Europe's balance of power issues. Turkey had no choice in the matter:

> [F]or the Turks, the most important feature of the post-war world was its bipolarity, and the fact that the United States and Soviet Union were the only two players who really mattered ... [Turkey] could not opt out of the Cold War [because it] was unable to play one European power off against another.
> *(Hale 2000: 109)*

Revisionists

Revisionists, in contrast, blame the US for the Cold War. In particular, they trace US bellicosity to its history of state-building. It was in the 1890s, during an economic crisis, "when Americans thought that the frontier was gone, they advanced and accepted the argument that new expansion was the best, if not the only, way to sustain their freedom and prosperity" (Williams 1962: 26). According to this narrative, "when combined with the ideology of an industrial Manifest Destiny, the history of the Open Door Notes became the history of American foreign relations from 1900 to 1958" (Williams 1962: 39–40). This narrative presents US foreign policy linearly from economic to political expansion. In this way, the revisionists tell a story much like the traditionalists. They may differ on the root causes of US foreign policy but they converge on the Western-centric catalyst that accounts for the Cold War. The West retains center stage in both accounts.

Narratives of Turkish foreign policy reproduce the revisionist narrative. Ataov (1970: 5) writes that "a cardinal truth of our century is that American leadership is still enhancing the traditional objective of the 1890s ... The Open Door Policy has enabled the U.S. to 'stabilize' the world in favor of the American metropolis and establish a new empire." And like both traditionalists and revisionists, he argues that Turkey's alliance with the West had been decided already because "the ruling circles of Turkey, having failed to develop the country, tied their hopes to the capitalist classes in the West" (Ataov 1970: 91). As such, "even before the famous Soviet notes[3] were submitted to Turkey, the country was ripe ... to take part in the Western world" (Turkkaya 1970: 92). Within this narrative, the existence of the Soviet "demands" were not in themselves the reason for wanting to become part of the Western alliance against the Soviet Union but it was rather because of the capitalist leanings of the state and the rising bourgeois class. Turkaya's narrative then reproduces not only the narrative of US foreign policy but also a narrative of inevitability with respect to Turkey becoming part of the Western alliance against the Soviet Union.

"Pericentrics"

"Pericentrics" bring in other actors in telling the Cold War tale. They begin with Great Britain but, over the course of the narrative, cite the importance of other actors as well. Britain, that quintessential player of world politics whose strategies had balanced power in Europe for over a century, had convinced America to abandon its Wilsonian ideals and join in the game of global power politics (Anderson 1981: 10). Under the slogan of "Shifting the Burden," the Truman Doctrine stepped up to replacing Britain with the US as the keeper of balance of power in Europe. In effect, the US adopted policies that were initially commenced by Britain but which later proved crucial in setting up the Cold War. For example:

> The United States adopted an approach in Greece that the British had employed since 1944. The administration also accepted Churchill's conviction, first expressed in 1943, that the post-war menace was Russia.
> (Anderson 1981: 179)

Sever (1997) brings in Turkey to the story of the Cold War. It presents Turkey as a key actor that convinces the US of the Soviet threat. The narrative builds on the story of Russian aggressiveness and Turkey's efforts to prevent Soviet expansion by convincing allies of the threat's urgency. "The Turkish government," Sever (1997: 26) writes, "had urged Washington to take a firm stance towards the Soviet Union by sending a series of reports ever since the end of the war." Now, Great Britain comes to agree with Turkey and attempts to persuade the US of the Soviet threat: "England already had doubts after the war as it had during, about whether cooperation with the Soviets could be continued" (Sever 1997: 242). In time, the US concludes the same.

This pericentric approach, however, actually reifies the "Cold War." Despite seeking agency for other actors, these accounts subsume other possible narratives. The landscape of the story about the Cold War may have extended but the time frame and characterizations themselves remain the same. European history, also, remains the same.

"Structuralists"

Structuralists take a systemic approach to synthesize these different perspectives. Gaddis (1972) places the impending rivalry between the US and the Soviet Union within a context of the inter-state system. A power vacuum created after the Second World War leaves the two great powers in a security dilemma; consequently, the story of the Cold War centers on restoring a balance of power in the world and resolving its security dilemma. "The Cold War grew out of a complicated interaction of external and internal developments inside both the United States and the Soviet Union" (Gaddis 1972: 361).

This narrative continues the traditionalist and revisionist privileging of Europe's balance of power as the crux of the Cold War story. According to Leffler (1992: 504), "the Americans were caught in the classic security dilemma whereby the steps deemed essential to promote their own security clashed with the security imperatives of the adversary." The narrative may ascribe different priorities to different actors but the Eurocentric conception of world politics remains. European balance of power, once again, commands center stage.

Celik (1999) continues this systemic approach for Turkey. "[I]n the aftermath of World War II and the formation of a bipolar international system," she writes, "foreign policy decision-making in Turkey became largely defined by the role that Ankara played in the international system" (Celik 1999: xi) The nature of the international system, in short, determines a state's foreign policy decisions. "[T]he structure of the international system was such an important factor in determining Turkish foreign policy, changes in this structure were bound to alter the way in which Turkey interacted with other states" (Celik 1999: 151). In effect, a certain degree of inevitability confronted Turkey. The international system determined the scope of actions, so there could be no room for other kinds of maneuver. Note how Celik presents the Cold War as a fact of life. It does not require much debate in and of itself:

> [T]he United States had emerged from World War II as the strongest major power, and the Soviet Union soon became its ardent enemy. It was becoming clear to many nations in the world that they could not maintain cordial relations with both the United States and the Soviet Union now that the world had been divided into two opposing camps.
>
> *(Celik 1999: 35)*

Despite their intentions, structuralists reproduce a mainstream narrative about the Cold War. It reflects a linear history of European affairs and the need to once and for all solve the issue of the "balance of power" in Europe. There can be differences between the narratives with respect to which events are emphasized but the main terrain upon which events are inscribed does not alter. Whether traditionalist, revisionist, pericentrist, or structuralist a similar narrative of the Cold War is presented. These traditions stage history as a "natural" progression from US foreign policy to balance of power to the international system as the deciding context. And Turkish foreign policy, like that for all other players, must comply.

Alternative narratives

Lost in this discourse are other stories about the Cold War. The Cold War is taken to define the history of IR between 1945 and 1990 but different narratives can be written and different periodizations can be made, which highlight other aspects and where the "Cold War" plays a supporting role if any at all. Three different narratives will be considered. First, one that breaks down the 1945–1990 periodization in a manner that focuses on "other" possible grand narratives. As such, one possibility is to take the time frame commencing from the eighteenth century until the present as the "Age of Imperialism/Age of Empire" (Hobsbawn 1997).[4] In this narrative the privileged aspect or issue would be imperialism and events would be narrated with the aim of explaining imperialism. Hence in this narrative the Cold War becomes part of a larger picture of imperialism whereby it is only an aspect of imperialism and events in the time frame 1945 to 1990 do not prioritize Cold War issues but rather considers those issues as they relate to explaining imperialism.

A second possibility brings forth events from 1945 to 1990. It links them at times to pre-1945 or post-1990 time frames that depict continuities and demonstrates that neither 1945 nor 1990 were clear-cut ruptures. An alternative can be written by taking the Third World as the center of the story whereby the Third World emerges as an active actor that questioned and challenged the bipolar view of the international system. In this narrative, "non-alignment" and the "spirit of Bandung" attempted to create an environment where Third World countries did not have to belong to either camp. In this narrative the "Cold War" is not a global war encapsulating all aspects of the international system but *one* aspect of the international that was challenged. This narrative privileges events and issues such as decolonization and development, and discusses issues such as the extension of membership in the United Nations (UN) and the New International Economic Order (NIEO), issues that the Cold War could not explain.[5]

A third possibility for alternatives breaks down the linearity imposed upon the onset of the Cold War and the tale of "inevitability." For the Turkish case, the narrative can include the renegotiations and discussions surrounding the nature of democracy in Turkey and the debates on foreign policy between 1944 and 1950 that inscribed "inevitability" into events in order to legitimize subsequent decisions. Cos and Bilgin (2010: 44) argue that:

> whereas previous communications of the USSR were portrayed by Turkey's policymakers as bilateral exchanges that did not impair the state of "sincere friendship" between the two countries, the June 1945 message from Molotov was channeled to the public as "Stalin's demands," that is, a threat to Turkey's sovereign existence and territorial integrity.

The aim of such a narrative would not only be to underline the problematic nature of the "inevitability" ascribed to the onset of the Cold War but bring forth a story of "Turkey" that is not embedded within and subsumed under the narrative terrain of the "Cold War."

Conclusion

De-centering Western-centric IR is an important agenda and deserves attention. But this attention remains focused on how the West created "fields," "concepts," and "theories" that constitute what should be a globally sensitive discipline. Such an approach places the West, once again, at the center of the IR narrative. This chapter problematizes the West's Western-centrism: it grants no agency or consideration to the non-Western actor. At the same time, this chapter opens for discussion an overlooked aspect of the debate: that is, the complicity of the non-West in reproducing this Western-centric IR. From this opening, perhaps new narratives about world politics can arise.

Without bringing in the non-Western actor into the story of IR's Western-centrism, even critiques of Western-centrism remain Western-centric. As such, any effort to deconstruct the Western-centrism of the field remains incomplete because it takes as its focus only the West and does not problematize the complicities and reproductions of Western-centrism in other settings. In order to write narratives about world politics that do not reproduce Western-centric assumptions, it is necessary to not write a Western-centric story of Western-centrism and attempt to deconstruct Western-centrism globally.

Notes

1 See, for example, White (1973, 1978, 1987), Ankersmit (1983), Veyne (1984), Munslow (1997), and Jenkins (2003).
2 For more on the origins of the Cold War, see Leffler and Westad (2012).
3 The Soviet notes refer to a series of correspondences between Turkey and the Soviet Union. Molotov gave the initial message on March 1945 to Selim Sarper, Turkey's Ambassador to Moscow. The message informed Sarper that the Soviet Union would not extend the 1925 Treaty of Friendship and Non-Aggression. On June 7, 1945 Molotov made a series of "demands" that included the return of certain provinces, bases to be allocated to USSR, and an agreement to be reached on the status of the Straits. For more on the notes exchanged and the Straits question see Vali (1971).
4 For more on Empire and International Relations, see Barkawi and Laffey (2002).
5 For a narrative of these events, see Mortimer (1984); for a discussion of Bandung see pp. 6–23; and for a discussion of the NIEO see pp. 43–71. For a narrative of the emergence of the idea of Afro-Asian unity and its development also see Jansen (1966), especially pp. 19–50.

References

Acharya, A. and B. Buzan. (eds) (2010) *Non-Western International Relations Theory: Perspectives on and beyond Asia*. United Kingdom: Routledge.

Anderson, T. (1981) *The United States, Great Britain, and the Cold War, 1944–1947*. Columbia: University of Missouri Press.

Ankersmit, F.R. (1983) *Narrative Logic: A Semantic Analysis of the Historian's Language*. The Hague: M. Nijhoff.

Celik, Y. (1999) *Contemporary Turkish Foreign Policy*. Westport, CT: Greenwood Publishing Group, Incorporated.

Cos, K. and P. Bilgin. (2010) "Stalin's Demands: Constructions of the 'Soviet Other' in Turkey's Foreign Policy, 1919–1945." *Foreign Policy Analysis* 6(1): 43–60.

Cox, R. (1981) "Social Forces, States and World Orders: Beyond International Relations Theory." *Millennium* 10(2): 126–155.

De Certeau, M. (1988) *The Writing of History*. New York: Columbia University Press.
Gaddis, J.L. (1972) *The United States and the Origins of the Cold War: 1941–1947*. New York: Columbia University Press.
Hale, W. (2000) *Turkish Foreign Policy, 1774–2000*. London and Portland: Frank Cass.
Halle, L.J. (1967) *The Cold War as History*. New York: Harper and Row.
Hobsbawn, Eric. (1997) *The Age of Empire, 1875–1914*. London: Abacus.
Hobson, J. (2012) *The Eurocentric Conception of World Politics: Western International Relations Theory, 1760–2010*. Cambridge: Cambridge University Press.
Jansen, G.H. (1966) *Nonalignment and the Afro-Asian states*. New York: Praeger.
Jenkins, K. (2003) *Re-thinking History*. London: Routledge.
Jones, B.G. (ed.) (2006) *Decolonizing International Relations*. Lanham, MD: Rowman & Littlefield.
Leffler, M.P. (1992) *A Preponderance of Power: National Security, The Truman Administration and the Cold War*. Stanford, CA: Stanford University Press.
Leffler, M.P. and O.A. Westad (eds) (2012) *The Cambridge History of the Cold War: Volume 1 Origins*. Cambridge: Cambridge University Press.
Ling, L. (2014) "Hobson's Eurocentric World Politics: The Journey Begins." *Millennium: Journal of International Studies* 42(2): 456–463.
Mortimer, R. (1984) *The Third World Coalition in International Politics*. London: Westview Press.
Munslow, A. (1997) *Deconstructing History*. London and New York: Routledge.
Rigney, A. (1990) *The Rhetoric of Historical Representation: Three Narrative Histories of the French Revolution*. Cambridge: Cambridge University Press.
Sever, A. (1997) *Soguk Savas Kusatmasinda Turkiye, Bati ve Orta Dogu*. Istanbul: Boyut Kitaplari.
Shilliam, R. (ed.) (2010) *International Relations and Non-Western Thought: Imperialism, Colonialism and Investigations of Global Modernity*. Abingdon: Routledge.
Turkkaya, A. (1970) *NATO and Turkey*. Ankara: Sevinc Print House.
Vali, F.A. (1971) *Bridge across the Bosporus: The Foreign Policy of Turkey*. Baltimore, MD: Johns Hopkins Press.
Veyne, P. (1984) *Writing History*. Manchester: Manchester University Press.
White, H. (1973) *Metahistory: The Historical Imagination in Nineteenth-Century Europe*. Baltimore, MD: Johns Hopkins University Press.
White, H. (1978) *Tropics of Discourse: Essays in Cultural Criticism*. Baltimore, MD: Johns Hopkins University Press.
White, H. (1987) *The Content of the Form: Narrative Discourse and Historical Representation*. Baltimore, MD: Johns Hopkins University Press.
Williams, W.A. (1962) *The Tragedy of American Diplomacy*. New York: Del Pub Co.

PART III
Theory

9

THE POSTCOLONIAL PARADOX OF EASTERN AGENCY

John M. Hobson

The development of postcolonial/non-Eurocentric challenges to Western international theory has gained rapid pace within international relations (IR) studies since the late 1990s. These developments have revealed the Eurocentric foundations of international and international political economy (IPE) theory (Ling 2002; Blaney and Inayatullah 2010; Hobson 2012, 2013), while also developing empirical accounts and explanations of the rise and development of the international system/world economy (Hobson 2004; Suzuki, Zhang, and Quirk 2013). One of the posited antidotes to Eurocentrism that has emerged from this growing literature is the need to factor in the role of Eastern agency into our empirical accounts and theories of world politics/economics. This derives from the unreflexively held postcolonial axiom, derived from Edward Said ([1978] 2003), that Eurocentrism/Orientalism reifies the West by granting it exclusive agency in the world while denying the existence of Eastern agency pretty much outright. Moreover, Orientalists assumed that imperialism was the only means to bring inferior races into civilized modernity. However, on much closer inspection it turns out, I shall argue, that Eurocentric international theory offers a wide spectrum of positions on these matters, ranging from awarding Eastern peoples/societies very low levels of agency to moderate and even high or very high levels, all of which are framed within different normative conceptions of imperialism and anti-imperialism. Accordingly, this means that we need to be much more careful when treating Eastern agency as the antidote to Eurocentrism. This is not to say that Eastern agency is unimportant, for I believe that it is a crucial part of the antidote. But it is to say that we need to be much more precise when conceptualizing its place within non-Eurocentric theory. Hence the *paradox of Eastern agency*: that the perceived postcolonial/non-Eurocentric antidote to Eurocentrism/Orientalism is to "bring Eastern agency in" when it turns out that it was there in some form or another within international theory all along.

Key constituent discourses emerge when we unpack Said's highly reductive and monolithic conception of Orientalism. This chapter's argument is developed in three sections. Section one sketches as briefly as possible the various dimensions and component parts of Orientalism. The second section then sketches the various positions with regards to Eastern agency in the racist-imperialist and racist anti-imperialist literature while the third does the same for the imperialist and anti-imperialist Eurocentric institutionalist literature.

Unpacking and re-visioning Orientalism

To counter what I view as Said's double-reductive move, I begin by breaking down his concept of Orientalism into two component parts – scientific racism and Eurocentric institutionalism – and then sub-dividing these categories into their imperialist and anti-imperialist components (see Table 9.1).

In essence, Eurocentric institutionalism locates difference to the degree of rationality found within a society's institutions and culture. The West is proclaimed superior because it has supposedly rational institutions, while the East's inferiority is presented as a function of its alleged irrational institutions. Thus, while the West has for the last three centuries allegedly enjoyed *civilized* democracy/liberalism/individualism/science, conversely, the East is said to have endured or suffered *barbaric* Oriental despotism, or simply the *savage* state of nature alongside authoritarianism/collectivism/mysticism. By contrast, scientific racism places a strong degree of emphasis on genetics and biology as elements underpinning difference while often emphasizing the role of climate and physical environment. For some, the causal pendulum of race behavior swings towards the climatic/environmental pole, whereas for others it swings more towards the genetic pole. This multivalent archipelago of scientific racist discourses was far more heterogeneous than Eurocentric institutionalism and was fractured into all sorts of sub-discourses, including social Darwinism, Eugenics, Weismann's germ plasm theory, Mendelianism and, not least, Lamarckianism, some of which were complementary while others conflicted.

A crucial complicating factor of note is that some variants of scientific racism, specifically Lamarckianism, factored social behavior/practice into the mix alongside environment and climate when analyzing racial characteristics. Not surprisingly, this feature sometimes means that Lamarckian international theorists resemble various Eurocentric institutionalists in their analyses and political visions. J.A. Hobson's paternalist Eurocentric vision of imperialism, for example, bears many striking

TABLE 9.1 The four variants of generic Eurocentrism/Orientalism in International Theory

	Pro-imperialist	*Anti-imperialist*
Eurocentric institutionalism	(A) Paternalist	(B) Anti-paternalist
Scientific racism	(C) Offensive	(D) Defensive

TABLE 9.2 Alternative conceptions of Orientalism/Eurocentrism

	Said's reductive conception of Orientalism	"Non-reductive" conception of Eurocentric institutionalism and scientific racism
Relationship of Orientalism and scientific racism	**Inherent** Racism, especially social Darwinism and Eugenics, is merely the highest expression of imperialist-Orientalism	**Contingent** Racism and Eurocentric institutionalism are analytically differentiated even if at times they share various overlaps
The centrality of the "standard of civilisation"	**Yes**	**Yes**
Agency is the monopoly of the West	**Inherent** The West has hyper-agency, the East has none	**Contingent** The West always has pioneering agency, while the East ranges from high to low levels of agency; but where these are high they are deemed to be regressive or barbaric
Propensity for imperialism	**Inherent**	**Contingent** Can be imperialist and anti-imperialist
Sensibility: Propensity for Western triumphalism	**Inherent**	**Contingent** Racism is often highly defensive and reflects Western anxiety. Some racist thought and much of Eurocentric institutionalism exhibits Western self-confidence, if not triumphalism

similarities with the Lamarckian vision advanced by Paul Reinsch, as I show later. More generally, this means that at times the borderline between scientific racism and Eurocentric institutionalism is blurred or fuzzy.

Table 9.2 differentiates my reading from that of Said's. I have included all the key dimensions, the sum of which is that the relationship between scientific racism/Eurocentric institutionalism and the various dimensions concerning imperialism, Eastern agency, and Western triumphalism is much more important.

This article reveals the ontological place of Eastern agency found within the four key meta-narratives that usually go under the generic term of Orientalism. I extract these from the international theory literature in the West since 1760. Because post-1945 international theory takes on various Eurocentric institutional guises, I shall begin by providing a highly condensed discussion of pre-1945 scientific racism.

Eastern agency within anti-imperialist scientific racist international theory, 1850–1945

Here, we encounter a spectrum of positions with respect to Eastern agency within anti-imperialist racist thought. Three broad positions construct a continuum. At the far left-hand side lies those racists who denied Eastern races agency altogether. We encounter the likes of David Starr Jordan (in his pre-1919 works) and James Blair. They argue that the non-white races are incapable of auto-generating and are therefore mired in regressive backwardness and stasis. This vision deems the civilizing mission pointless given that these races are incapable of being uplifted – to wit Jordan's claim that

> the race problem of the tropics [is] perennial and insoluble, for free institutions cannot exist where free men cannot live. The territorial [imperialist] expansion now contemplated [by the US government] would not extend our institutions, because the proposed colonies are incapable of self-government.
>
> (Jordan 1901: 44; cf. Blair 1899: 18)

Moreover, Jordan presents a series of arguments that amount to the conclusion that empire is not worth the candle because it will serve ultimately to harm the colonial power and do nothing to help the inferior races abroad.

Moving rightwards to the mid-point of our continuum, we encounter the likes of Herbert Spencer and William Graham Sumner who awarded the Eastern races a higher, albeit "moderate," amount of agency. Spencer asserted that all races are capable of auto-generation even if some – namely the black races – would take a very long time, possibly centuries, before they would break through to modernity. As Spencer put it:

> The ultimate development of the ideal man is logically certain – as certain as any conclusion in which we place the most implicit faith; for instance that all men will die ... Progress, therefore, is not an accident, but a necessity. Instead of civilization being artificial, it is a part of nature [and is therefore open to all races].
>
> (Spencer [1851] 1864: 79–80)

Spencer in effect grants the Eastern races what I call "derivative agency," insofar as he believes that they will auto-generate into civilized modernity but only by following the "natural" path that had been pioneered by Europeans.

Spencer and Sumner also insisted that imperialism was dangerous both for colonizer- and colonized-societies. Spencer reveled in pointing out the hypocrisy of those left-wing racist-imperialists who criticized his own laissez-faire political economy as callous while in the next breath,

> you may hear them, with utter disregard of bloodshed and death, contend that it is in the interests of humanity at large that the inferior races should be exterminated and their places occupied by the superior races ... Not worthy of much respect then, as it seems to me, is this generous consideration of the inferior at home which is accompanied by the unscrupulous sacrifice of the inferior abroad.
>
> (Spencer 1881: 71)[1]

Moreover, while imperialism would hinder the non-white races equally it would lead to the "rebarbarization of (white) civilization," thereby causing a regression of Western civilization into the more backward and barbaric-coercive "militant society" (Spencer 1902: 157–200).

Finally, a third major strand of anti-imperialist (cultural-realist) racism can be found in the genre that is represented by the likes of Charles Henry Pearson (1894) and Lothrop Stoddard (1920). Here the Eastern races – specifically the yellow races of Japan and China as well as the Islamic brown races, which are also singled out by Stoddard – are granted very high levels of agency. While they view these races as capable of modernizing this goes hand-in-hand with the negative trope of what I call Eastern "predatory agency," for they view the rapidly developing yellow and brown races as posing a significant threat to white civilization, in particular, and world order, more generally. Both writers were extremely concerned by the Yellow/Brown Peril that batters the walls of the Western citadel. Their posited solution for the West is to retreat from empire – for the most part. Colonizing the yellow and brown races would only lead to negative blowback for the West, unlike Stoddard and especially Karl Pearson, and many other racists for that matter, viewed the colonization of the tropics as pointless, owing to the degenerative impact of the sun's actinic rays on the white race.

Eastern agency within imperialist scientific racist international theory, 1850–1945

Here again we encounter a continuum or spectrum of positions ranging from very low levels of Eastern agency to moderate and sometimes high levels. With regards to the latter position we encounter the likes of Alfred Mahan and Halford Mackinder. In Mackinder (1904) and Mahan (1897), we encounter the trope of "predatory" Eastern agency. Both of these authors convened the notion of the Yellow Peril, viewing the Chinese and Japanese as future threats to white racial supremacy. Unlike Stoddard and especially Pearson, however, their political response was to advance the cause of white racial imperialism as the means to counter and contain such a potential threat.

The other extreme denies Eastern agency outright. A range of racists embraced differing configurations of social Darwinism, Eugenics, and Lamarckianism. The likes of Theodore Roosevelt (1905), Benjamin Kidd (1898), and Winwood Reade (1864) believed, like many Social Darwinists, that the agency-less non-white races were destined simply to die out upon contact with the white races since they were incapable of adapting to civilized life conditions. I call this the "*indirect* racial exterminist" brand of racist-imperialism. Others argued for a "*direct* racial exterminism" through which the white races would renew their racial vitality by conquering the non-white races and actively destroying them – either through breeding them out of existence (Gumplowicz 1883; Ward [1903] 2002) or by wiping them out with the gun (Pearson 1905). And others too believed that the absence of Eastern agency meant that the white race was destined to spread and dominate the world (Dilke 1868; Seeley [1883] 1906).

Finally, the mid-point position can be found in the likes of Henry Sidgwick (1897), Paul Reinsch (1905), and Alleyne Ireland (1905). They paralleled the paternalist Eurocentrics, arguing in effect that the non-white races were imbued with "conditional agency," such that they could develop but *only on condition* that the white race colonizes them first and delivers the required rational institutions via the civilizing mission. But while their political stances were very similar to those of the paternalist Eurocentrics the difference hinged on the particular meta-narrative that underpinned their analyses. Thus, for example, while the theories of Hobson and Reinsch were very similar, the latter's advocacy of an empathic imperialism rested on the belief that Eastern progress is a function of the passing on of rational modes of behavior that are delivered by the West through the civilizing mission, which are then absorbed and passed on within the Eastern races through hereditary characteristics to subsequent generations. Hobson, however, believed that the passing on of rational institutions from the West enables Eastern peoples to undo the blockages not in their minds but in their irrational societal and political institutions. To understand this I now turn to consider the Eurocentric institutionalist literature. Because it has dominated since 1945, I shall spend more time considering it.

Eastern agency within imperialist Eurocentric institutionalist international theory

Imperialist Eurocentrism embodies a strong dose of paternalism, which awards Western societies a *pioneering agency* such that they can *auto-generate* or auto-develop through what I call the "Eurocentric logic of immanence" into modernity. Conversely, Eastern societies are granted *conditional agency* and are unable to auto-generate or self-develop. That is, Europe's *exceptional* institutional and cultural genius means that development into modernity was immanent from the outset (i.e., from ancient Greece onwards) and that the story of Europe's breakthrough into capitalist modernity was foretold or preordained – it was but a historical fait accompli or rite of passage. This discourse deems Eastern peoples to have a *latent* rationality such that full rationality was blocked from reaching the surface on account of their irrational institutions. Accordingly, at worst their societies could not develop and were destined to languish in stagnation (as in savage anarchic societies), or at best they would be caught within a kind of high-level agrarian equilibrium trap (as in some barbaric societies).

But a solution remains at hand. In this paternalist imaginary, the West must deliver the necessary rational institutions to the Eastern societies so as to surface their latent reason, thereby kick-starting their progressive development into modernity – otherwise known as the "white man's burden." Once the necessary institutions have been delivered, Eastern peoples and societies can develop autonomously thereafter. In this discourse, Eastern peoples are awarded "conditional agency" in that they *can* develop but only *on condition* that the West intervenes first through the civilizing mission. This form of Eastern agency is higher than that awarded by those racists who denied the Eastern peoples any agency whatsoever, though obviously far lower to the levels of agency that are awarded to the Europeans.

One point of note: there was a range of positions regarding the precise modus operandi of the civilizing mission. At the far left-hand side of the continuum we encounter the likes of John Stuart Mill ([1859] 1984) and Karl Marx ([1867] 1954), both of whom argued that imperialism should take a harsh, coercive form and that this was the only way that rational institutions could be delivered so as to kick-start Eastern development. Nevertheless, and somewhat paradoxically, while Marx approved of imperialism as the only means by which the Eastern societies could be released from their self-imposed stagnation, he was insistent that the brutality of imperialism was lamentable in a moral sense (Marx [1867] 1954: 703).

At the far right of the continuum, we encounter a series of thinkers who argued for a much more "empathic" brand of imperialism: one that was often tied in with what might be called "international government." This was first mooted in 1902 by J.A. Hobson in the second part of his famous text, *Imperialism: A Study* ([1938] 1968). Hobson believed that the solution to the exploitative form of empire, or what he called "insane imperialism," could be remedied not simply by income redistribution within the colonizer society but through what he called "sane imperialism," wherein national imperialisms would be supervised by an international government to ensure that the rights of the natives within the colonies would be upheld and they would be treated fairly and with dignity. This became the blueprint for inter-war paternalist Eurocentrism, which also embraced, in effect, the trope of *conditional* Eastern agency (Woolf 1920, [1928] 1933; Zimmern 1934; Angell 1937).

Finally, there is a range of thinkers who wrote before 1914 who are situated at the mid-point of the continuum. Surprisingly, some of them are conventionally associated with the cause of non-interventionism and anti-imperialism: Richard Cobden (1868), John Bright (1895), and Norman Angell (1913). Perhaps it is here where my reading will find resistance, possibly by various historians of Cobden. Thus it is important to note my conclusion: that Cobden's writings were politically schizophrenic. For there is no doubting the point that he spent much time criticizing empire and all manner of quotes could be marshaled in this respect. But he also advanced a clear paternalist Eurocentric analysis that is found on no less than 443 of the 991 pages in his posthumously published two-volume set, *Political Writings*. And it seems curious to say the least that some historians who have spent many years of their lives studying Cobden have seemingly failed to come across these crucial writings.

Intersecting these two radically different interpretations of Cobden is the issue of the Crimean War. The conventional interpretation suggests that Cobden's anti-Crimean War stance was symptomatic of his non-interventionist credentials *par excellence*. But there is a clear paternalist Eurocentric sensibility that led him to this conclusion. Turkey was not worth "saving" as its barbaric institutions – particularly its Oriental despotic state and its regressive Islamic religion – had laid waste to this "marvellous" country and its people (Cobden 1868: 19, 173–174). And from there Cobden delivers his paternalist-imperial message, declaring that

> we have no hesitation in avowing it as our deliberate conviction that not merely Great Britain, but the entire civilized [i.e., Western] world, will have reason to congratulate itself, the moment when [Turkey] again falls beneath the sceptre of any other European power whatever. Ages must elapse before its favoured region will become ... the seat and centre of commerce, civilisation, and true religion; but the first step towards this consummation must be to convert Constantinople again into that which every lover of humanity and peace longs to behold it – the capital of a Christian [civilised] people.
> *(Cobden 1868: 33)*

Thus Cobden positively endorsed a Russian colonial take-over of Turkey on the grounds that this Western civilizing mission would yield considerable benefits not just to Turkey but also to Europe in general and to Britain in particular (Cobden 1868: 33–37, 189–191). And, in typical Eurocentric style, he concludes that Turkish (Eastern) society was "unchanging and stationary" whereas Russian (European) society was "progressing" (Cobden 1868: 187–188). Interestingly, John Bright, another so-called non-interventionist Cobdenite, counselled similarly:

> We are building up our Eastern Policy on a false foundation – namely on the perpetual maintenance of the most immoral and filthy of all despotisms over one of the fairest portions of the earth which it has desolated, and over a population it has degraded but has not been able to destroy.
> *(Bright 1895: 14)*

In the post-1945 era, many IR theories embrace paternalist Eurocentrism. The classical pluralist wing of the English School, for example, argued that the expansion of European international society in the eighteenth and nineteenth centuries and running down to the 1960s was a progressive movement that helped solve the problem of deviant Eastern backwardness (Watson [1992] 2009; Bull 2000). While neorealist hegemonic stability theory and Keohane's neoliberal institutionalist perspective also rely on the formula of pioneering Western agency/conditional Eastern agency (Hobson 2012), this Eurocentric idiom has returned with a vengeance in the post-Cold War era mainly, though not exclusively, in the guise of liberal international theory. Indeed large swathes of liberal-inspired international theory have gone back to the future of the paternalist Eurocentrism of the period between *c.*1830 and 1945. The 1945–1989 era, dominated by the process of decolonization and the "bad name" that Hitler had given the cause of racism, saw *subliminal* Eurocentrism oust scientific racism, whereby terms such as empire, civilization, barbarism, savagery, and white racial supremacy were dropped in favor of their whitewashed equivalences: hegemony, "modernity versus tradition," and "core versus periphery." But after 1989 the E-word came back – "empire" – as did the

C-word – "civilization." And with the Soviet Union gone by 1991, the way was open for a reassertion of Western civilizational pride across the world and the "new imperialism" whereby the Rest would gloriously be remade in the image of the West (Fukuyama 1992; Rothkopf 1997; Rawls 1999; Ignatieff 2003; Cooper 2004) all of which was encased within the explicit or manifest Eurocentrism that had existed before 1945. Moreover, much of this was repeated within a large literature that I call "Western realism" (Ferguson 2004; Brzezinski 2004; Krasner 2004, 2008).

Eastern agency in anti-imperialist/anti-paternalist Eurocentric institutionalism

Once again we encounter a range of positions in the wide anti-imperialist Eurocentric literature. In the liberal schema we encounter Immanuel Kant (1970) and Adam Smith ([1776] 1937) who award higher levels of agency to Eastern societies than did their paternalist Eurocentric cousins. They argue that Eastern peoples have a *moderate* level of agency insofar as they are deemed to be capable of auto-generation. This plays into their stages model of development. Smith and Kant both believed that *all* societies and peoples would traverse the different stages of development *of their own accord*, thereby implicitly negating the need for a civilizing mission that, for paternalist Eurocentrics, is a vital pre-requisite for Eastern development. In this way Smith awarded the East what can be called *derivative* agency (wherein non-Western peoples would spontaneously develop into modernity but only by following the natural path that had been trailblazed by the pioneering Europeans). Important here is Smith's assumption that modern commercialism is congruent with (universal) human nature such that modern capitalism is immanent within the make-up of *all* societies, given his famous definition of human nature as "the propensity to truck, barter and exchange one thing for another" (Smith [1776] 1937: 13). That is, all peoples would converge eventually on this stage of development since it was simply part of humankind's universal human nature.

For Smith and Kant, all societies would converge upon a commercial society. But they would only do so by following the "natural" path that had been laid by the pioneering Europeans. In these respects Smith and Kant overlap with the racist perspective of Spencer and Sumner discussed earlier. A further point of overlap with Spencerean racism lies in Smith's and Kant's anti-imperialist arguments: intervention through imperialism would serve only to disturb in a negative fashion the developmental trajectory of both the colonized and colonizer countries. And they also abhorred the immorality and arrogance of Western imperialism, as did Spencer and Sumner (Kant 1970; Smith [1776] 1937: Book 4, Chapter 7).[2] Nevertheless, they rejected the *racist* basis of Spencer's theoretical architecture.

Another anti-paternalist theory that critiques Western imperialism is found in numerous classical Marxist works (bar Marx and Engels) (Lenin [1916] 1973; Hilferding [1910] 1985) and in much of modern neo-Marxism. In this genre, we encounter the idiom of an all-powerful Leviathanesque West that crushes the passive and inert East through imperialism, both in its formal and informal guises. Many readers might reason that a critique of the West and of Western imperialism would surely be congruent with an anti-Eurocentric approach. But it is perfectly possible to produce a critique of the West while maintaining a Eurocentric stance. In fact, in one crucial respect this classical Marxist and neo-Marxist approaches are yet more Eurocentric than Smith's and Kant's approach as well as the paternalist Eurocentrics, Marx and Engels, Hobson and Angell. For this genre awards the *lowest* levels of Eastern agency found in the majority of the Eurocentric and scientific racist genres already discussed.

Finally, the anti-imperialist theory of the "clash of civilizations," advanced by Samuel Huntington (1996) and William Lind (1991) awards very high levels of agency to the Eastern peoples. This approach very much takes us back to the future of pre-1945 racist cultural-realism that was advanced by Stoddard, C.H. Pearson, and others, though now dressed up in Eurocentric institutional clothing. Once again, Eastern agency is viewed as "predatory" insofar as various Eastern peoples – mainly the Muslims and the Chinese – pose a threat to Western hegemony and supremacy. And once again, the posited solution is to avoid Western imperialist universalism and batten down the hatches of the Western citadel to maintain a pure Western identity within a multicultural world.

Conclusion

The upshot of this chapter is that the traditional assumption that Western-centrism always denies agency to non-Western societies and peoples is in need of correction. While certainly some approaches (especially social Darwinism) deny non-Western agency outright, other variants of Eurocentrism grant moderate or high levels of agency. The Eugenicist scientific racists, Lothrop Stoddard and Charles Pearson, award the Yellow and Brown races very high levels of agency. True, some of this is presented as predatory/barbaric agency but they also assign significant levels of developmental capacity (as do their modern-day Eurocentric institutionalist contemporaries, Samuel Huntington and William Lind). Moreover, some argue that non-Western peoples can spontaneously develop into modernity (such as the Eurocentric institutionalists, Adam Smith and Immanuel Kant, who find their scientific racist equivalents in Herbert Spencer and William Sumner). Ultimately, though, what none of them do is question the centrality and autonomy of the West in either world development or world politics. Hence one core antidote to this Western-centrism lies in revealing the ways in which East and West mutually interact to shape each other as well as world politics through a non-Eurocentric dialogical approach.

Notes

1 See also Spencer ([1893] 1966).
2 For a fuller discussion see Hobson (2012: 62–66).

References

Angell, N. (1913) *The Great Illusion*. London: G.P. Putnam's Sons.
Angell, N. (1937) *The Defence of the Empire*. London: Hamish Hamilton.
Blair, J.L. (1899) *Imperialism, Our New National Policy*. St. Louis: Gottschalk.
Blaney, D.L. and N. Inayatullah (2010) *Savage Economics*. London: Routledge.
Bright, J. (1895) *The Public Letters of the Right Hon. John Bright*. London: Sampson Low, Marston & Co.
Brzezinski, Z. (2004) *The Choice*. New York: Basic Books.
Bull, H. (2000) "The European International Order." In K. Alderson and A. Hurrell (eds.), *Hedley Bull on International Society*, 170–187. London: Palgrave Macmillan.
Cobden, R. (1868) *Political Writings*, 2 Volumes. London: William Ridgway.
Cooper, R. (2004) *The Breaking of Nations*. London: Atlantic Books.
Dilke, C. (1868) *Greater Britain*, 2 Volumes. London: Macmillan.
Ferguson, N. (2004) *Colossus*. Harmondsworth: Penguin.
Fukuyama, F. (1992) *The End of History and the Last Man*. London: Hamish Hamilton.
Gumplowicz, L. (1883) *Der Rassenkampf*. Innsbruck: Verlag der Wagner Schen Univ. Buchhandlung.
Hilferding, R. ([1910] 1985) *Finance Capital*. London: Routledge & Kegan Paul.
Hobson, J.A. ([1938] 1968) *Imperialism: A Study*, 3rd edition. London: George Allen & Unwin.
Hobson, J.M. (2004) *The Eastern Origins of Western Civilisation*. Cambridge: Cambridge University Press.
Hobson, J.M. (2012) *The Eurocentric Conception of World Politics*. Cambridge: Cambridge University Press.
Hobson, J.M. (2013) "Part 1 – Revealing the Eurocentric Foundations of IPE: A Critical Historiography of the Discipline from the Classical to the Modern Era." *Review of International Political Economy* 20(5): 1024–1054.
Huntington, Samuel P. (1996) *The Clash of Civilizations and the Remaking of World Order*. London: Touchstone.
Ignatieff, M. (2003) "Empire Lite." *Prospect* 83 (February) (http://www.prospectmagazine.co.uk/2003/02/empirelite/) (Downloaded: October 5, 2008).
Ireland, A. (1905) *The Far Eastern Tropics*. Boston: Houghton, Mifflin & Co.
Jordan, D.S. (1901) *Imperial Democracy*. New York: D. Appleton & Co.
Kagan, R. (2008) *The Return of History and the End of Dreams*. London: Atlantic Books.
Kant, I. (1970) *Kant's Political Writings*. Edited by H. Reiss. Cambridge: Cambridge University Press.
Kidd, B. (1898) *The Control of the Tropics*. New York: Macmillan.
Krasner, S.D. (2004) "Sharing Sovereignty: New Institutions for Collapsed and Failing States." *International Security* 29(2): 85–120.
Kagan, R. (2008) *The Return of History and the End of Dreams*. London: Atlantic Books.
Lenin, V.I. ([1916] 1973) *Imperialism, the Highest Stage of Capitalism*. Peking: Foreign Languages Press.
Lind, William S. (1991) "Defending Western Culture." *Foreign Policy* 84: 40–50.
Ling, L.H.M. (2002) *Postcolonial International Relations*. Houndmills: Palgrave Macmillan.
Mackinder, H.J. (1904) "The Geographical Pivot of History." *The Geographical Journal* 23(4): 421–437.
Mahan, A.T. (1897) *The Influence of Seapower upon History*. London: Sampson, Law, Marston.
Marx, K. ([1867] 1954) *Capital*, Volume 1. London: Lawrence & Wishart.
Mill, J.S. ([1859] 1984) "A Few Words on Non-Intervention." In J.M. Robson (ed.), *Collected Works of John Stuart Mill*, Volume 21, 111–124. Toronto: Toronto University Press.

Pearson, C.H. (1894) *National Life and Character: A Forecast*. London: Macmillan.
Pearson, K. (1905) *National Life from the Standpoint of Science*. London: Adam & Charles Black.
Rawls, J. (1999) *The Law of Peoples*. London: Harvard University Press.
Reade, W.W. (1864) *Savage Africa*. New York: Harper & Brothers.
Reinsch, P.S. (1905) *Colonial Administration*. New York: Macmillan.
Roosevelt, T. (1905) *The Strenuous Life*. New York: The Century Co.
Rothkopf, D. (1997) "In Praise of Cultural Imperialism." *Foreign Policy* 107 (Summer): 38–53.
Said, E.W. ([1978] 2003) *Orientalism*. London: Penguin.
Seeley, J.R. ([1883] 1906) *The Expansion of England*. Leipzig: Velhagen & Klansing.
Sidgwick, H. (1897) *The Elements of Politics*. London: Macmillan.
Smith, A. ([1776] 1937) *The Wealth of Nations*. New York: The Modern Library.
Spencer, H. ([1851] 1864) *Social Statics*. New York: D. Appleton & Co.
Spencer, H. (1881) *The Man versus the State*. London: Williams & Norgate.
Spencer, H. ([1893] 1966) *The Principles of Ethics*, Volume 2. Osnabrück: Otto Zeller.
Spencer, H. (1902) *Facts and Comments*. New York: D. Appleton and Co.
Stoddard, T.L. (1920) *The Rising Tide of Color against White World Supremacy*. New York: Charles Scribner's Sons.
Suzuki, S., Y. Zhang and J. Quirk (eds.) (2013) *International Orders in Early Modern Europe*. London: Routledge.
Ward, L.F. ([1903] 2002) *Pure Sociology*. Honolulu: University Press of the Pacific.
Watson, A. ([1992] 2009) *The Evolution of International Society*. London: Routledge.
Woolf, L. (1920) *Empire and Commerce in Africa*. London: George Allen & Unwin.
Woolf, L. ([1928] 1933) *Imperialism and Civilization*. London: Hogarth Press.
Zimmern, A. (1934) *The Third British Empire*. Oxford: Oxford University Press.

10

JUSTIFICATION OF TRANS-CULTURAL INTERNATIONAL STUDIES

Gavan Duffy

In this chapter I propose an epistemological justification for construing international studies as a trans-cultural enterprise. Most international studies scholars would welcome a trans-cultural conception of our discipline. After all, nations and cultures regularly interact with and permeate one another. It's natural that a discipline concerned with global affairs would construe its mission as both international and trans-cultural. But an epistemological justification suggests more than just the dissemination and discussion of trans-cultural topics. It suggests and even requires that the discipline itself become trans-cultural in its institutions and practices, particularly its practices of inquiry. To do otherwise would be to foster a discipline engaged in the production not of knowledge, but of rationalization and regime apology.

If grounded in the Western epistemological tradition, my justification will have its greatest force. I will show that the Western tradition itself compels us to create a discipline not bound to that tradition. So I proceed by reviewing the central debate in modern Western epistemology. The most widely held contemporary positions in this debate present theory choice as a collective practice, conducted discursively among a community of inquirers. This outcome poses special problems for social sciences and particularly for those, like international studies, that traverse cultural bounds. I conclude by suggesting ways we might begin to address these problems.

Theories of theory choice

A justification accompanies any theoretical innovation. The proponent of any new theory must persuade others of its intrinsic merits and superiority over pre-existing competitors. Explicitly or implicitly, such a justification necessarily appeals to some meta-theory – a theory of theory choice – on the basis of which we adjudicate claims to the rightness of competing generalizations. So, on what theory of theory choice shall we rely?

The normative basis of theory choice

Before we can address this question, another question immediately arises. Do we require a theory of theory choice at a higher level of generality? That is, do we need a theory of choice to adjudicate competing theories of theory choice? If we do, we'll need a higher-level theory to adjudicate those theories and so on, forever.

Fortunately, we can sidestep this infinite regress. In selecting a theory of theory choice, we are selecting a normative principle for guiding our conduct in the business of selecting empirical theories. Therefore, we ask how we *should* adjudicate competing theories about what *is*. We should select this normative guidance in a principled way. That is, we should select guidance broadly consistent with the principles that guide us in other areas of life, our theory of the good. In so doing, we avoid the infinite regress.

Broad consensus surrounds the more desirable characteristics of theories. Most, regardless of any meta-theoretical allegiance, value such properties as clarity, consistency, parsimony, and fruitfulness for both practice and theory. Yet, because we often encounter trade-offs between these values, none can stand as the sole criterion of theory choice. We require more powerful guidance, a principle of a higher order, a maxim that can help us select among competing theories even in the presence of first-order trade-offs.

A theory's predictive capacity is by itself an inadequate indicator of its merit. We are interested not only in accounting for observed variations in dependent variables but we also seek an understanding of the underlying causal processes that produce such observations. Prediction certainly counts as valuable activity. However, the exclusive interest in prediction often betrays an interest in control. One learns to predict the values of dependent variables from the values of independent variables in order to control or engineer outcomes. That is, we learn how much we must change the values of independent variables in order to produce a change in the value of some dependent variable to some desirable level. When pursued in the natural sciences, this interest in controlling outcomes is ordinarily benign. But, when pursued in the human sciences, the interest in control becomes an interest in *social* control. We should question whose ends this control would serve.

Contemporary thinkers urge us instead to further "human emancipation" (Habermas 1984) or "human flourishing" (Putnam 1990: 135–141). I take these as closely related notions. One cannot be truly emancipated if one is not flourishing and one cannot flourish if one is not free from oppression, both externally administered and internally adopted. Together, they seem far more defensible normatively than whatever theory of the good might be invoked to justify anyone's interest in social control. They also have a heritage that spans the entire history of inquiry. Francis Bacon, who inaugurated modern empirical science, acted from the impulse to further human emancipation and flourishing. Bacon sought, through his inquiries, to predict the outcomes of natural processes and, from these predictions, to engineer solutions that further human flourishing by emancipating people from such natural ravages as famine, flood, and pestilence. One wonders what interest is served when methods for controlling nature are applied uncritically to humans and human societies.

In any event, I digress from my discussion of theories of theory choice. But I do so with purpose. I declare my affinity to the principle of human flourishing (or emancipation) as an underlying normative guide for choosing a theory of theory choice. This normative principle is consistent with the central Western norm of reciprocity, articulated in Christ's golden rule and Kant's categorical imperative. Because I wish to show that Western meta-theory requires a trans-cultural conception of international studies, it is useful, even necessary, that I adopt a normative principle for theory choice consistent with the Western tradition. Now I am ready to begin.

Lakatos' taxonomy

In recounting the debates that culminate in his own position, Lakatos (1970), drawing upon distinctions first advanced by Popper (1959, 1970) provided a taxonomy of epistemological frameworks. This scaffolding serves as a convenient platform upon which to construct an articulation of modern (post-Bacon) options with respect to theory adjudication. Lakatos presented a verbal account, which Figure 10.1 represents graphically as a series of distinctions.

The first branching distinguishes passivist from activist theories of knowledge. Passivists (i.e. classical empiricists) viewed knowledge as the imprint of nature on a perfectly inert mind, the *tabula rasa*. Activists understood that empirical observation required the active application of our expectations, concepts, and theories. But passivists considered mental activity only as a source of distortion.

Conservative Activism

Lakatos distinguished conservative from revolutionary activists on the basis of their attitudes towards conceptual structures. Conservatives believed that we apply basic

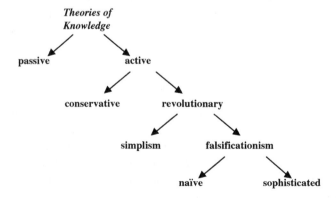

FIGURE 10.1 Lakatos' epistemological typology

human expectations to create conceptual structures that make sense of the world. We thereby make the world our world. However, once we acquire these conceptual structures, they virtually acquire us. Our theoretical commitments so constrain our expectations, conservative activists argued, that we misperceive experiences at odds with them. Revolutionary activists, however, granted us the capacity to break out of the conceptual prisons we erect. Most revolutionary activists would agree that our expectations can and often do cloud our perceptual judgments. Nevertheless, they credited us with the ability, albeit limited, to suspend or transcend our conceptual frames and to reformulate them when we deem necessary.

Lakatos' depiction of conservative activism amply fits verificationism. Verificationists treated theories, once verified empirically, as valid for all time and no longer subject to test. They deemed any verified theory a secure foundation for subsequent inquiry. Consequently, verificationists expected knowledge to grow in a unilinear, ever-progressing fashion, as successive generations of scholars erect new theories atop the edifice of theories their intellectual forebears had bequeathed to them.

If the spectacular supersession of Newtonian mechanics sounded verificationism's death knell, Karl Popper (1959) delivered the decisive blow to conservative activism. Popper cited Hume's problem – the fallibility of inductive inference – to demonstrate this proposition:

Proposition 1: *All theories are equally unverifiable*

Suppose our theory is that "all swans are white." No matter how many theory-confirming white swans we muster, we can never verify our theory. The next swan may well be non-white. No inductive inference is ever secure.

Popper disallowed recourse to probability. We cannot say that a theory is probably valid no matter how many verifying instances (and no matter how few falsifying instances) we muster. Given n, a finite number of confirming observations, in an infinite universe the probability that the next instance will confirm the theory is mathematically undefined, but infinitesimally close to zero: $n/\infty \approx 0$.

We cannot say that our theory about swans being white is probably verified, regardless of the number of white swans we have seen. Not only are all theories equally unverifiable, but:

Proposition 2: *All theories are equally improbable*

Verificationism encountered other troubles. Consider the "paradox of the ravens." If an observation of a black raven counts as a confirming instance of the theory that "all ravens are black," then so does an observation of any non-black non-raven, such as a white tennis shoe or a yellow banana. Because the statement "all ravens are black" is logically equivalent (by the contrapositive) to the statement "all non-black things are non-ravens," any non-black non-raven counts, as much as any black raven, as a confirmation of the theory that "all ravens are black."

Another difficulty for verificationism stems from its theory of meaning: "the meaning of a sentence is its method of verification." With this theory of meaning verificationists sought to demarcate meaningful statements – those that could be verified – from metaphysical statements, which verificationists took to be meaningless. They wanted to deny the cognitive significance of any proposition that fails to contribute to the prediction of our sensory stimulations (Putnam 1990: 139–140). They thereby dismissed as meaningless all metaphysical considerations. But the verificationist theory of meaning itself fails in just this way and so, on its own terms, lacks meaning.

Although verificationism predates them, the most recent advocates of verification were the logical positivists of the early twentieth century. Many international studies scholars today call themselves positivists, but few, if any, are verificationists. Generally, these "positivists" are actually falsificationists (discussed below) of one variety or other. This is an unfortunate source of continuing confusion.

Revolutionary Activism: Conventionalism

The school of French conventionalism bridged conservative activism (verificationism) and revolutionary activism. For conventionalists, the theoretical natural sciences provided no picture of nature, but only a logical construction. On this perspective, observations cannot falsify theories. Scientists rely on theories in order to observe or, more precisely, measure an observation scientifically (Popper 1959: 78–81). So long as observation theories were no more than systems of statements adopted by convention, scientists may freely modify them whenever recalcitrant observations threatened the theory under test. Conventionalists would effectively insulate favored theories from empirical disconfirmation.

Falsificationism

With falsificationism, Popper offered a remedy. Whenever scientists proposed a theory, they would state the conditions under which they would give it up. That is, if the theory were true, then it would have such-and-such empirical consequences. If these expected consequences failed to appear, *modus tollens* dictated the theory's rejection. If, however, the consequences did appear, the theory could not be accepted. To do so would be to affirm the consequent, a logical fallacy. A theory, for which the predicted empirical consequences were confirmed, could be accepted only provisionally. Some clever scientist may later refute the theory using better data, a more sophisticated test or superior acuity. Popper thereby devised a meta-theory founded on deductive inference. His falsificationism did not share the fallible inductive foundation of verificationism. Just as importantly, Popper's falsificationism, contra conventionalism, explicitly banished theoretical commitment beyond the bounds of good scientific practice.

Yet Popper's logical thesis did not describe actual scientific practice. Kuhn (1970), supported by much historical evidence, characterized normal scientific practice as "puzzle-solving" activity. Scientists in normal periods investigate the ramifications of their most well-corroborated theories. When this activity produces anomalies – results consistently at odds with the paradigm theory – a crisis threatens the complacency of the puzzle-solvers. Even then, because they are committed to it, they tend to defend the paradigm theory against any rivals who propose an incommensurable formulation that putatively resolves the anomaly. The incommensurability of the new paradigm – its poor fit with the terms of the old paradigm – inhibits its adoption among the adherents to the old. Scientific revolutions typically succeed less by the conversion of the current generation of scientists to the new paradigm and more by their replacement with a new generational cohort. Popper thought he had identified immutable rational standards that underpinned all scientific choice and discovery. But Kuhn's review of actual scientific practice indicated that no such standards existed.

Kuhn described theory choice as an irrational process more akin to gang warfare than to reasoned deliberation. This conclusion is unacceptable to many because it undermines the argumentative force of scientific results. If scientific choices are irrational, why should policymakers, for instance, place any weight on scientist's arguments? Lakatos (1970) endeavored to save science from irrationalism by elaborating falsificationism in light of Kuhn's critique. He pitched his "methodology of scientific research programs" as a more sophisticated understanding of the meta-theory Popper had proposed. In actuality, Lakatos proposed a new formulation that amounted to a major retrenchment. Lakatos abandoned theory as the main unit of epistemological significance. Theories cannot serve in that capacity, as any theorist may simply add a *ceteris paribus* condition to salvage a favored theory by incorporating an exception to the conditions of the experiment that putatively falsified the theory.

Lakatos made the "research program," or series of theories, the unit of epistemological significance. Adherents to a research program posited a "hard core" of fundamental propositions from which a "negative heuristic" diverts attention to a "protective belt" of "refutable variants." These scientists apply *modus tollens* to the variants and never to the hard core. A "positive heuristic" provides hints and suggestions on how to develop this protective belt. Lakatos required that each step in the belt's development be content-increasing, demonstrating a "consistently progressive theoretical problem shift." Now and then, the increase in content should be retrospectively corroborated, indicating the research program's "intermittently progressive empirical shift."

In enclosing falsificationism within this conceptual envelope, Lakatos deprived it of an important feature – a usable standard of theory choice. Popper had provided such a standard. He would reject a theory if the empirical evidence falsified it. But, if scientists failed to falsify the theory, he would accept it, but only provisionally and only so long as refutation efforts failed. Lakatos rejected the instant rationality implicit in Popper's "naïve" understanding of falsificationism. He recognized that budding programs require lenient treatment, as an early refutation may prevent such a program from discovering its most defensible formulations. Conversely, Lakatos argued that a more mature program might only appear to have been refuted: a cleverer inquirer with better measures, designs, or tests may later vindicate the program by refuting the refutation. So, for Lakatos, judgments regarding the validity of research programs can be made only in long hindsight.

Feyerabend noted that postponing such judgments entirely deprived falsificationism of its claim to rationality: any defender of a program subjected to refutation may simply deny the ripeness of a challenge to the progressiveness of the research program. "[I]f you are permitted to wait," Feyerabend asked, "why not wait a little longer?" For instance, consider Vasquez' (1997) depiction of (international studies) realism as a degenerating research program. Realists can respond that, however poorly realism may explain recent political history (e.g. the end of the Cold War), we should suspend judgment on its merits as a research program pending a forthcoming retrospective corroboration. A realist proclamation of corroboration, and thus also a progressive empirical shift, would follow the next appearance of world political events consonant with a realist understanding.

Thus, the standards that Lakatos advanced ultimately failed to address the substance of Kuhn's criticism of falsificationism, which had motivated Lakatos to devise them in the first place. Lakatos, contended Feyerabend (1970: 215), presented the apparatus of sophisticated falsificationism as merely a "verbal ornament, as a memorial to a happier time when it was still thought possible to run a complex and often catastrophic business like science by following a few simple and 'rational' rules." The effort to identify immutable rational standards had once again failed because advocates of the dominant theory can always ask critics to wait. Thus,

Proposition 3: *All theories are equally unfalsifiable*

Relativism

Because he considered Western rationality a willing tool of Western imperialism (Preston 1997: 5), Feyerabend found cause to celebrate the "methodological anarchism" that he believed the failure of falsificationism implied. Whether he adopted it on his own or whether his critics drove him to it, Feyerabend championed a scientific relativism that would endear him to postmodernists, many of whom also find ideology and oppression masquerading as rationality.

Ironically, the irrationality of postmodernism can nourish the oppression it rhetorically abhors. Rational argumentation, after all, serves as the sole check on brute power in setting public policies. If we have no rational standards of theory choice, political force prevails as reason recedes. Theoretical formulations with the most powerful advocates win the tenured positions, the research funding, and the capacity to reproduce intellectually. Historically, reason has undeniably been deployed in the service of oppressive, imperialistic, and authoritarian ends. But one should blame those who have so deployed it and those who had allowed it to be so deployed. Blaming reason itself seems wholly misplaced. Worse, given the alternative, blaming reason seems downright dangerous.

As a second irony, their relativism classes postmodernists, with verificationists, as conservative activists. Verificationists thought all verified knowledge secure. Once verified or proven true by observation, we need never revisit any formulation. Verificationists thought their knowledge, because verified, always consisted of true propositions. For relativists, however, no proposition can lay claim to truth, only truth relative to someone's conceptual framework erected from her subjective experiences. Neither, then, is open to criticism: verificationists because they believe themselves already in possession of the truth and the relativists because they have no notion of truth.

Putnam argued that Feyerabend's relativism, like all relativism concerning truth, is self-refuting. If one claims that truth is relative, Putnam (1981: 119–124) would counter that "truth may be relative for you, but it isn't relative for me." This demonstrates the subjectivist fallacy of claiming truth to be relative. Once two conversants have such an exchange, nothing more can follow. "It is a presupposition of thought itself that some kind of objective 'rightness' exists" (Putnam 1981: 124). The moment that one asserts that "truth is relative," one makes a truth claim. But, if truth were actually relative, why would one bother to make such a truth claim? The very act of issuing the truth claim that truth is relative effectively refutes the notion that truth is relative. For truth-relativists, intellectual discourse becomes pointless.

Truth-relativism sometimes attracts adherents among those who would welcome a more trans-cultural international studies. At first blush, relativism seems an appropriate way to express the notion that thinkers from widely differing cultural backgrounds may and often do come to different conclusions, even from the same body of evidence. But we do not need to follow truth-relativists into cloud-cuckoo-land in order to make this point. We can insist that there is a singular truth to any matter but, at the same time, allow that there may be a plurality of conceptions used to approach it and to describe it. That is, we can accept conceptual relativism as we reject truth-relativism. Across cultures and even across individuals within cultures, experiences vary. As a consequence, concepts and their contents also vary. In conversation, we mutually adjust our conceptual structures. We each make the contributions of the other comprehensible within a conceptual framework we have acquired through our (differing, yet overlapping) life experiences.

However irresponsible, irrational, and self-refuting it may be, Feyerabend's truth-relativism flowed from falsificationism's inability to articulate rational standards of theory choice. Compared to sophisticated falsificationists, who maintained foundational standards they all but acknowledged to be non-existent, Feyerabend was at least consistent. But a return to conservative activism – this time in relativist guise – need not have been the response to falsificationism's failure. One might instead have stayed within revolutionary activism, where an alternative was already available.

Simplism/Pragmatism

To the side of this debate over falsification resides another school of revolutionary activism. Lakatos lumped two approaches together, naming them "Duhem-Quine simplism" (Hesse 1976). Both Duhem and Quine are considered "holists." In his formulation, Duhem (1906) held that, in any experiment, the individual research hypothesis is never singly under test. Also tested are all the ancillary propositions that comprise the experimental setting – the observation theories on which it relies, its background assumptions, the measures it employs, etc. In Quine's (1951) later formulation, however, hypothesis tests always concern the entirety of human knowledge. This follows from his observation that the meanings of the terms of any proposition rely upon other propositions in a web of beliefs. Ultimately, in this way, any single proposition implicates all others, from the most mundane to the central propositions of logic and mathematics. From this perspective, one can salvage any hypothesis by simply reformulating other propositions in the web of our beliefs.

Each time we test a hypothesis, for Quine, all our knowledge is at stake. Fitting any new experience into our knowledge requires some adjustment to the web of our beliefs. Ordinarily we need to affect at most only small adjustments at the web's periphery. Sometimes, but only rarely, the integration of a new set of experiences requires adjustments closer to the web's core, necessitating additional adjustments and reformulations elsewhere in the web. These would be akin to what Kuhn termed "scientific revolutions," in which a new paradigm displaces the old. In any event, for Quine, we make these adjustments in order continually to maximize the coherence, or goodness-of-fit, of the whole of our knowledge. Since extended by Putnam, this perspective is today more widely known as "pragmatic realism" or simply "pragmatism."

The approach is considered realist in that it holds that well-corroborated scientific results describe the world as it is. They are not, as conventionalists would have it, just one of innumerably many descriptions. In other words, pragmatism is not truth-relativist. Scientists endeavor to understand reality as it really is. Yet, because concepts are often relative to each scientist's personal and professional background, theory choices become matters of collective deliberation and not individual contemplation. What is the rational standard against which such choices are made? From the pragmatic perspective, scientists ask whether proposed theoretical propositions would maximize the coherence of the web of our beliefs. Pragmatism thus does not provide the instant rationality that naïve falsification offered. But it does provide a rational standard, of which sophisticated falsificationism left us bereft.

Practical considerations for international studies

The collective and deliberative nature of theory choice presents difficulties for social science generally, and most particularly for those social sciences, like international studies, that transcend cultural bounds. The difficulty arises among the social sciences because they differ fundamentally from the natural sciences. I find it useful to convey this difference by referring to Aristotle's *aitia*, or (loosely speaking) the causes, reasons, or explanations of objects, events, or processes. Aristotle's main presentation of *aitia* appears in his *Physics* (Barnes 1984; Moravscik 1981).

130 Gavan Duffy

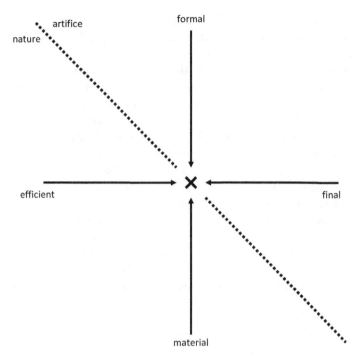

FIGURE 10.2 Aristotelian *aitia*

Aristotle understood any empirical entity, depicted as X in Figure 10.2, to be the joint product of four distinct *aitia*:

- *Efficient cause* refers to the Humean concept of cause. Efficient cause is "the primary source of the change," or "what makes of what is made and what changes of what is changed." If X were a sculpture, for instance, the efficient cause would be the sculptor's chiseling.
- *Material cause* we might consider to be the effects of composition on the (efficient) causal power of X. Material cause refers to "that out of which a thing comes to be and which persists … e.g., the bronze of the statue, the silver of the bowl." For a sculpture, then, in our recruitment of students, in our support for research projects, in our development of data and texts, and in every aspect of our discipline. To do otherwise would be to short-change the enterprise. I am arguing, then, for the rationalization of international studies as a discipline, a top-to-bottom overhaul aimed at producing rational knowledge about how the world works, considering the perspectives and traditions of all – the colonized as well as the material cause would be its medium, e.g., the marble or granite.
- *Formal cause* refers to the shape, form, or concept of X. It is, for Aristotle, "the form or the archetype, i.e. the definition of the essence and … the parts [*genus* and *differentia*] in the definition." The formal cause of a sculpture, then, is the idea of the sculpture in the mind of the sculptor.

- *Final cause* refers to the contribution of the ends of purposeful agents in producing X, or, for Aristotle, "that for the sake of which a thing is done." The final cause of a sculpture would be the intended effect of the sculpture on its beholders.

I have added a diagonal in Figure 10.2 to demarcate the natural sciences and the social sciences. Natural scientists concern themselves strictly with efficient and material causes of objects (and events and processes) found in nature. They do not treat formal and final causes. Social scientists, on the other hand, concern themselves with all four causes of the artefacts they study. In a sense, natural scientists have it easy. They need only investigate efficient and material causes. Final causes do not concern them because the entities they study are not teleological: they do not act in ways designed purposefully to produce desired outcomes. Neither do formal causes concern them. Communities of natural scientific inquirers can impose meanings by convention. They need not worry about meanings from the perspectives of the objects of their investigations, because these objects are oblivious to those meanings.

Social scientists very much concern themselves with intentions and meanings, with final and formal cause. But intentions and meanings receive interpretation only from within a cultural context. Each interpretation is embedded within a cultural milieu composed of features that themselves arise from an earlier milieu and that represent the latest way-station along a culture's historical trajectory. Consequently, the venues within which the truth claims of trans-cultural social sciences, e.g. international studies, are tested and redeemed must encourage the full participation of scholars across those cultures. More than this, we must produce diversity at all stages of knowledge production colonizer. Only in this way can we build a discipline that can help us all live better, more fulfilling and more peaceable lives. The alternative is more regime apology.

Conclusion

Knowledge is our sole bulwark against the unreasonable demands of the tyrant. For knowledge to have persuasive force, it must be rational. There exists no mechanical or formulaic rational standard for choosing between theories.

We necessarily submit claims of scientific truth to the community of experts for discursive redemption (or rejection). Accompanying such claims are offerings of support for the claim, consisting of arguments that acceptance of the claim would improve the global coherence of our knowledge. In the social sciences, because meanings vary cross-culturally and because intentions are subject to interpretation, discursive redemption can be rational only to the extent that the community of experts remains open to the variety of cultural perspectives that comprise the global community. What seems coherent to one scientist, owing to beliefs incidental to her biography, may seem less coherent to another scientist with a different biography. They must work this out discursively.

This feature of social science applies with particular importance to international studies. This discipline's subject matter transcends cultures. Scholars often investigate activities in which disparate cultural traditions interact with one another. Others find themselves in position to advise political practitioners on issues of foreign policy. Under these conditions, we cannot afford to allow representatives of a relatively small subset of the world's cultures to control judgments regarding the validity of social theories of world politics.

Imagine the echo chamber that such a state of affairs might produce. A history of capital exploitation and colonial domination produces a dominant international relations theory. Its advocates control of the offices and resources of the discipline. Their views predominate amid the councils of state leaders. They insist that only their theoretical formulations capture the real nature of world politics. They marginalize advocates of alternative formulations by characterizing them "idealist" dreamers who do not share the dominant group's "realism." State leaders produce foreign policies and take actions that presuppose the truth of the dominant group's formulations. They thereby create conditions that render those formulations self-fulfilling prophecies.

This nightmare scenario does not deviate much from the state of the discipline until relatively recently. Since the end of the Cold War, the discipline has moved discernibly in the right direction. With the improvements in telecommunication and transportation technologies that have accompanied globalization, international studies has recently become much more international and trans-cultural. And a sizeable segment of the discipline does not engage in political rationalization and regime apology. We do far better than we did only 40–45 years ago, when faculty from my own graduate department were devising techniques in support of efforts to prop up a cadre of thugs that dominated a small country in Southeast Asia (Oren 2003). But still, much room for improvement remains.

We could construct an international studies that is oriented towards achieving consensual analyses of human communities and their problems and formulating consensual collective actions for overcoming them. Our research products should increasingly include voices from the ranks of the colonized, even if we diminish (but surely not eliminate) voices of the colonizers. More generally, our deliberative associations and journals should find ways to open themselves to perspectives that have heretofore been closed out. Instead of dismissing new and alien ideas out-of-hand, scholars should go out of their way to engage them. Reward structures could be established to incent trans-cultural engagement. In the final analysis, a discipline that self-consciously promotes trans-cultural engagement would promote inter-cultural *modus vivendi* and dampen frustrations that culminate too often in political violence.

References

Barnes, Jonathan, trans. (1984) *The Complete Works of Aristotle*. Revised Oxford Translation. Princeton: Princeton University Press.

Duhem, Pierre. (1906) *The Aim and Structure of Physical Theory.* Philip P. Wiener, trans. Princeton: Princeton University Press.

Feyerabend, Paul K. (1970) "Consolations for the Specialist." In Imre Lakatos and Alan Musgrave (eds), *Criticism and the Growth of Knowledge*, pp. 91–196. Cambridge: Cambridge University Press.

Habermas, Jürgen. (1984) *Theory of Communicative Action.* Thomas McCarthy, trans. Boston: Beacon Press.

Hesse, Mary. (1976) "Duhem, Quine and a New Empiricism." In Sandra G. Harding (ed.), *Can Theories Be Refuted?*, pp. 184–204. Dordrecht: D. Reidel Publishing Company.

Kuhn, Thomas S. (1970) *The Structure of Scientific Revolutions.* Chicago: University of Chicago Press.

Lakatos, Imre. (1970) "Falsificationism and the Methodology of Scientific Research Programmes." In Imre Lakatos and Alan Musgrave (eds), *Criticism and the Growth of Knowledge*, pp. 91–196. Cambridge: Cambridge University Press.

Moravscik, J.M.E. (1981) "How Do Words Get Their Meanings?" *Journal of Philosophy* 78: 5–24.

Oren, Ido. (2003) *Our Enemies and US: America's Rivalries and the Making of Political Science.* Ithaca: Cornell University Press.

Popper, Karl. (1959) *The Logic of Scientific Discovery.* New York: Harper & Row.

Popper, Karl. (1970) "Normal Science and Its Dangers." In Imre Lakatos and Alan Musgrave (eds), *Criticism and the Growth of Knowledge*, pp. 51–58. Cambridge: Cambridge University Press.

Preston, John. (1997) *Feyerabend: Philosophy, Science, and Society.* Cambridge: Polity Press.

Putnam, Hilary. (1981) *Reason, Truth and History.* Cambridge: Cambridge University Press.

Putnam, Hilary. (1990) *Realism with a Human Face.* Cambridge, MA: Harvard University Press.

Quine, Willard Van Orman. (1951) "Two Dogmas of Empiricism." *The Philosophical Review* 60: 20–43.

Vasquez, John. (1997) "The Realist Paradigm and Degenerative versus Progressive Research Programs: An Appraisal of Neotraditional Research on Waltz's Balancing Proposition." *American Political Science Review* 91: 899–912.

PART IV
Articulations

11

ANTI-COLONIAL EMPIRES

Creation of Afro-Asian spaces of resistance

Clemens Hoffmann

> Africa [is] the cradle of the world's systems and philosophies
> *(J.E. Casely Hayford 1911)*

At first sight, contemporary Turkey and Ethiopia have very little in common. Turkey is a middle-income country with a strong industrial base and a developed state infrastructure. It has transformed from a recipient of aid to one of the largest donor countries: a "rising power" running a budget surplus with growth figures rivalling those of China. Ethiopia, on the other hand, has a legacy of violent conflict and secessions, mass poverty, hunger, and repeated droughts, and will likely remain dependent on external aid for years to come.

Despite this obvious divergence, there are plenty of commonalities, too. Both states, located at the peripheries of their respective continents, feature strong imperial legacies and histories of dominating those regions through their strategic locations. Having successfully defended their sovereignty against imperial designs, borders, identities and socio-political conditions were not directly imposed qua colonial fiat, making them cases of exception within Asia and Africa respectively (Tibebu 1996).[1] Agency, in other words, was not denied but sharpened defensively by an expanding Europe. Despite some dramatic territorial reconfigurations and social change "from above," the two states of Turkey and Ethiopia demonstrate a certain level of continuity in statehood reaching from their imperial to modern formulations of rule.

Yet despite the success in defending their independence and eventually gaining internationally recognized sovereignty, these states continued to be subjected to the surrounding power inequalities in the international system. Having undergone crisis-ridden "special paths" throughout the twentieth century and the Cold War, both states, located at the geostrategically central locations of the Straits and the Horn of Africa, respectively, came to occupy key roles as major US allies in otherwise highly volatile regions. Both now feature authoritarian developmentalist regimes gearing their economies towards greater integration into the world markets. Both see these ambitions tightly related to their (geo)political positions, overcoming periods of dependency and instability. Lastly, diplomatic and trade relations between the two countries themselves have steadily improved.

In contrast to those successful histories of resistance, literature on the postcolonial state usually focuses on the – continuing – experience of colonization. Anti-colonial struggles, the frequently violent process of winning political freedom from the imperial center, are thought to be half-successful at best. Multiple institutional colonial legacies and continued economic dependency mean that the vast majority of the world's polities are still subjected to structural power inequalities. A closer look at the conditions of postcoloniality reveals, indeed, that many struggles didn't so much generate independent states, but forms of neo-colonialism (Nkrumah 1965). Being subjected to those international power imbalances, the postcolonial state is likely to reproduce the inequalities and the continued social contradictions "within," inspiring allegations reaching from "internal colonialism" (Hind 1984) to structurally "weak" or even "failed" states.[2]

Having escaped outright colonial control and following their own "special paths," anti-colonial, or defensive states pose not only a formidable geopolitical but also an ontological challenge to the West's "constitutive will to [exercise] power over the Orient" (Said 2003: 222) and associated assumptions about its lacking agency. Engaging the history of their making through successful resistance serves as a guide for a positive reconstruction, or a conceptual "way out" of Eurocentrism. This addresses a conventional criticism of postcolonial theory as ultimately not offering theoretical alternatives beyond a powerful critique (Matin 2013). Moving beyond the structurally over-determined "post-colonial" agency-less condition, emphasizing anti-colonial *geopolitical* resistance aims to bring non-Western agency "back in." It does so not necessarily through an abstract re-formulation of the ontological West/non-West divide, but through the concrete historicization of late imperial anti-colonial struggles. Those agents, it is argued, should therefore be seen not just as passive recipients or emulators of a "defensive modernity" but as constitutive parts of a world order into the present (Anievas and Nisancioglu 2015: 40).

Starting from this recognition, the related Turco-Ethiopian histories of resistance enable an alternative understanding of world politics, namely one whereby anti-Western geopolitical encounters change the conceptual understanding of non-European agents as passive. Successful acts of resistance, usually written out of the narrative of Western domination as "aberrations," are made constitutive, rather than exceptional, cases in world history. They not only demonstrate the potential of resistance. Their global repercussions, in the form of anti-colonial pan-Islamism and pan-Africanism, produce Afro-Asian *spaces of resistance* conceptually. This normative commitment to alternative conceptual spaces de-naturalizes the modern international order generated and dominated by the West. Indeed, this order has always faced resistance and is, as a result, itself shaped by this negation from its inception.

This chapter's emphasis on the Ottoman-Turkish and Ethiopian polities as locales of resistance also defies the false dichotomy between "state-centered" and "social" (or "from below") levels of analysis. Institutions of political rule set the parameters within which social interactions, including those resisting, take place. Commitments to move "beyond" state-centrism never quite escape the spatio-temporal institutional confines within which political rule is organized and social life takes place as a result. Institutional strategies of social reproduction shape and frame agential power, including those "from below." This does not deny inevitable power inequalities and relations of domination within state structures, but rather to show how these struggles are, for the time being, intimately related to the reproduction of state power. In the two cases discussed here, this has both domestic and international consequences as both historical centers of geopolitical resistance produce their own internal and external contradictions, leading to allegations from internal authoritarianism to quasi-imperial expansion. The related histories of successful Afro-Asian anti-colonial struggles and their global reverberations are, therefore, not without contradictions, notably in the form of internal, regional, and global power projections by successful anti-colonizers.

This chapter will proceed by briefly elaborating on the meaning of the present historicization of postcolonial theory before looking into the Ottoman-Turkish and Ethiopian experiences in greater detail. Here, I identify two key geopolitical encounters, the Battle of Adwa in 1896 and the Ottoman Gallipoli campaign of 1915, as historical moments of successful resistance with meaning far beyond their individual contexts. Both histories, thus far neglected by IR historical scholarship, are then contextualized within their global contexts, namely the anti-colonial pan-Islamism of the late Ottoman Empire and the pan-Africanism still embodied in the notion of "Ethiopianism." These geopolitical encounters, I argue, have helped to generate global imaginaries of resistance, inspirational to many anti- and de-colonial struggles across the world to this day. Re-historicizing these related anti-colonial struggles and their long-term consequences and contradictions, finally, also helps to illuminate a more complex picture of the postcolonial world, replacing structural West/non-West, North/South, Colonizer/Colonized binaries with concrete and related historicized agencies of the colonial and the colonized alike.

Postcolonialism and the state

One of the core contributions of postcolonial literature is to write non-Western agency, missing in the dominant Western and Euro-centric accounts, into the narrative of world politics. While this has frequently involved a self-denial of agency in light of the West's overwhelming coercive power and universalizing tendencies, more recent work has taken up this challenge. One of the answers was to doubt the "purely" Western European origins of capitalism (Anievas and Nisancioglu 2013; Hobson 2004), emphasizing the sources of social change coming from the "East" and/or "South." The principal means of "emancipating" the thus far unheard of and unaccounted for histories of the South and the East was then to write them into the history of capitalist development. This was meant to address the "paradox of eastern agency" (Hobson 2014). John M. Hobson, in particular, argues that the multiple calls to re-invoke this agency were somewhat mistaken in trying to trace eastern agency as something emerging only as a result of the post-colonial struggle, having been previously "static." Hobson demonstrates how it was there all along – just that it has been left invisible and that postcolonial scholarship was in some ways complicit in obscuring it.

Hobson and others try to overcome this invisibility by historicizing the "eastern" contributions to Western modernity. These attempts are historiographically rich and well founded. Critically, however, they do little to illuminate Eastern agency in its own right. Non-European history only acquires meaning by writing it into the history of capitalist modernity, which is said to be a global, rather than Western, phenomenon from the outset. In other words, the transition from object to subject, the seizing of agency by the disenfranchised is conditioned upon a contribution to capitalist development. While this is a welcome contribution to the study of capitalist modernity, it comes at the expense of looking into the social histories of the "East" and the "South" in their own right and the ways in which they generate geopolitical spaces outside of and beyond the West.

This chapter offers such a historicization of non-Western agency in its own right. It does so without writing out Eastern agency from world historical dynamics, shaped by capitalist modernity. Similarly, instead of understanding it as a "pristine" or purifying form of resistance, this chapter further problematizes the internal social contradictions that this "Eastern agency" has naturally developed as part of a broader world political dialectic of resistance.

Nineteenth-century resistance and anti-colonial empires

Apart from having successfully fought wars of independence, the Ottoman Empire and "Abyssinia" (as Ethiopia is also known) produced much of their wealth by occupying important geo-strategic locations. In the case of the Ottoman Empire, its central position on the Silk Route and at the crossroads between the Eastern Mediterranean and the Black Sea is mirrored by Turkey's contemporary role as an energy transfer hub. Ethiopia's position at the Horn of Africa allowed control of the profitable Red Sea trade, including coffee, gold and slaves (Aregay 1988). With the opening of the Suez Canal this has been replaced by energy. While those geostrategically important positions strengthened both empires, these also made them vulnerable to geopolitical designs by outside powers, especially during European expansions. Reform and modernization processes reacting to those pressures were faced with various internal contradictions. Military and bureaucratic state classes not only had to deal with the vestiges of traditional society but also with issues of social and ethnic diversity. Maintaining control in the peripheries became particularly challenging. Military success over the would-be European colonizers earned them important international recognition (then as now the benchmark for sovereignty). However, this also engendered controversial regional geopolitical ambitions:

Ethiopia's expansions in Somalia and Eritrea continue to fuel allegations of regional imperialism, whereas "Ottoman imperialism" (Emrence 2011) is mirrored by Turkey's contemporary intention to create a "new Middle East" (Balcı and Yeşiltaş 2006).

The sick man's success: Ottoman reincarnation at Gallipoli

While the Ottoman Empire evolved from an expansionist "Tyrant" to a "Sick Man" in the West's perception during the nineteenth century (Çırakman 2002), Turkey itself is frequently described as a "bridge" country (Yarnık 2009), not least in the light of its EU accession aspirations. As a result, Turkey's position between "East" and "West" has received much academic and policy attention, which stands in contrast to its less reflected position between the "North" and the "South" (Deringil 2003). This relation, especially to its "Eastern" (but not so much its "Southern") neighbors has only recently attracted more interest insofar as it might signal a shift away from the "West" (Oğuzlu 2008). Frequently overlooked by postcolonial analysis (Göçek 2014), rather than being historicized with all its contradictions, Europe's relation with Ottoman/Turkish rule is either simplified as a "mirror image" (Müftüler-Bac 2000) or its Western orientation is taken for granted.[3]

Pan-Islamism

After expansion peaked in 1683, Ottoman rule entered a process of territorial decline. Its dual legitimacy from control of Mekka and Medina (Caliphate) and Istanbul/Constantinople (Eastern Roman Imperial successor state) suffered accordingly. Challenged by uprisings in its Christian majority peripheries combined with mainly Russian advances, Ottoman defensive modernization eventually merged with a political revival of pan-Islamism and a more one-sided emphasis on the Caliphate under Abdulhamid II (Karpat 2001). The First World War was subsequently fought as "jihad" by Sultanic decree, internationalizing the struggle against the Entente. This was particularly successful in British India (Özcan 1997) and Tanzania, leading to financial contributions and rhetorical admiration of the last Muslim state upholding the institution of the Caliphate while resisting Western occupation. Though many Indian Muslims also remained loyal to the Crown, it is clear that the resistance against the designs to divide the Empire and the Allied Occupation of Istanbul was observed with remarkable sympathies.

India's anti-colonial Muslims organized in the Klilafat Organization agitated in favor of preserving the Caliphate under Ottoman–Turkish rule. Ostensibly acting out of concern for the unity of the global *ulema*, its underlying purpose was to rally a pan-Indian Muslim constituency, without, however, intending to divide and ethnically separate India. Its core aim was adequate representation within congress – a bid supported by Gandhi and other Hindu leaders fully aware of British divide-and-rule policies intent on preserving national unity. Despite divisions within the Muslim constituency, the Ottoman struggle helped to induce a pan-Indian movement of solidarity, which, however, failed to attract movements beyond the subcontinent. Arab Muslims had entered the war on the side of the Western colonial powers, clearly perceiving Ottoman centralization as the greater "imperial" threat (Makdisi 2002).

Within this struggle roiled another. Struggle over control of the strategically important Dardanelles stands out for its symbolic value. Allied forces, mostly Australian and New Zealand contingents (or AZNAC) led by British commanders, fought an unsuccessful battle at the slopes of Gallipoli in 1915. The Ottoman army defeating a Western colonial force, the largest Empire on earth at the time, became a defining moment in the anti-Western struggle. The Caliphate had successfully defended not only its right to control one of the most important shipping passages but also its status as an independent actor in world politics. Beyond resisting its own domination, the Ottoman Empire also maintained its Muslim agency at a time of all-out inter-imperial warfare. The Ottoman's military effectiveness and motivation surprised the British high command, operating (much like Italy in Ethiopia) under an assumption of superiority and the related "backwardness" of enemy forces. Postcolonial studies of Gallipoli tend to focus on the relation between the British Empire and the colonial people dying on its behalf (Tranter and Donoghue 2007) while Turkish Republican historiography has long neglected Gallipoli along with its role in the First World War as part of an Ottoman heritage that was only recently reluctantly engaged (Turan 2014).

Despite being appalled by Mustafa Kemal Atatürk's secularism, his successful anti-colonial campaign during Turkey's War of Independence (1919–1923) was seen by Indian Muslims and others[4] as a logical continuation of the anti-Western struggle, making Atatürk the "ill lodged soul of the East still in search of a body" (Mishra 2012: 284). At a time when Britain and France still directly controlled the Middle East, maintaining the Caliphate one year into the Turkish Republic's laicist existence also maintained global Muslim support. Yet a Turkish "civilizing mission" both at home (Esenbel 1994) and abroad (Deringil 2003) increasingly compromised the already doubt-laden anti-imperialist credentials. During the republican period, Atatürk evoked civilizational themes, elevating the nationalist Turkish founding mythology of the "Hittites" to a "Central Asian" civilization relevant to the history of humankind as a whole. Such "Turkic" ethnic nationalism saw the forceful production of a homogeneous demographic around the Sunni Muslim majority leading to campaigns of ethnic cleansing, mass killings, and the oppression of minority populations to this day.

In sum, the late Empire and early Republic feature anti-colonial rhetoric and policies born out of a resistance against imperial territorial designs. This position contributed to (though it did not entirely cause) strong resentments against liberal-imperial powers as well as friendly relations with other "contender" states, including Germany (both before and after 1933), and the early Soviet Union. Realities of the postwar order and a continued self-identification as a European power brought Turkey back into the fold of those previously "unfriendly" powers.

Cold War dynamics such as Stalin's territorial designs on Turkey and the Korean War finally put an end to "contender state" aspirations and locked the Republic into a transatlantic future. This gradual entry into the Western hemisphere came at the expense of Turkey's anti-colonial credentials. Consciously and actively dissociating itself from its anti-colonial heritage, Turkey left Bandung publicly declaring the futility of anti-Western positions. Its pro-Israeli stance in the Arab-Israeli conflict damaged relations with many postcolonial nations that had previously supported and admired Turkey, further damaging already poor relations with most of the Arab world,[5] many of which were also members of the Non Aligned Movement (NAM). Turkey's role in the Cyprus crisis with its invasion and occupation in 1974 of a leading NAM country consolidated this split with the postcolonial world. Many postcolonial leaders were now clearly, if not entirely accurately, identifying Turkey with Western Imperialism.[6] The Cyprus invasion aside, Turkey's geopolitical role remained isolated, fortifying the second largest army within NATO against the dual threats of a Soviet invasion and continued regional instability. This has only recently been revised under the leadership of the Justice and Development (AK) Party, in power since 2002, showing a greater taste for regionally pro-active, if highly contentious, foreign policies.[7]

Ethiopia's dream

Like the Ottoman-Turkish state, Ethiopia's transformation is related to, but not determined by Western expansion. Once under the dual pressure from the Mahdist movement of Sudan (itself anti-colonial, fighting the Anglo-Egyptian condominium controlling Sudan at the time) and Italy's advances on the Red Sea coastline, a process of fiscal and military centralization similar to that of the Ottoman Empire, generated an uneasy alliance between a quasi-Absolutist imperial court and local landlords. Italy's designs on Abyssinia (as it was called in its colonial dictionary with reference to its biblical significance) were in turn determined by its experience as a latecomer. The Risorgimento and the subsequent rise of fascism resulted in an aggressive late entry in the Scramble for Africa, determining a taste for restoring its Roman imperial heritage.

Those imperial references fueled Italian expansionism with a false sense of superiority. Yet determined Ethiopian forces under Emperor Menelik twice stopped the Italian advance. First, in the highly symbolic battle of Adwa in 1896, a sense of superiority (much like the British in Gallipoli in 1915) obscured sound analysis of the well-equipped, trained, and effective Ethiopian troops. Victory at Adwa reminded the whole of Africa and the world that European expansion wasn't unstoppable. Apart from this global symbolic power (Milkias and Metaferia 2005), this event also earned Ethiopia the status of one of the first non-Western recognized sovereign states (Clapham 2002), capable of conducting its independent arms purchases.[8] Mussolini's revanchist invasion in 1935–1936 and the deployment of mustard gas earned the Ethiopian struggle further sympathies and inflated its symbolic value for a process of decolonization now already in full swing.

Though it fueled Ethiopia's international recognition as an anti-colonial power, the Italian invasion paradoxically also deepened internal contradictions. Eritrean and Somali forces had joined the Italian invaders due to grievances with the imperial court: the former had enjoyed lower taxes under Italian occupation, generating discontent upon the re-introduction of the Ethiopian centralized taxation system. Much of the Somali and Omoro population clashed with the developmental ambitions of a modernizing Empire. Their pre-capitalist semi-pastoralist subsistence economies came under attack by ambitions to expand irrigated agriculture and to recruit a labor force for a "civilizational" mission, exploiting the fertile, water-rich highlands for cultivating high-value crops, especially coffee.[9] A simplistic understanding of Ethiopia's internal contradictions would focus on the dominance of Christian subsistence farming over Muslim pastoralists, though ethnic and religious differences are much more complex and frequently only the surface expression of deeper socio-economic struggles. As a result, Omoro, Somalis, and others living under the "Yoke of Abyssinia" earn for Ethiopian imperial power the reputation of being just as oppressive as white colonialism (Jalata 2010). As with the Armenian, Kurdish, and Alevi questions in Turkey, these continued conflicting lines demonstrate that every process and project of emancipation is likely to generate its own internal and external contradictions.

Pan-Africanism

Those internal contradictions stand in stark contrast to Ethiopia's leading symbolic and political role in the pan-African movement, collectivizing the Ethiopian experience. The movement's philosophical foundations reach from romantic primitivism (accepting European charges of backwardness) to romantic gloriana (pointing out Africa's "civilizational" achievements) born of dream (poetry) and nightmare (imperialism) alike (Mazrui 1995). Ethiopian sources of pan-Africanism are similarly based on the "greatness of ancient Ethiopia" as a Christian heritage, the birthplace of the Queen of Sheba, the "cradle of civilization" and similar references (Geiss 1974: 133; Casely Hayford 1911; Lynch 1967: 250). After Adwa, the term "Ethiopia" not only acquires a meaning synonymous with "Black" Africa, based on Psalm 68:32: "Princes shall come out of Egypt – Ethiopia shall soon stretch out her hands unto God." "Ethiopianism" also developed as a political movement. Afro-American communities especially adopted this quasi-religion of "Ethiopianism" (Moses 1975; Shepperson 1953). The Haytian Emigration Society, for example, intended to build Haiti as the American pillar of the "Ethiopian Empire" (Geiss 1974: 133). Leading Pan-Africanists like W.E.B. DuBois frequently mixed the idea of Ethiopia with the institution of the Imperial court itself that he labelled "The Star of Ethiopia" (Dubois [1915] 1983). Marcus Garvey observed the contradictory realities in Ethiopia (or Abyssinia) and Haile Selassie's policies in particular, calling him a "failure of an Emperor who (famously) surrendered himself to the white wolves of Europe" (Garvey [1937] 1990: 739). "Ethiopia" and "Ethiopianism" kept their symbolic meanings, at times even portraying all black men as "Ethiopian." Though the conceptual uptake and its territorial referent were sometimes far removed from one another, Adwa certainly retained a strong symbolic power.

Ethiopianism and Ethiopia proper became associated with one another more closely again with the atrocities committed during Mussolini's invasion (Weisbord 1972). It was this second Italo-Abyssinian war that helped to consolidate an otherwise diverse and split pan-African movement leading to the foundation of the International African Friends of Abyssinia.

Today, Ethiopia headquarters the African Union, symbolizing both the ideational heritage of its struggle for Africanism and its contemporary influence over African politics in general. Beyond Africa itself, Ethiopia remains a key reference to many anti-colonial movements as well as the black rights movement in the Americas (Scott 1993).[10] As Garvey ([1937] 1990) had pointed out, it comes with a romanticization of Ethiopian internal politics overlooking multiple social contradictions and power inequalities, such as the current dominance of Ethiopian politics by the Tigray tribe despite a federal constitution and formal parliamentary democracy. None of the much longer-term historical references to Ethiopian greatness as a symbol of defying the West would be imaginable, however, without the more recent, early modern geopolitical encounter and repeated successful repulsion of a European imperial power.

Conclusion

Unlike Turkey, Ethiopia retained its anti-colonial credentials. While both contemporary states pursued aggressive growth strategies under authoritarian neo-liberal developmentalist regimes, Ethiopia is committed to a zero-carbon growth focusing on renewable energy production, whereas Turkey's focus on emissions-heavy construction and coal-fired energy production leads to accusations of being environmentally unsustainable. Both look for economic expansion in neighboring markets and project their power regionally wherever possible to secure those markets. At the same time, despite many diverging interests, both remain close allies of the US at geopolitically sensitive locations.

This short comparative history of anti-colonial empires and the spaces of resistance they create has demonstrated, first, that these anti-colonial histories are still relevant in contemporary world politics. Despite their formal alliances with the West, Turkey and Ethiopia maintain relatively high levels of independence, regional influence and stability within environments plagued by conflict and insecurity and, on the back of these circumstances, augment their global roles. Second, those different anti-colonial strategies and experiences can help to produce an alternative world political space materially, discursively, and relationally: Rather than being produced in and by the West (or merely contributing to the West), resistance is factored into the emergence of the international order from its inception. These processes are, however, not without internal contradictions. These find little expression in the respective global imaginaries they have helped to create. Historicizing successful anti-Western agency despite incomplete, patchy, and contradictory geopolitical "modernities" can help to re-think stale East–West divisions and ontological dichotomies. The conceptual and ideational understandings of world political alternatives are directly related to concrete, material histories. This shows, finally, that the conceptual apparatus of IR is only poorly understood if abstracted from concrete social relations, real-life struggles, resistance struggles, and social transformation, more generally.

Notes

1 Though exceptional, the Italian colonial heritage is clearly visible in Ethiopia where especially fascist Italy's Africa Orientale Italiana (AOI) left a strong mark, amongst others in Addis Ababa's city planning. See for example, Ponzanesi (2000).
2 For a critique of this concept see Bilgin and Morton (2004).
3 For an account on how Turkey's decidedly Western orientation was a reaction to its immaterial insecurities in being recognized as equal by the West during the late Ottoman and early Republican era, see Bilgin (2009).
4 Though some of the developments during Turkey's War of Independence irritated Indian Muslims, they saw Mustafa Kemal Atatürk's campaign by and large as one of defending Islam and Asia as a whole (Özcan 1997: 198).
5 Many Arab nationalists had blamed the Ottoman administration for inviting Zionist settler activities after the liberalization of the Ottoman land regime in 1858.
6 Cypriot and Arab leaders frequently compare the Palestinian and Cypriot experience of being occupied. This despite the fact that the crisis was caused by a *coup d'état* in an attempt to Hellenize the island (Enosis). Far from being a pro-Western manoeuvre, Turkey's occupation led to the collapse of the complicit pro-Western military junta in Athens and to US sanctions.
7 There is an active academic debate on the nature of Turkey's "new" foreign policy. A summary of this debate would exceed the scope of this chapter while a single reference wouldn't do justice to the breadth of the debate.
8 Initially, arms were purchased from Tsarist Russia, which appeared intrigued by the Ethiopian success story.
9 Incidentally, the coffee trade across the Red Sea was first cultivated under Ottoman rule, introducing this new commodity to European markets.
10 Contemporary US Hip Hop lyrics also make frequent references to Ethiopia or "the Ethiopian Queen."

Bibliography

Amin-Khan, Tariq. (2012) *The Post-Colonial State in the Era of Capitalist Globalization: Historical, Political and Theoretical Approaches to State Formation*. London: Routledge.

Anievas, Alexander and Kerem Nisancioglu. (2013) "What's at Stake in the Transition Debate? Rethinking the Origins of Capitalism and the 'Rise of the West.'" *Millennium-Journal of International Studies* 42: 78–102.

Anievas, Alexander and Kerem Nisancioglu. (2015) *How the West Came to Rule: The Geopolitical Origins of Capitalism*. London: Pluto.

Aregay, Merid W. (1988) "The Early History of Ethiopia's Coffee Trade and the Rise of Shawa." *Journal of African History* 29: 19–25.

Balcı, Ali and Murat Yeşiltaş. (2006) "Turkey's New Middle East Policy: The Case of the Meeting of the Foreign Ministers of Iraq's Neighboring Countries." *Journal of South Asian and Middle Eastern Studies* 29: 18–38.

Barkawi, Tarak. (2013) "War, Armed Forces and Society in Postcolonial Perspective." In Sanjay Seth (ed.), *Postcolonial Theory and International Relations: A Critical Introduction*, 87–105. London: Routledge.

Bilgin, Pınar. (2007) "'Only Strong States Can Survive in Turkey's Geography': The Uses of 'Geopolitical Truths' in Turkey." *Political Geography* 26: 740–756.

Bilgin, Pınar. (2009) "Securing Turkey through Western-Oriented Foreign Policy." *New Perspectives on Turkey* 40: 105–121.

Bilgin, Pınar. (2012) "Globalization and In/Security – Middle Eastern Encounters with International Society and the Case of Turkey." In Stephan Stettner (ed.), *The Middle East and Globalization: Encounters and Horizons*, 59–75. London: Palgrave Macmillan.

Bilgin, Pınar, and Adam David Morton. (2004) "From 'Rogue' to 'Failed' States? The Fallacy of Short-termism." *Politics* 24: 169–180.

Casely Hayford, J.E. (1911) *Ethiopia Unbound: Studies in Race Emancipation*. London: Cass.

Çırakman, Aslı. (2002) *From the "Terror of the World" to the "Sick Man of Europe": European Images of Ottoman Empire and Society from the Sixteenth Century to the Nineteenth*. Oxford: Peter Lang.

Clapham, Christopher. (2002) *Controlling Space in Ethiopia*. Oxford: James Currey.

Deringil, Selim. (2003) "'They Live in a State of Nomadism and Savagery': The Late Ottoman Empire and the Post-Colonial Debate." *Comparative Studies in Society and History* 45: 311–342.

DuBois, W.E.B. ([1915] 1983) "The Star of Ethiopia: A Pageant." In Herbert Aptheker (ed.), *Pamphlets and Leaflets by W.E.B. DuBois*, 161–165, 206–209. White Plains, NY: Kraus-Thomason.

Emrence, C. (2011) *Remapping the Ottoman Middle East: Modernity, Imperial Bureaucracy and the Islamic State*. London: I.B.Tauris.

Esenbel, Selçuk. (1994) "The Anguish of Civilized Behavior: The Use of Western Cultural Forms in the Everyday Lives of the Meiji Japanese and the Ottoman Turks during the Nineteenth Century." *Japan Review* 5: 145–185.

Garvey, Marcus. ([1937] 1990) "Editorial in The Black Man, March–April 1937: The Failure of Haile Selassie as Emperor." In Robert A. Hill (ed.), *The Marcus Garvey and Universal Negro Improvement Association Papers, Volume VII, November 1927–August 1940*, 739–742. Berkeley and Los Angeles: University of California Press.

Geiss, Imanuel. (1974) *The Pan-African Movement: A History of Pan-Africanism in America, Europe, and Africa*. London: Taylor & Francis.

Göçek, Fatma Müge. (2014) "Parameters of a Postcolonial Sociology of the Ottoman Empire." In Julian Go (ed.), *Decentering Social Theory*, 73–104. London: Emerald Group Publishing.

Hanioglu, M.Sükrü. (2001) *Preparation for a Revolution: The Young Turks, 1902–1908*. Oxford: Oxford University Press.

Hind, Robert J. (1984) "The Internal Colonial Concept." *Comparative Studies in Society and History* 26(3): 543–568.

Hobson, John M. (2004) *The Eastern Origins of Western Civilisation*. Cambridge: Cambridge University Press.

Hobson, John M. (2013) "The Other Side of the Westphalian Frontier." In Sanjay Seth (ed.), *Postcolonial Theory and International Relations: A Critical Introduction*, 32–48. London: Routledge.

Hobson, John M. (2014) "The Postcolonial Paradox of Eastern Agency." *Perceptions* 19: 212–234.

Jalata, Asafa. (2010) "The Ethiopian State: Authoritarianism, Violence and Clandestine Genocide." *The Journal of Pan African Studies* 3: 160–189.

Karpat, Kemal H. (2001) *The Politicization of Islam: Reconstructing Identity, State, Faith, and Community in the Late Ottoman State*. Oxford: Oxford University Press.

Lynch, Hollis R. (1967) *Edward Wilmot Blyden: Pan-Negro Patriot, 1832–1912: Pan-Negro Patriot, 1832–1912*. Oxford: Oxford University Press.

Makdisi, Ussama. (2002) "Rethinking Ottoman Imperialism: Modernity, Violence and the Cultural Logic of Ottoman Reform." In Jens Hanssen, Thomas Philipp and Stefan Weber (eds), *The Empire in the City: Arab Provincial Cities in the Ottoman Empire*, 29–48. Würzburg: Ergon Verlag.

Matin, Kamran. (2013) "Redeeming the Universal: Postcolonialism and the Inner Life of Eurocentrism." *European Journal of International Relations* 19: 353–377.

Mazrui, Ali A. (1995) "Pan-Africanism: From Poetry to Power." *Issue: A Journal of Opinion* 23(1): 35–38.

Milkias, Paulos and Getachew Metaferia. (2005) *The Battle of Adwa: Reflections on Ethiopia's Historic Victory against European Colonialism*. New York: Algora Publishing.

Mishra, Pankaj. (2012) *From the Ruins of Empire: The Revolt against the West and the Remaking of Asia*. London: Allen Lane.

Moses, Wilson J. (1975) "The Poetics of Ethiopianism: W.E.B. Du Bois and Literary Black Nationalism." *American Literature* 47: 411–426.

Müftüler-Bac, Meltem. (2000) "Through the Looking Glass: Turkey in Europe." *Turkish Studies* 1: 21–35.

Nkrumah, Kwame. (1965) *Neo-Colonialism: The Last Stage of Imperialism*. London: Nelson.

Oğuzlu, Tarik. (2008) "Middle Easternization of Turkey's Foreign Policy: Does Turkey Dissociate from the West?" *Turkish Studies* 9: 3–20.

Özcan, Azmi. (1997) *Pan-Islamism: Indian Muslims, the Ottomans and Britain, 1877–1924*. Leiden: Brill.

Ponzanesi, Sandra. (2000) "The Past Holds No Terror? Colonial Memories and Afro-Italian Narratives." *Wasafiri* 15: 16–19.

Said, Edward. (2003) *Orientalism*. London: Penguin.

Saul, John S. (1974) "The State in Post-Colonial Societies: Tanzania." *Socialist Register* 11: 349–372.

Scott, William Randolph. (1993) *The Sons of Sheba's Race: African-Americans and the Italo-Ethiopian War, 1935–1941*. Bloomington: Indiana University Press.

Shaw, Timothy M. (1982) "Beyond Neo-Colonialism: Varieties of Corporatism in Africa." *The Journal of Modern African Studies* 20: 239–261.

Shepperson, George. (1953) "Ethiopianism and African Nationalism." *Phylon* 14: 9–18.

Tibebu, Teshale. (1996) "Ethiopia: The 'Anomaly' and 'Paradox' of Africa." *Journal of Black Studies* 26: 414–430.

Tranter, Bruce, and Jed Donoghue. (2007) "Colonial and Post-Colonial Aspects of Australian Identity." *The British Journal of Sociology* 58: 165–183.

Turan, Ömer. (2014) "Turkish Historiography of the First World War." *Middle East Critique* 23: 241–257.

Weisbord, Robert G. (1972) "Black America and the Italian-Ethiopian Crisis: An Episode in Pan-Negroism." *Historian* 34: 230–241.

Yanık, Lerna K. (2009) "The Metamorphosis of Metaphors of Vision: 'Bridging' Turkey's Location, Role and Identity after the End of the Cold War." *Geopolitics* 14: 531–549.

12

FROM TERRITORY TO TRAVEL

Metabolism, metamorphosis, and mutation in IR[1]

Josuke Ikeda

Many observe today that international relations (IR) theory seems at a crossroad. One could interpret this observation in one of two ways: (1) a "crossroad" indicates a sense of intellectual indirection, a situation where IR theorists must make a choice as to where to go and what to believe in, or (2) a "crossroad" suggests a contact point where different people from different places meet, and then depart again into different directions. The latter could provoke a merger or a clash, or maybe nothing at all. What can be derived from these two understandings may be the quite mundane fact that merely standing at a crossroad is neither special nor inherently dynamic. Of course, "crossroad" serves as a metaphor in this context, indicating the discipline's travel since its establishment in 1919. However mundane it might have been, the discipline's theoretical exploration of global peace has been a long, and perhaps ongoing, journey.

This chapter explores the concept of "road-and-travel" in IR. Standing at its crossroad, the discipline is facing contemporary challenges in all three modes of intellectual inquiry: ontological, epistemological, and methodological. One point that differs from previous, similar challenges, however, is that the current inquiry targets the origin, or more precisely culture, of the discipline itself. Importantly, the inquiry contests the claim that IR started in Aberystwyth (Porter 1972) or Washington, D.C. (Schmidt 1998). These sites serve, rather, as goals or focal points to which all other traditions related to international/global life have been reduced. There is growing doubt, moreover, that Western/Westphalian IR can cover it all. And the answer so far seems to be quite easy: no. The term "global IR" (Acharya 2014) may seem redundant – after all, isn't IR already global? What it highlights is that IR may be global in reach but not in culture.

Here, real-life experiences with "road-and-travel" come to the forefront. A road-centered view of the world counterposes mainstream IR's territory-centered view; travel, too, enables one to cross borders and enter cultures, bringing the stranger and the native into mutual interaction. Such intercultural encounters help to change long-held assumptions and types of knowledge. The Self, the Other, and eventually the World all undergo change – and these changes occur from all directions. Observed from a global level, these changes could constitute a phenomenon of continuous change as well as continuous maintenance of the Self, the Other, and the World. This process resembles metabolism and possibly metamorphosis, whereby one's own body and mind undergo transformation. This chapter, in short, explores the idea of a global metabolism or metamorphosis for a post-Western, post-Westphalian IR.

"Westfailure" and its aftermath

Susan Strange (1999) first coined the term "Westfailure." Strange used it to refer to Westphalia's problematic reliance on excessive capitalism. I use this term, in contrast, to emphasize Westphalian IR's treatment of Self and Other. Developed primarily in the West, IR remains relatively ignorant of or mistreats the non-West. Issues of identity, culture, and civilization are at stake. Some take a "non-Western" approach by presenting a diversity of IR scholarship around the globe (Tickner and Waever 2009; Acharya and Buzan 2009; Shilliam 2010; Tickner and Blaney 2012). Various "national schools" have appeared subsequently (Inoguchi 2009; Zhang and Buzan 2012; Zhang 2012). Others advocate a "post-Western IR" that questions IR's foundational tenets in theorizing (Shani 2007, 2008; Vasilaki 2012). To them, the "Westfailure" problem reflects an identity politics in the discipline that almost equates with nationality. Non-Western IR theorists, accordingly, always have *at least* two stories to tell: one that centers on a master narrative of Western IR; another, on national or regional schools of non-Western IR. Pluralism plays an important part in post-Western IR (Vasilaki 2012), accompanied by a method to "provincialize" (Shani 2008; Vasilaki 2012) or compare (Chen 2012) theories so as to prevent any totalizing projects.

Bringing the non-West (back) into IR is not new. Along with underdevelopment theory, writers such as Ari Mazrui raised different standpoints from Western-based politics (Mazrui 1967, 1976). Some ground-breaking works in the 1980s examined how the West intellectually treated the non-West. These included critical assessments of "the standard of civilizations" (Gong 1984) and encounters or "entries" of the latter into the former (Bull and Watson 1984). Importantly, intellectual dismissal of the non-West in IR did not mean its occurrence in actual global dynamics as documented in world history. Different state-systems, like the Hindi system (Altekar [1958] 2009), are recognized as suzerain (Wight 1977) even when they did not count intellectually in the study of IR.

This time, however, non-/post-Western IR theorists seem to be enjoying some sustained success. In asking why no international theorizing exists outside the West, non-/post-Western IR has broadened the theoretical vista to include different cultural traditions. While some are based on established (and therefore closer to Western) sets of theories (e.g., Buzan and Gonzalez-Palaez 2009; Quayle 2013), others especially in East Asia (e.g., Acharya and Buzan 2009) identify some unique ideas for theoretical development. Together with the rise of national schools (in particular, the Chinese School), these suggest possibly new directions for theorizing about the world.

Nonetheless, these movements suffer a major drawback. In the name of non-/post-Western IR, they re-enact Western intellectual activity. At least two aspects of this can be observed. Regardless of which movement one endorses, non-Western or post-Western IR, it is *critical* in nature. Indeed, all academics agree: no intellection could qualify as academic without criticality. It is an activity to stop and reflect, to ask if the current situation is acceptable and reject received knowledge as given. Criticality comes from the European Enlightenment (Gay 1979) that sought to "struggle against the absolutist state" (Eagleton [1984] 2005: 9). Here, criticality contests the totality of IR: its theorizing of a unified picture of the world, or its universal approach and methodology. Against this background, many call for pluralizing or "democratizing" the discipline (Chen 2011).

A second aspect of Western intellectual activity involves insertions of *political* moments. There is an intimacy between the rise of criticality and political activism. Modern critical thinking started as chats on plays, music, and literature – in short, culture – which eventually nurtured a public sphere (Habermas 1991). Being critical comes to stand for being political. Paraphrasing Clausewitz on war, Eagleton ([2003] 2004: 29) states that criticality continues "politics by other means."

A problem arises with criticality and politics in tandem. Eagleton ([1984] 2005: 12) labels it an "irony of criticism": while showing "resistance to absolutism ... the critical gesture is typically conservative and corrective." In this sense, non-/post-Western IR suffers from a similar conservatism by building on this Western intellectual tradition and ethos. The word "corrective" also suggests attempts to reform the discipline. Therefore, both non- and post-Western IR may become "reformist" as incremental change is again the tenet of Enlightenment criticality (Eagleton [1984] 2005).

Put differently, a language game emerges. Considering the whole intellectual space as a game set by the West, all attempts to oppose the game may have meaning only through using particular language such as "critique" or "politics" that is already defined by the West. Accordingly, the "reformers" almost never reach the point of exiting the game or reconstituting it.

A typical example comes from Japanese IR during the interwar and wartime periods (Ikeda 2011). Basically, Japan's wartime regime and its advocacy of the Greater East Asian Co-Prosperity Sphere appropriated a non-Western IR project. Its character thus became both old and new, radical and conservative. It was new and radical by proposing a different worldview apart from the Westphalian or Versailles one; yet it was also old and conservative by enacting the same Western epistemology and ontology about world affairs. Major works by Royama (1940), Kamikawa (1944), and others have shown how the Co-Prosperity Sphere extended the Schmidtian idea of the political or the *Grossraum*, and therefore could not qualify as a non-Western approach in the strictest sense. Note, also, the (in)famous "Kyoto School" of Philosophy. Its historical and philosophical critiques and arguments

(Nishida [1940] 1950; Koyama 1939; Suzuki 1939) ended up reinforcing the wartime regime (Kosaka et al. 1943). While intensive research has already been done on the Kyoto School (Goto-Jones 2005, 2007; Shimizu 2011, 2015), a paradox remains: while some of the School's critiques had been fundamental in highlighting an asymmetry between the West and the non-West, Japanese IR still became complicit with the country's wartime regime. The history of the Kyoto School shows how a discourse that initially sought to critique might turn out in an opposite way, becoming "conservative and corrective."

An alternative language game for IR? The idea of road-and-travel

We may restart the work by focusing on the idea of change. We can summarize the current mode of IR theorizing as a triad: order/stability (mainstream IR), replacement (non/post-Western IR), and change (post-Western IR 2.0). This chapter's proposed framework belongs to the third: a second-generation (2.0) version of post-Western IR. Its point of departure is *change*, not replacement. It is important to differentiate one from the other, as previous attempts at change have shifted the emphasis only from one pole to another given a pre-set dichotomy (e.g., Western vs non-Western). How can we transform this dichotomy?

Let us build an alternative language game for IR that is free of the Western/Westphalian culture of critique and politics. This does not mean only proposing a post-"international," post-Western IR: it must also entail a post-theoretical theorizing. This is an act of theorizing that requires more or less some generalization with an elaborated flow of logics, supported by various facts. However, it is also post-theoretical as its intention is to break through the very condition of such a language game. Here, a different question arises. On the one hand, one cannot discard theory simply because it may be Western in critique or politics. On the other hand, attempts at a post-"international" theory may fall into the same pitfalls if we do not take the nexus of the critical and the political into consideration. For this reason, we may need to momentarily leave theory and seek a post-theoretical direction.

Elsewhere (Ikeda 2014), I presented a picture of a road-based, instead of territorial-based, IR. It extends the notion of "worldism" (Ling 2002; Agathangelou and Ling 2009; Ling 2014) that sees the world in terms of multiple relationships, contestations, and other kinds of interaction among mainly cultural actors. A simple observation from worldism is that intercultural dynamics occur at an everyday level among ordinary people. I propose a road-based framework to understand such interactions.

Historically speaking, a road serves three functions: (1) a type of physical infrastructure, (2) a norm, and (3) an exchange. The first is the most concrete while the third, the least. What comes in between highlights a "road complex."

The first characteristic of a road is its physical geography. Roads link spaces and places through networks of activity. A famous example is the Silk Road: it traded spices and even slaves while transmitting various religions like Buddhism, Islam, and Christianity. Today, highways, airplanes, and the digitized road of the Internet represent a contemporary version of the Silk Road. They all serve as infrastructure for human sociality, if not friendship, even if hostile groups can use the same road to conquer others. Regardless of outcome, roads portend interactions and deserve to be considered as sites of minimum sociality. Empires may have initiated roads to connect towns, capitals, and eventually outside territories. That merchants may have also developed road systems for their own purposes is no less important. But these routes often extended beyond territorial borders, forming a road system closer to a "network" of social relations based on a flow of persons along with commodities.

The second layer comes from the first: roads as a norm. Trade and religion set up norms as they travel along roads. Norms of trade are connected to notions of value, exchange, and, of course, profit, but other relevant ideas like fairness, equality, and freedom were added later. More energetic were the norms of religions. Originally a strong faith towards sacred authority and ways to express such faith, the overall character of religious norms has extended from a sense of self-centeredness, eventually intertwined with altruism. In this way, the road sets an imaginary route to ethical destinations. Daoism(道) refers to "the way" as a road. It has a moral dimension, guiding people to proper living. A similar understanding can be found in the Confucian "doctrine of the mean" (中庸). The middle-ness of a road also appears in Buddhism by Nāgārjuna. Aristotle exhibits a similar tendency by recognizing the essence of his ethos as a "via media" – interestingly, the Greek word *mesotes*, or Golden Mean in English, did not start out with road as a nuance but acquired it after its translation into Latin: i.e. "middle of the road." This brief comparison tells us that the idea of the road as a norm suggests a path to a moral ideal. In addition, the road as a practiced norm creates a specific site for learning. In ancient Greece, all roads led to the Academy of Plato and Aristotle; in Islam, to the Mosque; in Hindustan, the ashram; in medieval Europe, the abbey; and in China and other Asian cultures, to temples and shrines. These were sites of religion but they also worked as educational institutions to disseminate knowledge among people. Here, we see a linkage between the normative concept of the road, its institutions, and the activities (especially intellectual) that it fostered. This leads us to the third category of the road as a process.

What people do on the road (process) is just as important as what it is (infrastructure) and what it conveys (norms). This praxeological aspect of the road entails two questions: (1) what one does, generally, and (2) how these activities differ across cultures, in particular. Here the idea of "travel" appears. People come and go on the road. They move across cultures and, in so doing, embark on a process to know how people live differently in different parts of the world. Travel thus collects human interactions. Travel memoirs often give us insight into ancient, pre-modern, and modern interactions. One could invoke Marco Polo (Latham 1958) or Ibn Battuta (Mackintosh-Smith 2003). It is also worth remembering that travel had a variety of meanings. Almost in tandem with travel are explorations and missions. Their purposes encompassed more than mere traveling, including economic exploitations and religious and political suppressions.

When people travel, encounter becomes a key phenomenon. It enables moments when one identifies the Other, the World, and one's Self. Interactions always presuppose both the multiplicity of human beings and their differences with and among one another. Exchanging things and sharing ideas may occur in such encounters, each filling what the other lacks.

Within this context, learning deserves attention. Learning can be a process of mutual supplement through thoughts, values, and practices. Suzerain states in East Asia dispatched monks and scholars to learn the latest developments in Buddhist thought, while Ibn Battuta travelled around the Islamic world partly to learn law, politics, and other elements of his society. Christian scholars studying in the abbeys ushered in the "thirteenth century revolution" (Steenberghen 1955) when the West learned of Islamic interpretations of ancient Greek thought. Processes of encounter and learning facilitated all of the above.

Language plays a vital role. Exchange and learning is possible only on the minimum condition of mutual communication. But even here, exchanges can sometime distort or be interpreted different ways, both intentionally and unexpectedly. In addition, the term language entails linguistic and social aspects. Thus it is still possible that one may communicate with the other with the same language in former sense, but cannot do so in the latter. The Conquistador's brutality in Latin America can be one example of what could occur if people had little means of communication to know each other.[2] An opposite case may also be observed in Europe's encounter in the East Indies and North Africa, where a common language facilitated rules and agreements (Alexandrowicz 1967, 1973).

Another vital component of communication is translation. A cannot understand B without C's translation between them. If we accept language and reality as mutually constitutive, different ideas about translation can give us greater insight into each. For instance, the Japanese philosopher Hajime Nakamura (1974) argues the impossibility of translation as the duplication of original thought. Instead, he focuses on surfacing and heightening the gap between original and translated ideas, as it often entails a process of rejecting contingent elements while sharing and clarifying their common components. Another instance closer to IR comes in treating translation as a cultural, rather than linguistic, means of establishing cosmopolitanism (Delanty 2009). We are now shifting from "whether-or-not" translation is possible to "how," and the kind of change or result that may follow. The idea of road-and-travel may provide some clues to the social and praxeological settings to understanding encounters among cultures.

Towards a worldist approach of global metabolism/metamorphosis

In sum, the concept of road-and-travel implies the possibility of another approach for IR. It departs from the basic conditions of the discipline: namely, the sovereignty of states, territoriality, knowledge, and methodology. As partially mentioned, the road-and-travel perspective comes close to L.H.M. Ling's worldist approach (Ling 2002; Agathangelou and Ling 2009; Ling 2014) but with more stress on the random changeability of the Self, the Other, and the World. The metaphor of travel tells us that such change may occur at an everyday level, and it is especially through activities of encounter and learning that we can facilitate intercultural change. Importantly, the phenomena of travel, road, encounter, and learning are *inter*cultural – it is not endemic only to the "West" or the "non-West." These do not purport to replace particular worldviews even as the dynamics involved entail critical reflection.

Road-and-travel may present fresh thinking for globalizing IR. It is important to recall that the dynamics seen in the road complex are related to changes. The complex describes grand processes of continuous change among Selves, Others, Cultures, and the World; it does not serve any particular critical or political purpose. Finally, the road crosses territories. Traveling requires going back and forth and in between. The inner and inter-territorial culture of road-and-travel suggests that the whole world keeps alive through continuous "inbounds" and "outbounds" of people, actions, information, and anything else. Such dynamics resemble life in the human body: it changes at all times through inputs and outputs.

It is at this point that the road complex theory of the world most resembles an idea of global metabolism leading to global metamorphosis. Order, if there is one, is never stable but just the opposite: change accounts for order or, simply, order is change. As our nutritional intake both maintains the body and yet it is not the same as keeping the body's status quo, the inner interactions among different cultural areas may keep the world as such even as their characters, identities, and (re)actions are always changing.

This picture of global metabolism may be compared to that of the human body. Human growth aggregates various types of circulations – flows of air, food, nutrition, blood, and others. It can be compared with human mobility in the world, as well, through travel. As these constitute the whole order of the human body, human travel and interactions support the whole structure of the world. The latter, however, is less physical than the former. Social meanings construct the various components of the world, such as states and their relationships.

The worldist approach to global metabolism and/or metamorphosis may thus present different pictures of the world, while also sharing some core concepts in IR. Particularly important is worldism's understanding of what has been regarded as static. Order, as well as what constitutes order like states and territoriality, become changing elements. This renders fluid borders and identities of the Self, the Other, and the World. That said, two possible questions still remain. One is: can global metabolism provide an approach for change or the status quo? This comes from the very character of metabolism: order is change while change is order. For some critical thinkers metabolism is a frustrating concept as its pace of change is incremental and its ultimate purpose is to keep the status quo. Therefore, a second question arises: could the metabolic approach accompany another idea of further change, such as metamorphosis and even mutation? Ideas about global metabolism, metamorphosis, and mutation would help to understand how the world is changing, and the road-and-travel based approach may be a good way to introduce them.

Conclusion

It is not still clear if IR as a discipline needs an alternative framework right now. Yet a growing number of scholars are not satisfied with existing accounts. How can we understand this gap and, if we want to, fill it? These are interesting and tough questions. This chapter has attempted to offer one view on the situation. The crux of the matter is as follows: 1) IR theory is facing an intercultural challenge which requires an intercultural answer; 2) ongoing propositions of non/post-Western IR are not quite intercultural, as their scope and methods still tend to be either local/national or Western; 3) what can be proposed, instead, is to start from a multiplicity of cultures and peoples operating at an everyday level; 4) the concept of road-and-travel can link them directly and explain how the world is constantly changing; and finally, 5) global metamorphosis offers such a picture of change.

It is important to note that the global metamorphosis approach suggests two possible directions for changing IR theory. One is post-critical, and another is post-political. They overlap with one another, but remain fundamentally different. The former tries to forget the critical moment; the latter, the political. Crucially, it does not mean to reject criticism or political actions. Rather, this chapter claims that the ways and methods of being critical and political need to be scrutinized from an intercultural perspective. To do so, one needs to stop seeing the critical/political as given. The road-and-travel concept offers a temporary retreat from the critical/political, while, at the same time, authorizes a full investigation of critical methodology and its practical application in different cultures. Comparative political theory (Dallmayr 2010) can provide an important supplement to this intercultural development of IR theory or the establishment of global IR, if there is to be one.

Notes

1 Earlier versions of this chapter were presented at an international workshop for this book project in Ankara, Turkey, as well as at the Annual Convention of Japan Association of International Relations in Fukuoka, Japan. The author would like to express his gratitude to his hosts for financial, institutional, and intellectual support on those two occasions. Lastly, this chapter is part of the author's KAKENHI-fund project (Category: Start-up/Number: 26884022).
2 In his famous lecture on the Indies, international lawyer Francisco de Vitoria argued that the Spaniards did not have a reason to resort to war simply if the announcement were made and the Indies did not receive it. But he also mentioned that if the Indies refused to hear the preachers they would commit a sin. In addition, Vitoria argued that the Indies "are bound to receive the Christian faith" if the preachers were put with "reasonable arguments" and "persuasive demonstration" (Vitoria 1917: 144).

References

Acharya, Amitav. (2014) "Global International Relations and Regional Worlds: A New Agenda for International Studies." *International Studies Quarterly* 58: 647–659.
Acharya, Amitav and Barry Buzan (eds). (2009) *Non-Western International Relations Theory: Perspectives on and beyond Asia.* London: Routledge.

Agathangelou, Anna M., and L.H.M. Ling. (2009) *Transforming World Politics: From Empire to Multiple Worlds*. London: Routledge.

Alexandrowicz, Charles Henry. (1967) *An Introduction to the History of the Law of Nations in the East Indies*. Oxford: Oxford University Press.

Alexandrowicz, Charles Henry. (1973) *The European-African Confrontation: A Study of Treaty-Making*. Leiden: A.W. Sijthoff.

Altekar, Anant Sadashiv. ([1958] 2009) *States and Government in Ancient India*. Delhi: Motilal Banarsidass.

Bull, Hedley and Adam Watson. (1984) *The Expansion of International Society*. Oxford: Oxford University Press.

Buzan, Barry and Ana Gonzalez-Pelaez. (2009) *International Society and the Middle East: English School Theory at Regional Level*. London: Palgrave.

Chen, Ching Chang. (2011) "The Absence of Non-Western IR Theory in Asia Reconsidered." *International Relations of the Asia Pacific* 11(1): 1–23.

Chen, Ching Chang. (2012) "The Im/Possibility of Building Indigenous Theories in a Hegemonic Discipline: The Case of Japanese International Relations." *Asian Perspective* 36: 463–492.

Dallmayr, Fred. (2010) *Comparative Political Theory: An Introduction*. London: Palgrave.

Delanty, Gerard. (2009) *The Cosmopolitan Imagination: The Renewal of Critical Social Theory*. Cambridge: Cambridge University Press.

Eagleton, Terry. (1984/2005) *The Function of Criticism*. London: Verso.

Eagleton, Terry. (2003/2004) *After Theory*. London: Penguin Books.

Gay, Peter. (1979) *The Enlightenment: An Interpretation*. New York: W.W. Norton.

Gong, Gerrit. (1984) *The Standard of "Civilization" in International Society*. Oxford: Oxford University Press.

Goto-Jones, Christopher. (2005) *Political Philosophy in Japan: Nishida, the Kyoto School and the Co-Prosperity*. London: Routledge.

Goto-Jones, Christoher (ed.). (2007) *Re-politicising the Kyoto School as Philosophy*. London: Routledge.

Habermas, Jurgen. (1991) *The Structural Transformation of Public Sphere*. Cambridge, MA: MIT Press.

Ikeda, Josuke. (2011) "The 'Westfailure' Problem in International Relations Theory." In Shiro Sato, Josuke Ikeda, Ching Chang Chen, and Young Chul Cho (eds), *Re-examination of "Non-Western" International Relations Theory* (Kyoto Working Paper on Area Studies, no. 118), 12–42. Kyoto: Center for Southeast Asian Studies, Kyoto University.

Ikeda, Josuke. (2014) "The Idea of the 'Road' in International Relations Theory." *Perceptions* 24(1): 153–165.

Inoguchi, Takashi. (2009) "Why Are There No Non-Western International Relations Theories? The Case of Japan." In Amitav Acharya and Barry Buzan (eds), *Non-Western International Relations Theory: Perspectives On and Beyond Asia*, 51–68. London: Routledge.

Kamikawa, Hikomatsu. (1944) "Sekai Shin-chitujo Ron [「世界新秩序論」 On New World Order]." In Magota Hideharu (ed.), *Nihon Kokka Kagaku Taikei* [『日本国家科学大系』], Series on Japanese Science of the State, Volume 14, 1–86. Tokyo: Jiotsugyo no Nihon-Sha.

Kosaka, Masataka, Keiji Nishitani, Iwao Koyama and Shigetaka Suzuki (1943). Sekaishi-teki Tachiba to Nippon [『世界史的立場と日本』 World Historical Position and Japan] (Tokyo: Chuo Koron-sha).

Koyama, Iwao. (1939) *Bunka Ruikei-gaku* [『文化類型学』, Cultural Typology]. Tokyo: Kobun-do.

Latham, Ronald (trans.). (1958) *The Travels of Marco Polo*. London: Penguin Books.

Ling, L.H.M. (2002) *Postcolonial International Relations: Conquest and Desire between Asia and the West*. London: Palgrave Macmillan.

Ling, L.H.M. (2014) *The Dao of World Politics: Towards a Post-Westphalian, Worldist International Relations*. London: Routledge.

Mackintosh-Smith, Tim (ed.). (2003) *The Travels of Ibn Battutah*. London: Pacador.

Mazrui, Ari. (1967) *Towards a Pax Africana: A Study of Ideology and Ambition*. Chicago, IL: University of Chicago Press.

Mazrui, Ari. (1976) *A World Federation of Cultures: An African Perspective*. New York: Free Press.

Nakamura, Hajime. (1974) *Kodai Shisou* [Ancient Thought]. Tokyo: Shunju-sha.

Nishida, Kitaro. ([1940] 1950) "Nihon Bunka no Mondai [「日本文化の問題」 On Japanese Culture]." In *Nishida Kitaro Zenshu* [『西田幾多郎全集』 Nishida Kitaro Works], *Volume 12*, 277–434. Tokyo: Iwanami Shoten.

Porter, Brian. (1972) *The Aberystwyth Papers: International Politics 1919–1969*. Oxford: Oxford University Press.

Quayle, Linda. (2013) *Southeast Asia and the English School of International Relations: A Region-Theory Dialogue*. London: Palgrave.

Royama, Masamichi. (1940) *Sekai no Henkyoku to Nihon no Sekai-seisaku* [『世界の変局と日本の世界政策』, Changing World and Japan's Global Policy]. Tokyo: Gansho-do. In Japanese.

Schmidt, Brian. (1998) *The Political Discourse of Anarchy: A Disciplinary History of International Relations*. New York: State University of New York Press.

Shani, Giorgio. (2007) "'Provincializing' Critical Theory: Islam, Sikhism, and International Relations Theory." *Cambridge Review of International Studies* 20(3): 417–433.

Shani, Giorgio. (2008) "Towards a Post-Western IR: The Umma, Khalsa Panth, and Critical International Relations Theory." *International Studies Review* 10(4): 722–734.

Shilliam, Robbie (ed.). (2010) *International Relations and Non-Western Thought: Imperialism, Colonialism and Investigations of Global Modernity*. London: Routledge.

Shimizu, Kosuke. (2011) "Nishida Kitaro and Japan's Interwar Foreign Policy: War Involvement and Cultural Political Discourse." *International Relations of the Asia-Pacific* 11(1): 157–183.

Shimizu, Kosuke. (2015) "Materializing the 'non-Western': Two Stories of Japanese Philosophers on Culture and Politics in the Inter-war Period." *Cambridge Review of International Affairs* 28(1): 3–20.

Steenberghen, Hans Van. (1955) *The Philosophical Movement in the Thirteenth Century: Lectures given under the Auspices of the Department of Scholastic Philosophy, the Queen's University, Belfast*. London: Nelson.

Strange, Susan. (1999) "The Westfailure System." *Review of International Studies* 25(4): 345–354.

Suzuki, Sigetaka. (1939) *Ranke to Sekaishi-gaku* [『ランケと世界史学』, Ranke and the Study of World History]. Tokyo: Kobun-do.

Tickner, Arlene B. and David L. Blaney (eds). (2012) *Thinking International Relations Differently*. London: Routledge.

Tickner, Arlene B. and Ole Waever (eds). (2009) *International Relations Scholarship around the World*. London: Routledge.

Vasilaki, Rosa. (2012) "Provincialising IR? Deadlocks and Prospects in Post-Western IR Theory." *Millennium* 41(1): 3–22.

Vitoria, Franciscus de. (1917) *De Indis et De Ivre Belli Relectiones* (translated by John Pawley Bate) (Classics of International Law, edited by Ernest Nys). Washington, D.C.: Carnegie Institution.

Wight, Martin. (1977) "De Systematibus Civitatum." In Martin Wight, *Systems of States*, 21–45. Leicester: Leicester University Press.

Zhang, Feng. (2012) "The Tsinghua Approach and the Inception of Chinese Theories of International Relations." *The Chinese Journal of International Politics* 5(1): 73–102.

Zhang, Yongjin and Barry Buzan. (2012) "The Tributary System as International Society in Theory and Practice." *The Chinese Journal of International Politics* 5(1): 3–36.

13

EMPIRE OF THE MIND

José Rizal and proto-nationalism in the Philippines

Alan Chong

Colonialism and its enduring impacts have vanished from the international relations (IR) agenda on Asia.[1] Most scholars of and in the region tend to pursue Realist approaches to studies of security and diplomacy (Eaton and Stubbs 2006). With rational choice as a basic assumption, "culture" exists, at best, as a feature in the bureaucratic politics of Asian foreign policymaking. Research chokes, accordingly, since rational choice prohibits consideration of diverse inputs into Asian politics. As it has been argued elsewhere, there are Asian worldviews that both predate and deviate from Kantian and Humean calculations of interests and notions of the self.

In this chapter, I take a different tack. I probe into the frames of politico-cultural struggles created by Western colonialism in Asia. Here, I quote from Edward Said. On the co-constitutive relationship between a newly independent nation-state's political culture and its colonial past, he wrote:

> [C]ulture is in advance of politics, military history, or economic process ... [Revolutionary] changes cannot occur [however] ... unless the idea of empire and the cost of colonial rule are challenged publicly, unless the representations of imperialism begin to lose their justification and legitimacy, and, finally, unless the rebellious 'natives' impress upon the metropolitan culture the independence and integrity of their own culture, free from colonial encroachment ... [W]e should acknowledge that, at both ends of the redrawn map, opposition and resistance to imperialism are articulated together on a largely common although disputed terrain provided by culture.
>
> *(Said 1993: 241)*

In particular, I sample two popular novels by José Rizal Mercado, a pioneer Filipino nationalist. Of his peers, Rizal alone receives the conjoined labels of teacher, leader, and scribe of Philippine nationalism. His two novels, *Noli Me Tangere* and *El*

Filibusterismo, provide more than just historical and philosophical insight. Together, they depict colonialism through a panorama of characters who mirror colonial society's high officials, their acolytes, the pretentious half-Spaniards who aspire to be the social equal of the former, and the native Filipinos dubbed *"Indios."* Through this literary landscape, Rizal takes his readers through the ideological contradictions of Spanish colonialism, its psychological domination of the *Indios*, and Catholicism as Spain's instrument of administrative and intellectual oppression.

To Rizal, change must have a *positive* purpose. It cannot simply assuage the colonized's hatred of the colonizer. Violence, like fire, may be a good servant but a bad master; when uncontrolled, it can produce an apocalypse of ideals in place of genuine liberation. In particular, Rizal warns that throwing off the shackles of Western colonialism/imperialism remains incomplete. The new, post-revolution citizen must also prepare for the new, post-revolution nation.

Mercantilist Spanish colonialism (1565–1898), followed by postwar US hegemony (1898–1946), account for the Philippines. Much like the rest of colonized Asia, the Philippines as a nation and a state did not exist before this advent of the Western Other. Asian nationalists faced a dilemma, accordingly: how to declare a new state *and* denounce the Western colonialism/imperialism that set it up (Mulder 2012)? Rizal cautioned that indigenous leaders, as much as foreign ones, could reproduce colonial governance without addressing underlying structural injustices (Ayoob 1985); at the same time, wholesale return to a pre-colonial past could undercut any attempts at progressive change.

The "empire of the mind" prefaces the lessons offered by Rizal's writings.

Empire of the mind

Western colonialism/imperialism in South East Asia started in the 1500s. Europeans migrated to Asia to alleviate demographic and economic pressures at home. Yet they enhanced their life prospects in the new territories by turning the original inhabitants into secondary or marginal considerations in their own land (Thornton 1980). Treaties were signed without local consent or full knowledge of an imported "Westphalian system" (Abdullah 1970). Bound by earthly law and its principle of *pacta sunt servanda*, Westphalian treaty-making deviated from local worldviews rooted in cosmological notions of governance. Soldiers also accompanied these pacts, signaling the mix of war and peace in Westphalian diplomacy. Such were the stakes involved. An involuntary form of "international relations" emerged whereby one "state" came to occupy the territory and population of another.

To consolidate colonial control, the colonizers imposed a "modern" form of education. This is where the thought of José Rizal Mercado enlightens. Spanish colonialism had tethered the idea of a progressive Filipino society to the exploitative structures of the colonial state and its ideological handmaiden, the Church. Liberation from colonial rule, accordingly, must bridge the gap between a colonized mentality and its nationalist successor. Rizal suggested this adjustment through education. This was a painful path since education required breaking religious taboos while arming one's mind for a new set of ethics involving constitutional freedoms and resistance against corruption offered by power dressed as authority.

I look at Rizal's two novels, *Noli Me Tangere*, and *El Filibusterismo*. These offer a reading of Asian anti-colonialist thought to further universal explanations of the international relations of social adjustment (Scholte 1993). This perspective of IR takes as its starting point the nature of social relations within state-bounded societies and their transnational relations with peoples residing across other sovereign boundaries. IR is social since it arises as much from psychological adjustments between peoples through their thinking selves, as it is from the physiological needs between peoples. It is therefore extremely relevant to unpacking the impact of colonialism upon IR in the non-West. For my purpose, it accounts for why security regionalism and other forms of IR in Southeast Asia frequently produce incomplete solutions to interstate disputes and robust institution building (Acharya 2010). But first, a little historical context is necessary.

Church and State in the Philippines

Spain ruled the Philippines for nearly 360 years with a dual political system: Church and State. Both were designed to treat the native Filipinos, whether *mestizo* or *Indio*, as objects of exploitation. In the words of a historian:

> Native life under the colonial regime acquired a complexity not heretofore known. Each colonized Filipino was expected to live in a *pueblo* [village or urban district] for purposes of civil government; be part of a *doctrina* [religious district or diocese], for religious instruction; and of an *encomienda* [apportioned land granted to the original Spanish soldiers and settlers as rewards for their service] for the exaction of tribute, produce, and labour.
>
> (Francia 2014)

This was not merely a spatial and bureaucratic instrument of subjection. It also correlated with an ideological tyranny expressed through ecclesiastical despotism. As Nicholas Cushner puts it, the Spaniard represented a "centralizing force" that swept aside the pre-Hispanic ways of small village kinship-based communities (*barangays*) led by autonomous *datus* who came together only in face of a common enemy (Cushner 1971). Spanish administration joined the *barangays* into *pueblos, encomiendas,* and townships, often administered by a resident friar in the name of the *doctrina*. Each of these residential and municipal jurisdictions exacted taxes and labor from the *Indios*, especially in the vast rural areas. These institutions induced a culture of passivity or "indolence" amongst the native population – a popular target of Rizal's writings.

Church and State also jointly managed the colonial enterprise via the *patronato real* (royal patronage). The Papacy in Rome conceded this right to the kings of Portugal and Spain since the 1400s for spreading Catholicism throughout heathen lands. In the Philippines, the Spanish Crown pledged to support the Church financially while the latter granted the Crown the privilege of presenting clergy and bishops for appointment to the dioceses and churches across the colony. In practice, however, a number of pre-sanctioned powers granted by the Papacy to the various Catholic orders, such as the Franciscans, Augustinians, and Jesuits, allowed each to preach without fear or favor, and perform absolutions from social transgressions (Cushner 1971). In areas remote from the capital in Manila, friars reigned as substitutes for the Spanish Crown and its agents. The *patronato real* became an extended moral basis for friars to demand fees for hearing confessions, solemnizing marriages, and maintaining local parishes. Wielding the threat of Providential punishment and excommunication, the friar could demand from his local "flock" voluntary labor for assorted construction projects for his own benefit as well as the common interest in towns under his "charge." "God's calling," Francia writes, became "the cover under which Mammon could be served eagerly and faithfully. The early years of hardship and asceticism gave way to pampered living" (Francia 2014).

The various Catholic orders united in their educational mission: to teach the *Indios* only so much so they could be baptized. This helped to maintain religious authority, and by undeclared extension, Spanish colonial authority. For a wealthy few *mestizos*, a tertiary education abroad was a luxury that only they could afford; nonetheless, they ignited awareness of colonial subjugation distributed through pamphlets and nascent newspapers (Francia 2014). The seeds of rebellion had been planted.

Rizal's socialization

Rizal embodied these converging and conflicting forces. A *mestizo* of *Indio* and Chinese parentage, Rizal combined within him "middle class" privileges compounded by the social tragedy of being born a colonial subject. The Chinese community in the Philippines was enriched by trade, especially rice and other foods, and assimilated by converting to Catholicism and marrying locally, usually with *Indio* women (Francia 2014). The Spaniards relied on the Chinese as a mainstay of the comprador economy. With their accumulated wealth, the Chinese *mestizos* bought land from the *encomiendas* or profited by leasing out their land to *Indios* to cultivate cash crops.

José Rizal could have stayed a privileged landowner. But this was a young man incensed with the injustice meted out to three Spanish priests in 1872 on the grounds that their liberal-leaning views had predisposed their charges and Filipino priests to disturb public order and corrupt public morality. The Spanish Revolution of 1868 afforded a brief interlude that precipitated the incident (Francia 2014). During three years of revolutionary government in Madrid, the liberal-leaning Carlos Maria de la Torre was appointed Governor General of the Philippines. He lifted numerous bans on reformist currents on the ground and encouraged *mestizos* and *Indios* to consider legal guarantees of a more liberal political and social climate. The end of forced labor and other exactions in the countryside appeared in sight. But reactionaries amongst the old order rescinded any possibility of reform. On

January 20, 1872, the *Indio* employees of the Cavite Arsenal rebelled against the reinstitution of forced labor and murdered seven Spanish officers over two days of violence. Three Spanish priests were accused of fanning the flames of Filipinization. Reactionary friars persuaded the new right-wing Governor to sentence these priests to death for sedition. Overnight, the three enlightened Spanish clergymen became martyrs for Filipino nationalism. Against this background, we can appreciate Rizal's development as a pioneer of anti-colonialism.

Rizal, the author

Part autobiography, the *Noli* masquerades as a work of fiction. It is 1887: a young man, whose deceased father was a native landowner under Spanish colonial authority, returns home after obtaining a gentleman's education in Europe. He succeeds to his father's honorific title and becomes Don Crisostomo Ibarra. Spanish colonial officials, as well as the "half-breed" or *mestizo*, Filipino landed gentry and officialdom, are curious about the young man's manners, political views, and social outlook. Much as Ibarra's homecoming is an opportunity to reconnect with the officially approved colonial high society, both *mestizos* and *Indios* turn to the young man as a benign alternative to their current patron-client networks in the country. Right from the start, Ibarra finds the Catholic religious adjutants to Spanish civil authority, that is, the friars, bishops and even *mestizo* priests, an ideological wall to his aspirations to improve the lot of the Filipino people. Ibarra discovers his own restlessness against Spanish tutelage and the narcotized nature of colonial high society and establishes communication with *mestizos* and *Indios* who seek to overthrow Spanish authority. Ibarra counsels caution, suggesting a gentle petitionary course of reform towards the powers that be, but he remains sympathetic to those who embrace an armed solution to colonial oppression. Ibarra gets tarred in the process as an insurgent and *appears* overcome by a Spanish counter-attack at the end of the novel.

Noli's sequel, *El Filibusterismo* (*Fili* for short), sees Ibarra "resurrecting" himself into a determined, armed revolutionary. This time, Ibarra adopts a perfect disguise to navigate between colonial high society in the city and armed revolutionaries in the countryside. He reinvents himself as Simoun, an American Jewish jeweler pandering to the material fancies of high society and the lower strata of *mestizos* and *Indios* alike. Simoun/Ibarra now plots a bomb attack at a party attended by the Governor and times it with an armed uprising. Ultimately, Simoun/Ibarra fails, dying an even more embittered nationalist while vowing eternal opposition to colonialism. In these pages, Rizal produced stunning passages of nationalist introspection and intellectual sparring with the powers that be. Here, art imitated life. Rizal himself died at age 35 in front of a Spanish firing squad after years of persecution for his novels.

To make a state

Rizal's writings ask: How deeply does the colonial state affect the civilization of its subjects? Rizal himself had spent much of the 1880s abroad in Europe and corresponded with a number of intellectuals there. His writings expressed a heartfelt desire to uplift the material and spiritual lot of the *Indios*. By extension, he was also upbraiding the colonial government for grossly neglecting the constitutional rights and responsibilities of its subjects. This might suggest the blossoming of political liberalism in Rizal; but it can also be read as the emergence of a proto-nationalist experimenting with comparative politics. In chapter 3 of the *Noli*, cryptically titled "The Dinner," the seniors and friars around the table ask Ibarra which of the countries he visited in Europe most appealed to him. In the tone of polite conversation he replies:

> After Spain, my second homeland, [I admire] any country in free Europe ... Speaking frankly, what is surprising in those peoples, laying aside the national pride of each one ... before I visit a country I endeavour to study its history, its exodus – if I may call it that – and after that I would find it understandable. I always found that the prosperity or the misery of a people is in direct proportion to its liberties or concerns, and consequently to the sacrifices or selfishness of its ancestors.
>
> *(Rizal 2006)*

Insulted by the allusion to friar dominance in the colony's administration, one Franciscan retorts: "And you have not seen more than that? ... It is not worth squandering your fortune in order to learn so little. Any schoolchild knows that!" (Rizal 2006). Ibarra resists a counter-response to this bold-faced denial of the Church's oppression in the countryside but writes afterward in his private journal:

> In the Philippines, the most useless person in a supper or feast is the one giving it: to begin with, the master of the house can be thrown out into the street and everything will proceed as usual. In the actual state of things it is almost for the good of the Filipinos not to be allowed to leave the country or to be taught to read.
>
> *(Rizal 2006)*

Anguish mixes with irony here. Ibarra laments the residual goodwill of the Filipino people "hosting" Spanish rule despite the latter's cruelties. "The Dinner" thus serves as an analogy of how colonial Spain is losing legitimacy in the eyes of one awakened subject when the "guest" abuses its "host." In an aside, an elderly Spaniard, holding the bureaucratic appointment of a *Teniente*, admits to Ibarra the rot within:

> We Spaniards who have come to the Philippines are unfortunately not as we ought to be. I say this for one of your grandfathers as well as for his enemies. The continual changes, the state of demoralization in the higher spheres, favouritism, the shortness and the cheapness of travel are responsible for everything. To this country come the dregs of the [Iberian] peninsula and if one arrives a good man, soon he is corrupted in the country.
>
> *(Rizal 2006)*

Like Rizal in real life, Ibarra inherits his late father's wealth and proposes to avail himself of the good graces of the few enlightened Spaniards willing to listen to his plan to build a modern school. Ibarra is fortunate to find a kindred spirit in the reigning Governor of the Philippines who promises to protect him from reactionary Franciscans. Yet the enlightened Governor finds it necessary to maintain appearances in keeping the balance of power between Church and State:

> Here we cannot laugh at these things in public as we do on the [Iberian] Peninsula or in cultured Europe. Withal in the future, be more prudent. You have pitted yourself against the religious orders which, because of their importance and their riches, need to be respected. But I will protect you because I like good sons; I like for them to honour the memory of their fathers; I too have loved mine and God alive! I don't know what I would have done in your place.
>
> *(Rizal 2006)*

However, the fiery anger of Elias, the *Indio*, severely tests Ibarra's hopes of patient reform in the colonial state:

> I did not think you had such a poor [i.e. misinformed] idea of the government and of the country. Why don't you despise one and the other? What would you say of a family which lives in peace only because of the intervention of a stranger? A country that obeys because it is deceived, a government which commands because it resorts to deception, a government which does not know how to inspire love and respect for its own sake! Begging your pardon, Sir, I believe that your government is stupid and suicidal when it rejoices in that belief.
>
> *(Rizal 2006)*

Elias fronts for the common, partially educated *Indio*, dispossessed of his family land and taxed beyond relief by friar administrators, and neglected by the Governor in Manila. Ibarra's acrimonious dialogue with him eventually turns into a revolutionary strategy but only after being educated in the miseries of Elias' family and personal histories. Hence, by the time that Rizal's pen transforms Ibarra into the fanatical Simoun in *Fili*, the imagery of revolution is stark, bloody, and hints at derangement. In these words, Ibarra arrogates to himself the role of an avenging Savior purifying the intimate "you," the Filipino nation-to-be:

> Within a few days ... when from her four sides flames burn that wicked city, den of presumptuous nothingness and the impious exploitation of the ignorant and the unfortunate; when tumult breaks out in the suburbs and there rush into the terrorized streets my avenging hordes, engendered by rapacity and wrongdoing, then I will shatter the walls of your prison; I will snatch you from the clutches of fanaticism; white dove, you will be the phoenix that will be reborn from the glowing ashes.
>
> *(Rizal 2006)*

One might observe that Rizal advocated revolution as a final resort only. Change must be paced and timed with the aptitude and character of those in government and the people governed. Even in face of rulers' glaring "sins" of omission, oppression and the like, reform was the more thoughtful response, born of comparative knowledge and level-headed rationality. Revolution was not to be taken lightly (Torres 2014). Rizal had, in all probability, adopted messianic and apocalyptic terms to describe revolution to convey its potentially uncontrollable horrors. After all, revolution meant wanton violence despite its initially idealistic promise (Brinton 1965). Behind Rizal's political inclinations, as manifested in the two novels, was a keen awareness that political change must be measured against its consequences and the human commitment needed to ignite it.[2]

Educating subject peoples for the nation

Throughout the two novels, Rizal imparted an urgency to educate – not unlike his European contemporaries, Karl Marx and Friedrich Engels. The masses in slumber were inadequate material for igniting the anger that would drive reform, let alone revolution. Rizal appreciated this only too well. The *Indios* and *mestizos* could not conceive of themselves a nation until they took pride in and ownership of their teacher–student relationship. This, in turn, meant empathy in each other's mission: the student to learn how to contribute to society; the teacher, to understand the needs of the children and to set off appropriate sparks of inquiry in their minds. Rizal's hectoring tone verges on a tutelary authoritarianism for the purpose of emancipating the illiterate and semi-literate *Indios* and *mestizos* from the Church's nearly absolute monopoly of education. Once the former are made aware of alternatives to the clergy's Gramscian-like pedagogies for reproducing subjection, only then can serious thinking for the state after independence be productively conceived. Rizal's depiction of Ibarra's chance encounter with a schoolmaster in his father's ancestral hometown of San Diego illustrates the systematic demoralization of the Filipino educator:

> [O]ne poor single teacher cannot fight against prejudices, against certain influences. The school would need, first and foremost, to have a place of its own, not as it is now, where I teach beside the parish priest's carriage under the convent house. There, the boys, who like to read aloud, naturally bother the Padre. At times, he would come down upset, especially when he has one of those attacks; he shouts at them and insults me at times.
>
> *(Rizal 2006)*

The metaphor of place is evocative: education by locals for the locals must still concede to the whims and fascism of the colonial Church. The schoolmaster's double life of putting up a politically correct and submissive face to the gaze of colonial power breeds ironically a secret determination to examine alternative visions, becoming Gramsci's "organic intellectual" in service of counter-hegemonic change (Gramsci 2000):

Since that day when I was so grossly insulted, I examined myself and I saw myself actually an ignoramus. I made myself study Spanish day and night, and all that had to do with my profession. The old philosopher lent me some of his books; I read what I could lay my hands on, and I analysed what I was reading ... I saw errors where before I saw only truths, and truths in many things which seemed errors to me.

(Rizal 2006)

Religion, culture and civilizing the masses

In his political pamphlets, Rizal underscored Spain's destruction of Filipino traditions, especially poetry, songs, and laws. Spanish colonialism rendered anything "foreign and incomprehensible" as inherently superior. Yet, in Rizal's romantic imagination, Spain was not the irreconcilable enemy in the recovery of Filipino dignity. In the *Noli*, Rizal sought to awaken in his readers the subtlety with which hatred of colonial injustice might trap the mass of the oppressed into despising all forms of colonial tutelage. Witness, for instance, the rhetorical exchange between Ibarra's ambivalently naïve belief in colonialism's civilizing mission and the *Indio* Elias' blind hatred of how colonialism dispossessed his agricultural livelihood and those of his ancestors. Ibarra asks Elias to reconsider his hatred of the Church by recalling how religion has guided Filipinos from moral error in their daily lives and the good priests who shielded the helpless from the "tyrannies of civil power." Elias replies that while he could not argue against Ibarra's historical and philosophical logic, he insists that Filipinos, as sons of the soil, had paid "too expensive" a price for this moral and social guidance (Rizal 2006).

This form of materialist and instrumentalist anti-colonialism had constantly shadowed Rizal's preferred mode of enlightened nationalism. The latter is one that distinguishes the value of the good in relation to the varying degrees of the evil. Friar colonialism had civilized the Filipino by at least introducing schools and basic literacy, but it had in the process wantonly displaced local culture with a foreign one. The comparisons made with Spain's "cultural denial" of its Jewish and Islamic heritage are deliberately invoked to castigate Spain's double standards in eviscerating the Philippines' pre-Hispanic culture (Rizal 2006). Elias makes a second point: Spain's Catholic culture also exploited the locals economically. Piety became associated with consumptions of Catholic trinkets, leading to a commodity fetishism of religion.

By the time Rizal composed *Fili*, he had grown disillusioned with the ability of ordinary Filipinos to divine the nobler dimensions of colonialism. Through the voice of Simoun, as a vengeful Ibarra-turned-revolutionary, Rizal taunted his terrorist comrades, along with the reader, with a call for the cleansing of the ignorant, angry masses. Simoun brazenly applauds the silence of world opinion in the face of mass cruelties perpetrated by nationalist revolutionaries in making the United States of America, Portugal's plunder and subjugation of the Moluccas, and Britain's imperialist acquisition of Australia and New Zealand achieved by massacring scores of native inhabitants (Rizal 2006). Clearly, Simoun verges on approving the practice of genocide by the imperialist powers even though he is making a case for purifying mass culture for a respectable nationhood. Those who long to establish self-determining nation-states ought to be worthy of the quest by renovating their cultures and keeping what is progressive. These include awareness of a universal God and a standard of universal human rights. Nationalism by the people for the people needs to be owned by them. Simoun reflects on this point as he lies dying in the house of a sympathetic *mestizo* priest:

> The school of suffering tempers; the arena of combat strengthens the soul. I do not mean to say that our freedom is to be won by the blade of the sword; the sword enters very little now in modern destinies, yes, but we must win it, deserving it, raising the intelligence and the dignity of the individual.
>
> (Rizal 2006)

After Simoun dies, Padre Florentino throws over a cliff the departed's "revolutionary war chest." Padre Florentino speaks poetically of the need to await a worthy revolutionary, when his people are ready for the proper form of violence for constructing a genuinely independent state:

> When for a holy and sublime end men should need you, God will draw you from the breast of the waves … Meanwhile there you will not distort right, you will not foment avarice.
>
> (Rizal 2006)

Conclusion

Rizal warns us of the *incompleteness* of anti-colonial nationalisms. Revolution may eject the physical trappings of alien rule but, to be whole, it must also decolonize the mind. To do so, we need to sift the positive educational legacies of colonialism and graft new identities onto it. When one scans the Asian international relations landscape, accordingly, one invariably concludes that political and economic regionalism can, at best, be a work in progress.

Southeast Asia's semi-democracies and authoritarian states, for instance, proudly proclaim nationalist credentials when displaying martial prowess but fail to realize they may be recycling colonialism under the banner of "independence." Take, for instance, Malaysia's internecine controversies over how vernacular education should be supported, or Thailand's and Vietnam's curbs on "free and critical thought" on the Internet and other social media, or Singapore's obsession with revising the ruling party's history of anti-communism. Nationalism within the Association of Southeast Asian Nations (ASEAN) states needs to heed Rizal's admonition about straightjacketing education for political purposes.

To Rizal, nationalism must germinate organically. It must arise from the idealistic hearts and minds of the self-motivated person who aspires towards a dignity found only through self-sacrifice, and not through the factory-like processes of an industrialized nationalism.[3]

Notes

1 Recent exceptions include Jones (2006) and Shilliam (2011).
2 In this regard, one senses a resonance in the way that ASEAN states today adopt particularly procrastinating approaches to reforms of state and nation (Chong 2011). For instance, ASEAN's constantly gentle reproach of Cambodia, Myanmar, and Thailand for abuses in democratic procedure and treatment of political opposition perfectly illustrate accommodation of an incomplete nationalism.
3 I owe this point of reflection to discussions with Rene Escalante of the Department of History, De La Salle University, in Manila, Philippines (Escalante 2014). One can contrast Rizal's conception of an organic nationalist with Ernest Gellner's treatment of industrial-era nationalism (Gellner 2006).

Bibliography

Abdullah, M., 1970. *The Hikayat Abdullah*. Kuala Lumpur: Oxford University Press.
Acharya, A., 2010. *Whose Ideas Matter? Agency and Power in Asian Regionalism*. Singapore and Ithaca: ISEAS and Cornell University Press.
Ayoob, M., 1985. The Primacy of the Political: South Asian Regional Cooperation (SARC) in Comparative Perspective. *Asian Survey*, 25(4), pp. 443–457.
Bauman, Z., 1998. *Globalization: The Human Consequences*. New York: Columbia University Press.
Brinton, C., 1965. *The Anatomy of a Revolution*. Third ed. New York: Vintage Books, Random House.
Capie, D., 2013. Structures, Shocks and Norm Change: Explaining the Late Rise of Asia's Defence Diplomacy. *Contemporary Southeast Asia*, 35(1), pp. 1–26.
Chew, E.C., 1991. The Foundation of a British Settlement. In E.C. Chew and E. Lee, eds., *A History of Singapore*. Singapore: Oxford University Press, pp. 36–40.
Chong, A., 2011. A Society of the Weak, the Medium and the Great: Southeast Asia's Lessons in Building Soft Community among States. In A. Astrov, ed., *The Great Power (mis)Management: The Russian–Georgian War and its Implications for Global Political Order*. Farnham: Ashgate, pp. 135–158.
Chong, A., 2012. Premodern Southeast Asia as a Guide to International Relations between Peoples: Prowess and Prestige in "Intersocietal Relations" in the Sejarah Melayu. *Alternatives: Global, Local, Political*, 37(2), pp. 87–105.
Collins, A., 2013. *Building a People-Oriented Security Community the ASEAN Way*. Abingdon: Routledge.
Cushner (S.J.), N.P., 1971. *Spain in the Philippines: From Conquest to Revolution*. Quezon City, Manila; Rutland, VT: Institute of Philippine Culture – Ateneo de Manila University; Charles E. Tuttle Company.
Eaton, S. and Stubbs, R., 2006. Is ASEAN Powerful? Neo-Realist versus Constructivist Approaches to Power in Southeast Asia. *The Pacific Review*, 19(2), pp. 135–155.
Escalante, R., 2014. (Professor of History, De La Salle University) Interview, December 16, 2014.
Francia, L.H., 2014. *A History of the Philippines: From Indios Bravos to Filipinos*. New York: The Overlook Press.
Gellner, E., 2006. *Nations and Nationalism*. Oxford: Blackwell.
Gramsci, A., 2000. The Southern Question. In *The Modern Prince and Other Writings*. New York: International Publishers, pp. 28–54.
Guerrero, L.M., 2007. *The First Filipino: A Biography of Jose Rizal by Leon Ma. Guerrero*. Manila: Guerrero Publishing.

Jones, B. G. ed., 2006. *Decolonizing International Relations*. Lanham, MD: Rowman & Littlefield.

Ling, L., 2014. *The Dao of World Politics: Towards a Post-Westphalian, Worldist International Relations*. Abingdon: Routledge.

Mahbubani, K., 2008. *The New Asian Hemisphere: The Irresistible Shift of Global Power to the East*. New York: Public Affairs.

Mulder, N., 2012. The Insufficiency of Filipino Nationhood. In *Situating Filipino Civilisation in Southeast Asia: Reflections and Observations*. Saabrucken: LAP Lambert Academic Publishing GmbH, pp. 29–63.

Rizal, J., 1996. *El Filibusterismo: Subversion. A Sequel to Noli Me Tangere*. Makati City (Manila): Bookmark Incorporated.

Rizal, J., 2006. *Noli Me Tangere*. Makati City (Manila): Bookmark Incorporated.

Said, E.W., 1993. *Culture and Imperialism*. London: Chatto and Windus.

Scholte, J.A., 1993. *International Relations of Social Change*. Milton Keynes: Open University Press.

Shilliam, R., ed., 2011. *International Relations and Non-Western Thought: Imperialism, Colonialism, and Investigations of Global Modernity*. Abingdon: Routledge.

Thomas, M.C., 2012. *Orientalists, Propagandists and Ilustrados: Filipino Scholarship and the End of Spanish Colonialism*. Minneapolis: University of Minneapolis Press.

Thornton, A., 1980. *Imperialism in the Twentieth Century*. London: Macmillan Press.

Torres, V., 2014. (Doctor, Department of History, De La Salle University) Interview, December 16, 2014.

14

THE KOREAN WAVE

Korean popular culture at the intersection of state, economy, and history

Jooyoun Lee

Many consider the "Korean Wave" an exemplar of "soft power." The Korean Wave refers to a global popularity of South Korean cultural products since the 1990s. Through TV dramas, K-pops, entertainment programs, films, and video games, the Korean Wave has galvanized attention in Asia and elsewhere. The concept of soft power comes from Joseph Nye (2004). He differentiates it from the more familiar, material-based notion of "hard power" in international relations (IR). To Nye, soft power helps to shape the preferences of others without coercion; it mobilizes cooperation without resort to threats. Analysts of Asia find soft power increasingly appealing, especially its implications for foreign policy (Wang and Lu 2006).

The notion of soft power, however, explains only partially. The Korean Wave entails more than simply amassing culture to serve national ends; it reflects a complex mix of linkages between the state and the economy within a context of history. After all, South Korea transitioned from a former Japanese colony to a postwar "developmental state" to become one of two Asian members (the other is Japan) of the club of advanced, industrialized countries, the Organisation for Economic Co-operation and Development (OECD), yet verged on collapse when the Asian Financial Crisis hit at the end of the last century – all the while operating within a context of militarized division between North and South. These complexities, I submit, extend beyond the Korean experience: they echo the experiences of not just other Asian countries but the global South, more generally.

This chapter draws on postcolonial insights to examine the Korean Wave. It sheds light on Korea's historical specificities as well as their implications for other countries that had experienced similar histories of suffering in the context of global and regional colonial/social power relations. Soft power presupposes sharply drawn national boundaries by viewing culture as a property or resource exclusively held by a state to influence others. Here, however, I posit that movements of culture constantly reshape geopolitical borders. In particular, I draw on L.H.M. Ling's

(2002) analysis of the Asian Financial Crisis and Homi Bhabha's (2004) identification of a postcolonial "third space." Both account for the South Korean state's "cultural turn" after the crisis. The state stayed away from the economy, as demanded by neoliberal restructuring from the International Monetary Fund (IMF). But the government turned, instead, to an alternative venue not anticipated by neoliberals: that is, culture. Not only did it provide another means of economic recovery focused on the culture industry but also helped Korea as a nation and a state recuperate its sense of lost national manhood – especially at the hands of an iconic Western institution like the IMF.

I begin with a brief overview of the Korean Wave and the neoliberal backdrop to its development in South Korea in the 1990s. Next, I draw on Ling's (2002) analysis of the Asian Financial Crisis (1997–1998) to understand its racial, gender, and cultural dynamics, and how these contributed to the Korean Wave. Then, I turn to Bhabha's notion of a third space to reflect on the evolution and effects of Korean popular culture. Finally, I analyze how Korea's historical experience of suffering appeals to other countries with similar paths. This chapter concludes with some thoughts on the theoretical implications of the Korean Wave for IR.

The Korean Wave

Chinese media first coined the term "Korean Wave" (*hanliu* in Chinese, *hallyu* in Korean) in the late 1990s. It describes a surge in popularity of Korean cultural products in Asia primarily through TV dramas and pop music at the time (Hogarth 2013). A Korean TV drama series, *Winter Sonata*, started the craze. Aired in Korea in 2002, NHK BS broadcast the drama series a year later in Japan and it became the country's first Korean mega-hit. *Winter Sonata* also won widespread fandom in other Asian countries such as Taiwan, Vietnam, and Uzbekistan (Mori 2008; Ryoo 2009).[1] Another mega-hit followed in 2003. *Dae Jang Geum* (*Jewel in the Palace*) also became a global success. Aired in China in 2005, *Jewel*'s fever affected even high officials. When China's former General-Secretary of the Communist Party, Hu Jintao, met with the visiting head of South Korea's Yeollin Uri Party, Hu told his guest, "It's a pity that I cannot watch *Jewel in the Palace* every day because I am so busy" (Cai 2008: 101).

Korean pop music (K-pop) lags not far behind. Its popularity resonates all the way to Latin America. Brazilian media began to pay attention to K-pop when more than 5,000 fans gathered in São Paulo to see a South Korean boy band, MBLAQ, in 2011. Fans came from Asia, Europe, and Latin America to attend a concert held by the South Korean agency, YG Entertainment, in Seoul in August 2014. YG's artists included Gangnam Style star, Psy, and the boy band, Big Bang (Ng 2014). Notably, Psy's *Gangnam Style* became the first YouTube video to reach 1 billion viewers in December 2012, surpassing *Baby* by Justin Bieber (Gruger 2012); to date, it has reached over 2 billion viewers. This prompted YouTube to upgrade the maximum view limit to more than 9 quintillion in December 2014 (BBC News 2014).[2] *Gangnam Style* brought K-pop into global attention as never before, making South Korea "unquestionably an important player in the global pop culture industry" (Armstrong 2014: 34). Evidently, the song rewrote the history of YouTube and global pop music.

YouTube contributed greatly to this phenomenon. But South Korean entertainment companies, including SM Entertainment, JYP and YG Entertainment, also helped by implementing a systematized production system to make stars so that they are ready to go global. Young trainees go through several years of training, including singing, dancing, and acting, before their debut on the global stage (Ono and Kwon 2013). The sections that follow offer a broader picture of understanding the surge of Korean popular culture in the context of neoliberal globalization and beyond.

The Korean state and neoliberal globalization

An in-depth analysis of the Korean Wave reveals a complex set of relations between the state and the economy, especially given South Korea's position in the tide of neoliberal globalization. Under its authoritarian government, South Korea tightly regulated cultural products, including imports and exports. Directed against North Korea, popular culture until the 1980s aimed at sending out anti-communist messages. When the Kim Young-sam administration took office in 1993 as the first civilian government, a culture-promoting policy replaced the previous policy of cultural regulation (Lee 2013). The following year, the government established the Cultural Industry Bureau within the Ministry of Culture and Sports to promote Korea's culture industry on the global stage. A report from the Presidential Advisory Board on Science and Technology noted that profits made by the Hollywood blockbuster, *Jurassic Park*, equaled the value of 1.5 million sales of Hyundai cars on the international market (Shim 2006: 32).

A regional market seemed open, also. Driven by the growth of a new urban middle class, Asian economies wanted easier access to cultural products from other countries (Kim 2013a). In the 1970s, for instance, media imports in China accounted for less than 1 percent of those programs aired by China's Central Television Station (CCTV); by the late 1990s, this number had jumped to 20–30 percent (Shim 2008).[3] From this basis, South Korea's culture industry was able to reach out to more audiences than ever in Asia – until the Asian Financial Crisis hit in the late 1990s.

Crisis, power, and national humiliation

At the beginning of 1997, a record number of *chaebols* declared bankruptcy (Lee 2011; Jwa and Yi 2001). By October, the economic downturn had drastically deteriorated. Conditions for short-term borrowing from overseas lenders turned unfavorably for Korean commercial banks. For the biggest seven banks, the rollover rate was severely brought down to 59 percent from 87 percent in one month. In November, influenced by a contagion effect, foreign investors withdrew $580 million from the South Korean bond market, and long-term borrowing from overseas lenders had grown by $560 million but repayment on short-term overseas loans amounted to $5 billion (Lee 2011). Cornered, the Korean government requested financial support from the IMF on November 21, 1997 and received emergency funding in December.

The crisis induced the worst economic downturn in South Korea's modern history. From the 1970s to the 1990s, South Korea had proudly identified as one of the Four Tigers.[4] The country received praise internationally as a model of economic growth for other developing countries. Scholars and policymakers alike credited the *chaebols* as the main engine of growth. Now, the financial crisis was reducing South Korea into a cautionary tale of *unhealthy* capitalism.

The IMF concluded that *chaebol* recklessness caused the country's economic ruin. The international organization thus targeted the *chaebols* for structural adjustment programs, seeking to dismantle them not only from each other but also, more significantly, from the state. The Asian Financial Crisis supposedly centered on the "objective," "material" nature of global capitalist competition but it conveyed, also, an important *symbolic* message – especially to those suffering from the crisis.

"National humiliation" flooded Korea with the IMF bailout (Shim 2006). South Korea's economic collapse raised serious questions about whether a *chaebol*-dominated economic model could still be viable. The *chaebols* were bitterly shaken – so was the nation's dependence on them.

"I lead, you follow"

Here, Ling's (2002) analysis helps to explain the crisis from inside and below. An implicit logic of "I lead, you follow," she writes, has always underwritten global capitalist development. It casts Western capitalism as a source of dynamic, industry-building "creative destruction"; whereas Asian capitalism, in contrast, is riddled with "crony capitalists" who collude with effeminate, bribe-seeking officials, producing "poor governance." Accordingly, the Asian Other "needs cure/therapy from the healthy, masculine, doctor/scientist West" (Ling 2002: 127). Such unbridled self-congratulation, Ling further argues, stems from Western wariness of *real* competition from the Asian Other. After all, Asian capitalism – of which South Korea's was emblematic – had graduated from a "formal" mimicry of copying Western capitalism in form to a "substantive" mimicry of internalizing Western capitalism in *substance*. Put differently, the Asian Other had shifted from "hyperfeminized subordination to hypermasculinized competition" (Ling 2002: 118). The Asian Financial Crisis, however, offered an opportunity to restore the previous order.

Given these terms of hypermasculine economic competition, the South Korean state *had* to reclaim its national manhood. And culture was the answer.

Popular culture, government policy, and the retrieval of national manhood

Following the crisis, the South Korean government focused on exporting popular culture to recuperate the country's economic health (Kim 2013a). President Kim

Dae-jung, who took office in February 1998, was the first president elected from the opposition party. It marked South Korea's first regime change in modern political history. Taking advantage of this historic moment, President Kim announced a budget of $148.5 million to sponsor the culture industry (Shim 2006). The government subsequently made available a variety of subsidies, grants, tax breaks, and screen quotas to promote Korean culture for overseas markets (Nam 2013).

The succeeding Roh Moo-hyun administration continued this policy. At his inauguration in 2003, President Roh proclaimed three goals for foreign policy: (1) build up a community between South and North Korea, (2) pursue comprehensive security in Northeast Asia, and (3) strengthen soft power. These policy goals came to be known as the "Era of Peace and Prosperity in Northeast Asia Initiative" (Munhwa Ilbo 2003). To achieve these goals, values including cultural affinity with other Asian countries, moral legitimacy in the region, democratization, the growth of civil society, cultural power through *hallyu*, and enthusiasm toward education were identified as ingredients of South Korea's soft power (DongBukA Shidae Uiwonhoe 2005). The Korean Wave satisfies all of these goals. Since 2005, *hallyu* has received systematic support from the government, involving various ministries and agencies (Kim 2006). The Hallyu Support Group was established in 2005 as an inter-governmental body tasked with boosting cultural policy across relevant agencies including the Ministry of Culture and Tourism. In addition, the Hallyu Policy Advisory Committee was founded as a non-governmental body to channel grassroots voices to governmental agencies (Samsung Economic Research Institute 2005b).

The nation's sense of humiliation and the government's desire to retrieve its national manhood gave rise to a systematic cultural policy. Instead of bowing to the will of the liberal capitalist order by staying out of the economy, as demanded by the IMF, the South Korean state stayed viable by guiding its culture industry. In effect, the Korean Wave opened up an interstices or "third space" of negotiated culture.

A third space

In *The Location of Culture* (2004), Bhabha develops the notion of a third space. It highlights culture as a haven of interstices whereby "the overlap and displacement of domains of difference" (Bhabha 2004: 2) can transform into creative hybridities. Culture, in short, does not stand still. Bhabha notes that "the 'inter' – the cutting edge of translation and negotiation, the inbetween space … carries the burden of the *meaning* of culture" (Bhabha 2004: 56, my emphasis).

The Korean Wave offers such a third space. It provides a location where Asian and Western values as well as practices can interact. Korean popular culture appeals to Asian audiences, specifically, but also non-Western societies, generally, by offering "traditional" values like the concept of fate or pre-destination, and Confucian tenets like filial piety and other family relations (Hogarth 2013). Korean dramas also do not portray romantic relationships in a graphic, sexual way (Kim 2013b).

Middle-aged, Japanese women loved *Winter Sonata* because the drama series brought back the good old days when society valued "pure love" (Shim 2008). Another recent mega-hit is *Byul-eso on Kudae* (*My Love from the Star*, 2013–2014). It tells of an alien who lands in Korea during the *Chosun* period (1392–1910). Over the next 400 years, he lives as a human being but doesn't age. In contemporary Korea, he falls in love with a famous actress. The drama revolves around the theme of eternal love transcending time and space. These Asian components have won acceptance and popularity in other, non-Western countries in contrast to Hollywood/US dramas usually centered on Western values, such as individualism, commercialism, and sensationalism (Hogarth 2013). More pointedly, these dramas show what it means to be a *real* man.

Dissolving borders

Bhabha's "third space" entails productive instability and capacities. No relationship, accordingly, could remain unaffected. The Korean Wave, for instance, has blurred boundaries. More than selling, marketing, and consuming cultural products, *hallyu* has created complex spaces that defy the simple boundaries of neoliberal globalization *and* the developmental state. Of note is that *hallyu*'s global popularity depends on an intimate interaction between Asian values and Western technology.

The Internet, for instance, expedited the instant popularity of *My Love from the Star*. Audiences throughout the globe could access the drama series immediately after its broadcast on Korean television. Relatedly, many acknowledge that the core of *hallyu*'s success lies in the competitiveness and diversity of its cultural products. *Hallyu* not only markets dramas, films, music and online games but also cuisine, cosmetics, and Korean lifestyles. Furthermore, Korean films emulate the production process of the US film industry, forming close ties with global banking and financial industries. Learning from Hollywood, Korean films rely on investments from the financial sector and marketing strategies including quick and sensational selling (Nam 2013). Collaboration and partnerships between the media and other culture industries follow, often involving producers, directors, and actors across national borders (Iwabuchi 2013). K-pop skillfully emulated the rhythms and styles of popular US music trending globally. This emulation was key in appealing to a wider audience beyond Asia (Nam 2013; Hogarth 2013).

The Korean Wave has boosted tourism for Korea. Visitors from China and Japan, for instance, increased by almost 47 percent in the first half of 2004 (Samsung Economic Research Institute 2005a). The Korea Tourism Organization registers 12.2 million tourists from abroad generally in 2013, showing an increase of 9 percent from the previous year (Tang 2014). The South Korean government is keen to exploit this surge in tourism due to the Korean Wave. On February 13, 2014, the City of Seoul designated and announced 120 places and 7 theme courses connected to *hallyu* as travel attractions (The Korea Foundation for International

Culture Exchange 2014). The Korea Tourism Organization also offers plot synopses and information on the main characters of diverse Korean dramas.

For instance, *My Love from the Star* sparked a rage for *chimaek* or "chicken and beer." Korean fried chicken restaurants saw an increase in their takeout orders in many parts of Asia. Some fans decided to visit South Korea to experience the actual taste of *chimaek* in a Korean fried chicken restaurant. Intensified by the drama series, the fever for *hallyu* made South Korea the third most popular destination for mainland Chinese tourists after Hong Kong and Macau in 2014 (Lee 2014), with an increase of 66 percent of Chinese visitors to South Korea in the first five months of 2014 (Yonhap News Agency 2014).

Conflict transformation

Another unexpected byproduct of the Korean Wave is the ability to *transform* conflicts. For instance, tensions between Korea and Japan have had a long historical legacy. Given its former colonial history, Korea and Japan had developed mutually negative images. For over a millennium, Koreans had held the view that Japan was "small and insignificant" (Armstrong 2014: 5). Added to this were more recent, bitter memories of Japanese occupation. As Asia's first country to modernize at the end of nineteenth century, Japan, in turn, viewed Korea as inferior and backward. But *Winter Sonata* changed the image of South Koreans among Japanese in a dramatically positive way, enhancing a general interest in Korean culture, language, and tourism. Many think that the drama series contributed more to the relationship between South Korea and Japan than the FIFA World Cup, which the two countries co-hosted in 2002 (Mori 2008; Ryoo 2009). Japan and South Korea eventually came to share the event after fiercely competing to host it. Before then, the World Cup had never been held in Asia, and it had never been hosted jointly. The event offered an opportunity for the region's traditional enemies to cooperate at a bilateral level (Longman 1996).

The enormous success of *Winter Sonata* in Japan was largely due to the fact that it evoked a sense of nostalgia for the past. The self-sacrificing love of Bae Yong-joon, the male lead, captured the hearts of the audience, boosting tourism and learning of the Korean language (Hogarth 2013). This nostalgia and an awareness of common ground eventually eroded the idea that Japan is superior to other Asian countries (Iwabuchi 2013). This is why many consider that Korean popular culture did more to smooth the relationship between two, long-standing rivals than the world's largest single sporting event. In effect, *Winter Sonata* led to a deeper understanding and cultural affinity between Korea and Japan.

The relationship between South Korea and Vietnam has entered a new phase as well. The Vietnamese still remember South Korean military forces in the Vietnam War, fighting against their Liberation Army (Shim 2006). However, since the two countries signed an Agreement on Cultural Cooperation in 1994, culture has drawn them closer in various ways. Vietnamese society now wants more Korean cultural products. In 1992, bilateral trade between Vietnam and South Korea amounted to $490 million; by 2006, it had climbed to $4.85 billion (West 2008). *Hallyu* has positively transformed the image of South Korea and Koreans among the Vietnamese (Lee 2005).

Similarly, the people in Taiwan felt betrayed when South Korea shifted its diplomatic recognition from Taipei to Beijing in 1992. But the Korean Wave has changed the atmosphere. Korean hot-pot shops and BBQ restaurants have replaced Japanese noodle restaurants as a favorite eating spot. The taste of Korean kimchi was even added to Kentucky Fried Chicken's hamburgers and Pizza Hut's pizzas in Taiwan. Foreign cosmetic brands, such as Olay (US) and DHC (Japan) now hire South Korean actresses to advertise their products (Huang 2011).

These developments exemplify the porousness between so-called "enemy" and "friend," underscoring that relationships between countries are not always static. Nor are they determined exclusively by military dominance, alliance, or material interests at the state level, as mainstream IR approaches would predict. Rather, *people's everyday lives* can transform geopolitical enmity into cultural affinity.

Cultural fever from a non-great power

Conventional IR does not recognize Korea as a major regional or global player. Traditionally, Chinese influence and its Confucian civilization pervaded the region. Korea adopted Confucianism as an ideology and based its centrally administered, bureaucratic state on that of China's. The *Koryŏ* dynasty (918–1392), for instance, followed the Tang dynasty's model of culture, ritual, religion, and music (Kang 2010). And from 1910 to 1945, imperial Japan occupied and colonized Korea. Historically, then, Korea's geopolitical location has placed it at a crossroad between vested, powerful interests, ranging from China and Russia to the North, Japan to the East, and the US across the Pacific in the West.

The Korean Wave, however, rebuts this geopolitical logic. Indeed, Korea's historical colonial victimhood has served as an essential source of *global* acceptance and appeal. People all over the world identify with the Korean sense of *han* – that is, a deep-seated sense of grief and suffering (Nye and Kim 2013). It articulates Korea's suffering after its partition from the Second World War followed by a devastating civil war (1950–1953). Poverty was so rampant that it was embedded in the sentiment of *han*, even after general prosperity came with rapid industrialization in the 1960s. Among the hit songs of a Korean boy band, G.O.D., is a song called "To My Mother." In it, the narrator reminisces about when he was young and his family did not have enough money to eat out. He had to cook instant noodles, *Ramyon*, for himself while his mother went to work. Sick and tired of eating *Ramyon*, he begged his mom to go out to a restaurant. She gathered up all the money she had and ordered *Jajangmyon* for her son in a Korean-style Chinese restaurant, and did not eat any herself. When her son asked his mom why she was not eating, she replied by saying that she did not like it so that her son could eat as much as he wanted. He was so happy with *Jajangmyon* then. Later, he looks back on this moment and tells his mom how much he regrets not telling her how much he loved her before.

Shim (2006) considers this song an example of cultural appropriation: that is, how a rap song about a sacrificing mother contrasts with rebellious lyrics usually adopted by boy bands. But I look at how *han* appeals to Koreans (and other non-Western peoples) due to the legacy of war, poverty, and the nation-as-family.

The sacrificing mother embodied a shared experience: how special it was for most Korean families to eat out. Those in poverty who could not afford rice had to survive with *Ramyon*. The Korean-style Chinese restaurant was the most popular type of restaurant available to ordinary Koreans. They often asked for *Jajangmyon*, a Korean-style Chinese noodle dish. The song illustrates how tough life was and how most people struggled to survive on a daily basis. Going out for *Jajangmyon* was a rare opportunity.

Many societies in the global South must still grapple with poverty. Equally important, many in the global South have suffered Western and/or Japanese occupation and colonialism. These historical experiences and awareness have generated sentiments of bitterness, similar to Korean *han*. Evoking the shared historical anguish of poverty and oppression, the song appeals to Koreans as well as larger audiences throughout the globe by connecting to the sensibility of sadness.

Conclusion

The Korean Wave reveals complex interactions among diverse forces, especially those of the state, the economy, culture, and history. This complex picture refutes any single perspective for understanding the global surge of popularity for Korean culture. Although the concept of soft power is useful, it fails to attend to the historical and postcolonial context of the Korean Wave and why it appeals to so many outside the usual, geopolitical boundaries. Korean popular culture allows people in different national and regional locations to realize mutual understanding based on border-crossing, third spaces. This suggests that culture is not exclusively possessed by one nation as a property or structured only by geopolitical interests. Rather, culture has the capacity to cross borders, reaching out to people across politically demarcated boundaries of race, gender, and ethnicity. Such interactive hybridization invariably stretches, reshapes, and perhaps transforms our unconsciously tamed, boxed-in imaginations.

The South Korean government turned to culture to repair its national manhood threatened by the Asian Financial Crisis. The Korean Wave did so by creating a multitude of third spaces, including hybridizing Confucian content with Western technology. But in the process, the Korean Wave also *redefined* the original categories and terms of global capitalist competition. Enemy vs Friend no longer seemed to matter or serve a productive purpose. This applied especially to collaborations between Asian content and Western technology. Among Asian countries still marred by the experiences of the Second World War, the Korean Wave also enabled another kind of transformation. It found common cause among all those who had suffered colonial oppression and postwar poverty. This shared awareness motivates a universal sense of cultural acceptance and enjoyment.

This story of the Korea Wave bears many implications for IR theory. Many find in IR a deep and abiding Eurocentrism. It fosters a "tendency to deny the very legitimacy and worth of non-Western values, traditions, practices, struggles, discourses, and thought" (Jones 2006: 12). Colonized cultures thus feature in IR as "victims of a static past of unchanging custom and tradition, virtually immune to history" or "in a process of 'decline'" (Narayan 1997: 16). This analysis of the Korean Wave, however, challenges the pessimism of this critique.

First, the fact that the Korean Wave appealed widely in Asia, specifically, but also the global South, generally, discloses how historical awareness and non-Western values are extensively shared across the globe. This sensibility reinforces a regional connectedness within Asia, forming a sense of an extended self. Second, the Korean Wave challenges the idea of Western imperialism as ubiquitous and incapable of change or transformation, leaving Western culture as the only dominant force in the world. Empirical evidence, as provided by the Korean Wave, indicates otherwise. As Bhabha notes, the intervention of a third space "quite properly challenges our sense of the historical identity of culture as homogenizing, unifying force, authenticated by the originary Past" (Bhabha 2004: 54). Third, the Korean Wave shatters a mainstream assumption, started by Hegel and reinforced more recently by Francis Fukuyama (1992) that Asia remains "outside" of history or is merely catching up with it. The Korean Wave shows, instead, the possibility of *rewriting* history (with a small "h") from a non-imperial perspective. Power relations require far more sophistication and subtlety than a presumed dichotomy between the Great Powers vs Weak Powers, Hypermasculine Competition vs Hyperfeminine Subordination, and lastly, West and Rest.

Notes

The author would like to thank L.H.M. Ling for her helpful comments on earlier versions of this paper and her editing of it.

1 In 2005, *Winter Sonata* aired for the first time in the Middle East (Nye and Kim 2013). The drama received an explosive response. In Egypt, more than 300 viewers organized a fan club and launched a "Winter Sonata" website. In response to Egyptian fans' request, KBS (Korean Broadcasting System) introduced an Arabic version on the drama's website. Since then, Korean dramas, including *Dae Jang Geum (Jewel in the Palace)* and *Kaul Donghwa (Autumn Fairy Tale)*, have attracted local audiences. It has been noted that the popularity of Korean dramas among locals in Arab countries can be attributed to shared cultural elements, including "conflicts between in-laws portrayed in Korean dramas" and societal values that respect parents and elders (The Korea Tourism Organization 2005; Korea.Net 2010).
2 The view limit was raised to 9,223,372,036,854,775,808.
3 As of 2007, China has the world's largest TV market, with more than 378 million TV households (Nam 2013).
4 In addition to South Korea, the Four Tigers included Taiwan, Singapore, and Hong Kong.

References

Armstrong, Charles K. (2014) *The Koreas*. New York and Abingdon: Routledge.
BBC News. (2014) "Gangnam Style Music Video 'Broke' YouTube View Limit." December 4 (http://www.bbc.com/news/world-asia-30288542) (Downloaded: June 28, 2015).
Bhabha, Homi K. (2004) *The Location of Culture*. London and New York: Routledge.

Cai, Jian. (2008) "China's First Taste of the Korean Wave." In *The Korea Herald* (ed.), *Korean Wave*, 100–101. Gyeonggi: Jimoondang.
DongBukA Shidae Uiwonhoe (The South Korean Presidential Committee on Northeast Asian Cooperation Initiative). (2005) *Sae Jilseo-wa Hankook-ui Yeokkhal* (A New Order in Northeast Asia and the Role of Korea). Seoul: DongBukA Shidae Uiwonhoe (The South Korean Presidential Committee on Northeast Asian Cooperation Initiative), August 30.
Fukuyama, Francis. (1992) *The End of History and the Last Man*. New York: The Free Press.
Gruger, William. (2012) "Psy's 'Gangnam Style' Hits 1 Billion Views on YouTube." *Billboard*. December 21 (http://www.billboard.com/articles/columns/k-town/1481275/psys-gangnam-style-hits-1-billion-views-on-youtube) (Downloaded: June 28, 2015).
Hogarth, Hyun-key Kim. (2013) "The Korean Wave: An Asian Reaction to Western-Dominated Globalization." *Perspectives on Global Development and Technology* 12(1/2): 135–151.
Huang, Shuling. (2011) "Nation-Branding and Transnational Consumption: Japan-Mania and the Korean Wave in Taiwan." *Media, Culture & Society* 33(1): 3–18.
Iwabuchi, Koichi. (2013) "Korean Wave and Inter-Asian Referencing." In Youna Kim (ed.), *The Korean Wave: Korean Media Go Global*, 43–57. London and New York: Routledge.
Jones, Branwen Gruffyd (ed.) (2006) *Decolonizing International Relations*. London: Rowman & Littlefield.
Jwa, Sung Hee and Insill Yi. (2001) "The Korean Financial Crisis: Evaluation and Lessons." In O. Yul Kwon and William Shepherd (eds), *Korea's Economic Prospects: From Financial Crisis to Prosperity*, 73–98. Cheltenham and Northampton: Edward Elgar.
Kang, David C. (2010) *East Asia before the West: Five Centuries of Trade and Tribute*. New York: Columbia University Press.
Kim, Dong-Taek. (2006) "Hallyu-wa Hankookhak (Hallyu and the Korean Study)." *Yuksa Bipyong* (The Critics of History). Spring: 213–240.
Kim, Youna. (2013a) "Introduction: Korean Media in a Digital Cosmopolitan World." In Youna Kim (ed.), *The Korean Wave: Korean Media Go Global*, 1–27. London and New York: Routledge.
Kim, Youna. (2013b) "Korean Wave Pop Culture in the Global Internet Age: Why Popular, Why Now?" In Youna Kim (ed.), *The Korean Wave: Korean Media Go Global*, 75–92. London and New York: Routledge.
Korea.Net. (2010) "Korean Wave Spreads in Middle East through TV and Tourism." June 3 (http://www.korea.net/NewsFocus/Society/view?articleId=81446) (Downloaded: June 26, 2015).
Lee, An-Jae. (2005) "Hallyu Yeolpoong-ui Haebu (Analyzing the Craze for Hallyu)." *Pyonghwa Forum* (Peace Forum) 21: 44–69.
Lee, Hye-Kyung. (2013) "Cultural Policy and the Korean Wave." In Youna Kim (ed.), *The Korean Wave: Korean Media Go Global*, 185–198. London and New York: Routledge.
Lee, Kyu-Sung. (2011). *The Korean Financial Crisis of 1997: Onset, Turnaround, and Thereafter*. Washington D.C.: The World Bank and the Korean Development Institute.
Lee, Woo-young. (2014) "Korea becomes Third Most Popular Destination for Chinese Tourists." *The Korea Herald*. December 29 (http://www.koreaherald.com/view.php?ud=20141229000911) (Downloaded: January 7, 2015).
Ling, L.H.M. 2002. "Cultural Chauvinism and the Liberal International Order: 'West versus Rest' in Asia's Financial Crisis." In Geeta Chowdhry and Sheila Nair (eds), *Power, Postcolonialism, and International Relations: Reading Race, Gender, Class*, 115–141. London: Routledge.
Longman, Jere. (1996) "Soccer; South Korea and Japan Will Share World Cup." *The New York Times*. June 1 (http://www.nytimes.com/1996/06/01/sports/soccer-south-korea-and-japan-will-share-world-cup.html) (Downloaded: July 2, 2015).

Mori, Yoshitaka. (2008) "Winter Sonata and Cultural Practices of Active Fans in Japan." In Chua Beng Huat and Koichi Iwabuchi (eds), *East Asian Pop Culture: Analyzing the Korean Wave*, 127–141. Hong Kong: The Hong Kong University Press.

Munhwa Ilbo. (2003) "Roh Daetongryong Uegyo Chonryak Mueonga" (President Roh's Foreign Policy). February 26 (http://www.munhwa.com/news/view.html?no=20030226010303230050040) (Downloaded: July 4, 2015).

Nam, Siho. (2013) "The Cultural Political Economy of the Korean Wave in East Asia: Implications for Cultural Globalization Theories." *Asian Perspective* 37(2): 209–231.

Narayan, Uma. (1997) *Dislocating Cultures*. New York: Routledge.

Ng, Gwendolyn. (2014) "Fans of K-pop Stars Are Willing to Spend Big Bucks to See Their Idols." *The Strait Times*. September 4 (http://www.straitstimes.com/lifestyle/music/story/fans-k-pop-stars-are-willing-spend-big-bucks-see-their-idols-20140904) (Downloaded: September 5, 2014).

Nye, Joseph Jr. (2004) *Soft Power: The Means to Success in World Politics*. New York: Public Affairs.

Nye, Joseph, Jr. and Youna Kim. (2013) "Soft Power and the Korean Wave." In Youna Kim (ed.), *The Korean Wave: Korean Media Go Global*, 31–42. London and New York: Routledge.

Ono, Kent A. and Jungmin Kwon. (2013) "Re-worlding Culture? YouTube as a K-pop Interlocutor." In Youna Kim (ed.), *The Korean Wave: Korean Media Go Global*, 199–214. London and New York: Routledge.

Ryoo, Woongjae. (2009) "Globalization, or the Logic of Cultural Hybridization: The Case of the Korean Wave." *Asian Journal of Communication* 19(2): 137–151.

Samsung Economic Research Institute. (2005a) "Soft Kanguk Uro Kanun Kil (*The Path toward Soft Power*)." *Issue Paper* March 23: i–xiii.

Samsung Economic Research Institute. (2005b) "Hallyu Chisokwha-rul Uihan Pangan (The Strategies for Sustaining *Hallyu*)." *Issue Paper* November 7: 20–31.

Shim, Doobo. (2006) "Hybridity and the Rise of Korean Popular Culture in Asia." *Media, Culture & Society* 28(1): 25–44.

Shim, Doobo. (2008) "The Growth of Korean Cultural Industries and the Korean Wave." In Chua Beng Huat and Koichi Iwabuchi (eds), *East Asian Pop Culture: Analyzing the Korean Wave*, 15–31. Hong Kong: The Hong Kong University Press.

Tang, See Kit. (2014) "Food and Fashion: How K-Drama Is Influencing Asia." *CNBC*. June 18. (http://www.cnbc.com/id/101767713) (Downloaded: June 23, 2014).

The Korea Foundation for International Culture Exchange. (2014) *Global Hallyu Issue* (54) February 27: 4–6.

The Korea Tourism Organization. (2005) "Korea Wave Hits Middle East." December 11 (http://english.visitkorea.or.kr/enu/FU/FU_EN_15.jsp?cid=289367) (Downloaded: June 26, 2015).

Wang, Hongying and Yeh-Chung Lu. (2006) "Soft Power in East Asia." Paper presented at the Annual Meeting of the Association of Chinese Political Studies.

West, Aviva. (2008) "The Korean Wave 'Will Never Die' in Vietnam." In The Korea Herald (ed.), *Korean Wave*, 50–51. Gyeonggi: Jimoondang.

Yonhap News Agency. (2014) "S. Korea Sees Surge in Visas for Chinese Tourists." June 9 (http://english.yonhapnews.co.kr/news/2014/06/09/0200000000AEN20140609007700315.html) (Downloaded: June 24, 2014).

15

ROMANCING WESTPHALIA

Westphalian IR and *Romance of the Three Kingdoms*

L.H.M. Ling[1]

State violence in Asia invariably resurrects the West's old saw about "Oriental despotism."[2] Basically, it accuses "Oriental" peoples of not knowing how to govern themselves. They resort to acts of violence and suppression whenever dissent arises, Eurocentrics claim, in contrast to the enlightened, democratic processes of the West. It's the same old story of the future vs the past, modernity vs tradition, liberal-democracy vs authoritarianism. To Fukuyama (1992), this realization signals "the end of history": *they* ("the Orient") must learn to be more like *us* ("the West"). Accordingly, more education, more supervision and, if necessary, more sanctions must follow. The West still rules.

Besides its inherent imperialism, this Eurocentric critique sees only half the picture. It fails to acknowledge a context to the problem: that is, the *international* sources of state violence. Gourevitch (1978) first raised this awareness in the late 1970s but from an elite-structural, not a subaltern-postcolonial, perspective. Palumbo-Liu (1994) describes this analytical lack as "white absence." It accounts for why the mainstream media in 1992, for example, focused only on the conflict between Koreans and blacks in the riots following the first Rodney King trial.[3] That is, "white absence" excuses from scrutiny the white power structure in which both minority groups must fight for survival *and* justice. As C. Chen points out in this volume, we must understand context to understand why a conflict persists and what we can do about it. Indeed, Westphalia's forced entry into world politics has left huge swathes of the globe dealing with "cartographic anxieties" that rationalize state violence both externally and internally, as Ahmed notes in his chapter on Assam. Emasculated by Westphalia as the degenerate, "sick" Oriental Other,[4] state elites felt compelled to proclaim to the Westphalian Self: "*We* are man enough to be just like *you*! We, too, can censor, jail, barricade and shoot."[5] (Eurocentrics fail to appreciate the comprehensiveness of postcolonial mimicry.) Indeed, state elites and Eurocentrics alike benefited from internalized imperialism. They could seem to be actively taking charge and solving problems without doing anything to transform the situation. Meanwhile, ordinary citizens have suffered and continue to do so. Yet Westphalia's impact on world politics remains hidden, overlooked, and untreated.[6]

Generations of leaders/thinkers in Asia have tried alternatives. National strategies have ranged from rejection (Qing China) to assimilation (imperial Japan) to hybridity (Nehru's India). Ultimately, each succumbed to larger, contextual forces.[7] Strategies directed internationally have fared no better. The 1955 Bandung Conference sought to neutralize Cold War rivalries between the US and the Soviet Union with Afro-Asian-Caribbean solidarity. In the 1970s, third-world states proposed a New International Economic Order (NIEO), reinforced by oil price hikes from the Organisation of Petroleum Exporting Countries (OPEC), to create a more equitable world economy for all. Each effort dissipated despite its early promise. Seven years after Bandung, India and China warred over borders drawn by former colonizers (Ling et al. 2016). Today, the World Social Forum (WSF) champions global change for the Global South. Founded in 2001 and committed to the proposition that "another world is possible," the WSF seeks to counter the neoliberal, globalizing interests of the World Economic Forum (WEF). The latter represents the globe's corporate, cultural, and political elites, gathering annually in the posh Swiss resort of Davos, whereas the WSF convenes at various locations in the Global South and welcomes the subaltern, the exploited and the oppressed (Hasso 2013). But is this *enough* (Ling and Pinheiro forthcoming)?

We need to re-envision international relations (IR) (Chen 2011). As history attests, neither domestic nor international reform *alone* can shift Westphalia's hegemony. Instead, we need to align the "outside" with the "inside" by anchoring both in a "regional world." In his call for papers for the 2015 meeting of the International Studies Association (ISA), Acharya (2014) defines a regional world as a "broader, inclusive, open, and interactive dynamic of regions and regionalisms. It is not just about how regions self-organize their economic, political and cultural space, but also about how they relate to each other and shape global order." Put differently, a regional world represents a way of life and living through time-honored traditions shared by neighbors. This would globalize IR for an already globalized world-of-worlds (Ling 2014). Not only would we finally see and hear from the "multiple worlds" (Ling 2002; Agathangelou and Ling 2009; Ling 2014) that make world politics but doing so would also "provincialize" (Chakrabarty 2000) Westphalian IR as, simply, another regional world. From this basis, we may curb, if not transform, Westphalia's "cartographic anxieties."

Let's try a thought experiment. I draw a regional world for East Asia based on the fourteenth-century Chinese epic, *Sanguo yanyi* (*Romance of the Three Kingdoms*; hereafter, *Romance*).[8] The epic remains popular today throughout the region, ranging from the vast Chinese mainland to Korea–Japan in the northeast and Hong Kong–Taiwan–Singapore–Vietnam in the southeast. The epic tells of the competition between three states – Shu, Wu, and Wei – for supremacy "under heaven" (*tianxia*). The epic covers the chaos that followed the Han Dynasty's decline (AD*c*.169) to the re-establishment of world-order under the Jin Dynasty (AD*c*.280). Besides books (Lam 2011), films (*Chi bi* [*Red Cliff*], 2008), and TV dramas (*Sanguo Yanyi* 1994, *Sanguo* 2010), the novel stays current through new social media such as *manga*,[9] *anime*,[10] computer games[11] and Internet discussions.[12] As B. Chen notes in his chapter, the President of Taiwan cast future relations with China in terms of the novel's opening line: "Long divided, the world will unite; long united, it will fall apart" (*tianxia da shi, fen jiou bi he, he jiou bi fen*). These words, along with the epic's other phrases, episodes and characters, echo throughout the region.[13]

To contrast *Romance* with Westphalia, I begin with Wendt's (1999) "three cultures of anarchy": Hobbesian enmity, Lockean rivalry, and Kantian friendship. I juxtapose these with comparable identities in *Romance*: Cao Cao[14] enmity, Zhuge[15] rivalry, and Liu Bei[16] brotherhood. I include three other identities that also signify the epic: strategic genius, political trickster, and ubiquitous narrator. (More could be added but these are the main ones.) Here, I draw on the latest (2010) televised version of *Romance*, titled *Three Kingdoms* (*Sanguo*).[17] I do so rather than draw directly from the novel to underscore the epic's currency in the popular imagination today within China and throughout the region. (The series also mirrors the novel closely.)[18] I conclude with the implications of a *Romance*-inflected regional world for globalizing IR.

Enemy, rival, friend

To Wendt, only three ideal-type cultures apply in (Westphalian) world politics. Hobbesian enmity, also noted as Machiavellian, evokes realist IR with the familiar characterization of world politics as an unrelenting "warre of all against all." Lockean or Grotian rivalry accords with liberal IR with its recognition of the capacity of norms and institutions, such as sovereignty, to curb Hobbesian tendencies. And Kantian friendship prefigures the rise of constructivist IR with its belief in the possibility of (collective) norms subsuming (individual) self-interest; accordingly, states could resolve disputes without resort to violence knowing that cooperation benefits all. "External norms," Wendt (1999: 288) writes on Kantian friendship, "have become a voice in our heads telling us that we *want* to follow them" (original emphasis).

Wendt bases these cultures on individual, Western psychology. Hobbesian/Machiavellian enmity, for instance, asserts a self-interested, competitive and murderous individual in the State of Nature now coded for world politics: "Self mirrors Other, becomes *its* enemy, in order to survive ... This gives enemy-images a homeostatic quality that sustains the logic of Hobbesian anarchies" (Wendt 1999: 263, original emphasis). Lockean/Grotian rivalry reflects the possessive individual who seeks, primarily, to protect property: "[The] neoliberal or rationalist explanation holds [that] states comply with sovereignty norms because they think it will advance some exogenously given interest, like security or trade" (Wendt 1999:

287). And Kantian friendship internalizes "Lockean culture": "Most states comply with its norms because they accept them as legitimate ... identify with them and want to comply. States are status quo not just at the level of behavior, but of interests as well, and as such [are] now more fully self-regulating actors" (Wendt 1999: 289). Wendt implies a progression here: states advance from Hobbesian enmity to Lockean rivalry to (it is hoped) Kantian friendship.

Cao Cao enmity, Zhuge rivalry, Liu Bei brotherhood

Romance offers a distinctive contrast. Not only does the epic interpret enmity, rivalry, and friendship differently but it also extends the roster of cultures to genius, trickster, and narrator.

Let's see how:

1 **Cao Cao Enmity**. Cao Cao (AD 155–220) serves as the key antagonist in *Romance*. A low-level official from a family associated with eunuchs,[19] Cao rises to become chancellor of the Han Dynasty in its dying years. To deflect charges of unseemly ambition, Cao never proclaims himself emperor – despite acting like one and holding the actual Emperor hostage. *Romance* depicts Cao as ruthless, conniving, and self-serving. For instance, Cao kills his kindly godfather, who had given him safe haven, for fear the old man would inadvertently spill the secret. But the epic also notes Cao's utmost competence, savvy, and – contrary to the times – emotional honesty. "I'd rather owe the world," Cao famously declares, "than have the world owe me" (*ning yuan wo fu tianxiaren, bu yuan tianxiaren fu wo*). Cao embodies a kind of self-aggrandizing power: his approach to enemies reflects agency, not Hobbes' situational inevitability or Machiavelli's amoral calculations or Wendt's existential mirroring. Cao decides on friend or foe depending on person and circumstance. At times, Cao allies with his main rival, Liu Bei (AD 161–223), only to discard such alliance when it no longer suits an immediate purpose. Cao also honors talent. He imprisons, and then releases, Guan Yu (Liu's right-hand man) due precisely to the warrior's famed ability with a halberd and his unswerving dedication to his "elder brother" (*da ge*), Liu Bei. When Guan Yu dies, Cao mourns grievously.

2 **Zhuge Rivalry**. The novel itself testifies to rivalry in world politics. All the characters and plots revolve around this central premise. For this reason, social scientists in the West take the "three kingdoms" as a metaphor for a multi-polar world politics (Niou and Ordeshook 1987; Lam 2011). But the plots and schemes in *Romance* do not simply carry out rule-bound self-interest or possessiveness, as Wendt suggests for Lockean/Grotian rivalry. Rather, decisions to ally or fight often reflect contending psychologies such as greed, ambition, fear, lust, jealousy, vanity, and brotherly love – often in the same individual. Still other times, alliances reflect norms of honor, duty, and righteousness. One episode shows Zhuge Liang, master strategist for Liu Bei, on a mission to persuade Sun Quan,[20] Prince of Wu, to ally with Liu against Cao. A long hallway of Sun's

ministers, generals, and advisers supposedly greet the master strategist when he arrives at the palace. Instead, each poses a searing question to Zhuge, as he walks down the hallway, as to why the state of Wu should agree to an alliance. Zhuge defeats each questioner by exposing a defect in his logic. Zhuge's final and winning argument, however, hinges on righteousness: "Are we not honorable men?"[21] The longstanding appeal of Romance rests not only on calculations of self-interest – certainly, these matter – but the epic also underscores a larger sense of what it means to go to war, sacrifice one's life, persevere despite repeated failures, and make the most of triumph that is, ultimately, momentary. The novel asks: What is it all *for*?

3 **Liu Bei Brotherhood**. The epic celebrates, above all else, brotherly love. It finds iconic expression in the relationship between Liu Bei ("first brother"), Guan Yu ("second brother"), and Zhang Fei ("third brother"), ordered according to age. Each supports, comforts, and protects the other, always. Even when Cao captures Guan Yu, hoping to recruit him, the latter returns to Liu's side at his first opportunity despite countless hazards along the way. The three men's oath of loyalty is legendary: "We ask not to be born in the same year, same month, same day (*bu qiou tong nian, tong yue, tong ri sheng*) but hope to die in the same year, same month, and same day" (*dan yuan tong nian, tong yue, tong ri si*). Cao commands in lonely isolation, in contrast, perhaps accounting for his frequent migraines. Advisers and ministers abound but they perform primarily as lackeys. Cao does not inspire the kind of brotherly love that Liu enjoys. For example, Liu values the brilliance of Pang Tong, a subsidiary character, despite the latter's ugly face and body. Here, the epic makes a subtle point: all the plotting and scheming, warring and fighting may thrill but it pales next to the succor and devotion of one's brothers-in-arms. Even conjugal love cannot compare. "Wives are like clothes" (*qizi ru yishang*), Liu jokes, "whereas brothers are like the palm of one's hand" (*xiongdi ru shouzhang*). This norm of brotherly love and loyalty in *Romance* contrasts starkly with Wendt's (1999: 305) notion of Kantian friendship. It may induce "a single 'cognitive region' [such as] … 'we-feeling,''solidarity,''plural subject,''common in-group identity,''thinking like a team,''loyalty,' and so on," but the state-as-person remains "pre-social" (Wendt 1999: 198). Like Hobbes' individual in the State of Nature, Wendt's state-as-person sprouts mushroom-like after a rain. There is little sense of identity *through* social relations, as demonstrated by the oath of eternal brotherhood between Liu, Guan, and Zhang.

4 **Strategic Genius**. We return to Zhuge Liang for another distinctive feature: strategic genius. Always elegantly attired in silk robes and waving a fan made of crane feathers (even in battle), Zhuge is Liu's master strategist and, later, his prime minister. In addition to military strategy, Zhuge is renowned for his overall genius as a scholar, thinker, and inventor. Two examples suffice. In the critical Battle of Red Cliff (*chi bi*), along the southern bank of the Yangzi River, Liu finds himself outnumbered by Cao's forces in men and ammunition. Defeat seems imminent but Zhuge finds an extraordinary solution. He has several small, straw boats made to send out in the thick fog of night towards the enemy's fleet.

Thinking Liu is attempting a sneak attack, Cao's admirals order thousands of arrows shot at the boats. Zhuge's men later retrieve the boats – and the arrows embedded in them – to use against the enemy next day. A second example comes from an episode titled "Empty City Scheme" (*kong cheng ji*). Sima Yi, now Great Commander under Cao's son, Cao Pi, advances towards Zhuge who is camped within a small city. Zhuge is caught by surprise, without adequate forces, yet he cannot run. He knows Sima's army can easily capture them. Instead, Zhuge leaves the city gate slightly ajar. He orders some men to casually sweep leaves outside. Zhuge stations himself atop the city gate, plucking the *guqin*, a zither-like instrument. The master strategist plays calmly, melodiously. *He must have lots of men armed to the teeth to play so well*, Sima guesses with his forces just beyond the city gate. Sima retreats and Zhuge is saved for another day. Westphalian IR has no narrative of genius in world politics. At most, it forwards the notion of (Western) hegemonic stability to justify the Eurocentric claim of "West knows best."

5 **Political Trickster**. A related but very different character in the epic is the political trickster exemplified by Sima Yi. He waits a lifetime before seizing power. Initially appointed to tutor Cao Pi, Sima lies low until his 70s, even feigning a coma, before making his move. When he does, Sima takes off his boot and sticks his bare foot on the neck of his now kneeling captive, Regent to the boy Emperor. Cao Cao, Sima explains, had once joked that the shiniest part of a man's body is his foot because it is always covered. Now, Sima declares, he can show the world his bootless foot. He has nothing more to hide. Sima's grandson eventually rises to become the founding Emperor of the Jin Dynasty, thereby reuniting China and ending the Three Kingdoms period. Again, Westphalian IR has no explicit counterpart to the trickster. What comes closest are stereotypes of the Other as "duplicitous" or "deviant" but with only negative outcomes such as "rogue" or "failed" states.

6 **Ubiquitous Narrator**. We cannot discount the role of the ubiquitous narrator in *Romance*. Not only does it relate all the events and characters that transpire over a century, but the narrator also provides a philosophy to understand them. Its opening line conveys the dialectics of time and power: "Long divided, the world will unite; long united, it will fall apart." The narrator draws on this outlook throughout the epic to account for the various alliances and their unravelling epitomized by the three kingdoms. Westphalian IR's closest version of a narrator comes from Waltz's (1979) identification of world politics as a "self-help system" that structures world politics so that there can be order without an orderer.

Romancing Westphalia broadens, while deepening, IR and world politics. It expands our repertoire of identities, norms, and practices for world politics today drawn from the rich histories and cultures of our pre-Westphalian past. From this basis, the postcolonial state may begin to recover from its "cartographic anxieties" induced by Westphalian hegemony. Still, it is the interaction between *Romance* and

Westphalia that makes the difference. Either on its own merely reproduces a mono-cultural hegemony. Indeed, both the conflicts and the compatibilities between Westphalia and *Romance* contribute positively to a globalizing IR.

Conflicts and compatibilities

Romancing Westphalia surfaces some counter-normative surprises (see Table 15.1). Let's see how:

1 **Compatibilities.** Westphalia and *Romance* match best in their treatments of friendship. Despite divergences in social ontology, whereby Kantian friendship is "pre-social" and Liu Bei brotherhood in *Romance* emerges from sociality, both value and propagate norms of cooperation, if not love. This bond may solidify and stabilize relations between East Asia and the West but it also causes a problem: it skews power and politics in favor of hypermasculinity/patriarchy. To truly globalize IR and give the feminized its due in world politics (Marchand and Runyan 2011),[22] we need feminist interventions to realize *human*, not just gender, priorities. Here, a second, albeit modest, compatibility between Westphalia and *Romance* helps. Lockean/Grotian rivalry proceeds from rules about possessing and protecting property; nonetheless, it does not deny or reject Zhuge's style of multiple and mobile negotiations, as suggested in *Romance*. An integrated understanding of rivalry could enhance cooperation by, for example,

TABLE 15.1 Westphalia and *Romance* compared

	Westphalian IR	Romance	Implications for globalizing IR and world politics
Enemy	**Hobbesian/Machiavellian** Homeostatic, self-mirroring murderous competition	**Cao-ist** Variable, agential self-aggrandizement	*Sophisticate* competition
Rival	**Lockean/Grotian** Rule-bound possessiveness	**Zhuge-ist** Multiple, mobile negotiations	*Dynamize* sovereignty
Friend	**Kantian** Internalized cooperation	**Liu-ist** Eternal brotherhood	*Feminize* interventions
Genius	(Hegemonic state)	**Zhuge-ist** Paradigm-jumping strategizing	*Contest* hegemony
Trickster	(Deviant duplicity, failed states)	**Sima-ist** Unknown factor	*Consider* transformative possibilities
Narrator	(Order without an Orderer: Self-help anarchy)	**Sanguo-ist** Dialectics of power	*Evaluate* power as a process over the long term

dynamizing sovereignty. The physical, the immovable, and the contemporary need not limit our understanding of sovereignty. Instead, sovereignty could take on, when needed, an older understanding of borders as relational, mobile, and longstanding (Ling 2003).
2 **Conflict.** Westphalia and *Romance* conflict most, not surprisingly, in the category of "enemy." Westphalia defines "enemy" as situationally compelled (Hobbes/Machiavelli) and stagnantly Self-mirroring (Wendt); whereas, in *Romance*, enemy-making depends on self-aggrandizement. This apparent conflict would seem to repel Westphalia from *Romance* but the two compatibilities identified above, friendship and rivalry, introduce some elasticity in the relationship. Accordingly, Westphalia's difference from *Romance* on "enemy" could *sophisticate* understandings of inter-state competition as agential, rather than induced, and variable, not homeostatic. With this range, murderous competition need not dominate.
3 **New Agendas.** The categories of genius, trickster, and narrator in *Romance* bring new identities and agendas to world politics. Zhuge's "genius" shows the value of challenging conventions and jumping paradigms: it contests hegemony. Sima's "trickster" reminds us to never presume and always consider the possibility of transformation. *Sanguo* "narrator" underscores the dialectics of time and power: politics is a process best evaluated over the long duration. The final outcomes rarely conform to initial expectations.

Conclusion

Nodes of compatibility and conflict weave through Westphalia and *Romance*. These show how two regional worlds, represented by their respective epics of world politics, could converge despite their differences. *Romance* also introduces new identities and agendas that inveigh upon us to seek emancipation, discard complacency, and watch out for developments in the long run. Equally significant, *Romancing* Westphalia highlights multiplicity in world politics. Not only do regional worlds vary tremendously and colorfully – *Romance* and Westphalian IR are but two, limited examples – but regional worlds also overlap and interact, as shown above, thereby producing ever more variations. IR and world politics both need to take these developments into greater account.

Recent developments in IR suggest that such conceptual bridging is taking place. Even without the benefit of *Romance*, Lacassagne (2012) finds the promise of relationality, *habitus*, and social interdependencies enriching IR. It can recognize that "[t]he civilizing process is not unilinear, there can be de-civilising processes ... major outbursts of violence, or a return to a state in which the external constraints take precedence over self-restraint." As Duffy notes in his chapter, the seeds of self-transformation already exist within Western social science.

My thought experiment now ends. It suggests that the gap between "the West" and "the Rest" can close in theory and in practice. Eurocentrics can no longer claim supremacy in civilization disguised as enlightened governance. Nor can postcolonials bemoan a "cartographic anxiety" that renders them victimized yet reactionary, oppressed but violent. We are, as Zhuge Liang shows, capable of far greater creativity.

Notes

1 I thank Chen Boyu, Kim Wookyung, Kim Youngwon, Thuy Do, and Kay Yamaguchi for helping me with the cultural artifacts of Romance in East Asia today. Special thanks, also, to Tan Chung for his insights on *Romance*.
2 For a brief review of the history of "Oriental Despotism" in European thought, see Minuti (2012).
3 These riots occurred in South-Central Los Angeles where African Americans dominated as residents but Korean Americans owned and operated many local stores. The first Rodney King trial exempted four white police officers of police brutality and racial animus despite a videotape showing them beating an unarmed black man, Rodney King, who laid prostrate on the ground. A second trial later reversed this sentence. For a full recounting of the incident, the trials, and the riots, see *The New York Times* (2013).
4 Eurocentrics labeled both Ottoman Turkey and Qing China as "sick men" in the nineteenth century. A cartoon from 1898 shows Turkey, as the "sick man of Europe," consoling China, the "sick man of Asia," at http://www.granger.com/results.asp?image=0014135&screenwidth=1274 (last visited December 15, 2013).
5 Nandy (1988) demonstrates how Indian elites internalized the British colonizer's hyper-masculinized, "undeveloped heart" to show their worth in British eyes *and* rule over domestic Others.
6 For a recent example, see Miller (2013).
7 Qing China suffered defeat and unequal treaties; imperial Japan, atomic devastation; and Nehru's India, Cold War power politics.
8 For a competent yet brief synopsis of the epic, see http://en.wikipedia.org/wiki/Romance_of_the_Three_Kingdoms [last visited December 15, 2013]. Other Chinese epics like *Shuihu zhuan* (*Water Margins*), *Xiyou ji* (*Journey to the West*), and *Honglou Meng* (*Dream of the Red Chamber*) have had a similar cultural impact on the region but only *Romance* deals explicitly with world politics.
9 See, in Japanese: http://mangafox.me/manga/sangokushi/ [last visited December 8, 2013]; in Vietnamese: http://www.sachbaovn.vn/doc-truc-tuyen/sach/tam-quoc-dien-nghia-tap-1-(truyen-tranh)-MUQwQTQ2MkI [last visited December 9, 2013].
10 See, in Japanese: *Kōtetsu Sangokushi* (2007).
11 See, in Korean: http://samleague.no3games.com/nmain.php; http://cafe.naver.com/scsamguk; https://itunes.apple.com/kr/app/id431552463; http://cafe.naver.com/samtactic [last visited December 10, 2013]; in Japanese: *Sangokushi Taisen* (2005, 2006); in Vietnamese: http://3d.3qc.vn/teaser/xich-bich.htm, http://luyengame.com/games/tamquocchi.html [last visited December 9, 2013].
12 See, "*Xin sanguo yanyi: zhong, e, mei*" ("New Romance of the Three Kingdoms: China, Russia, US"), *tianya shequ* (one of the biggest bulletin boards in China), September 30, 2010.
13 South Korea's president, Park Geun Hye, notes her love of the epic in her autobiography, at http://www.goodreads.com/book/show/18138421-the-exercise-of-my-despair [last visited December 10, 2013]. In Vietnam, daily discourse includes these phrases from the epic: e.g., "*Vợ chồng như quần áo, anh em như tay chân*" ("wives are like clothing; brothers are like the palm of one's hand"); "*Nhắc Tào Tháo, Tào Tháo đến*" ("speak of the devil [Cao Cao] and he appears"); "*Ba ông thợ may bằng một Gia Cát Lượng*" ("three stinky leather tanners can triumph over one Zhuge Liang [genius]"). Many temples in Vietnam also worship Guan Yu, a key character in *Romance*. He symbolizes the principled warrior/nobleman.

14 Cao is pronounced "Tsao" in Mandarin.
15 Zhuge is pronounced "Joo-guh."
16 Liu Bei is pronounced "Li-oh Bay."
17 To access the 2010 TV series with English subtitles, see http://the-scholars.com/view topic.php?f=5&t=21148 [last visited July 27, 2011]. A version dubbed in Turkish is available at http://www.youtube.com/watch?v=rD3hZkPTLfI [last visited December 12, 2013].
18 Slight differences appear. For example, the 2010 series does not include the novel's chapter, "Seven Times Caught, Seven Times Released" (*qi qing qi zong*). On this, see chapter 6 of Ling (2014).
19 Cao's father was the foster son of a favored eunuch in the Han Dynasty court.
20 Sun Quan is pronounced "Suin Chuan."
21 This is a paraphrase of the dialogue in the drama series. In the TV drama, "*Sanguo*" (2010), Zhuge asks: "Have we no ruler, no father (*wujun wufu*)?" Since the state equates with the patriarchal household in imperial China, the charge of "no ruler, no father" codes for sedition or disloyalty ("without patriotism, without filial piety" or *wu zhong wu xiao*).
22 These include any identity not deemed "masculine": e.g., women, the underclass, the informal economy and the non-Western Other.

References

Acharya, Amitav. (2014) "Call for Proposals: Global IR and Regional Worlds, A New Agenda for International Studies." (http://www.africadesk.ac.uk/news/2014/apr/25/international-studies-association-56th-annual-conv/) (Downloaded: July 9, 2016).

Agathangelou, Anna M. and L.H.M. Ling. (2009) *Transforming World Politics: From Empire to Multiple Worlds*. London: Routledge.

Chakrabarty, Dipesh. (2000) *Provincializing Europe: Postcolonial Thought and Historical Difference*. Princeton: Princeton University Press.

Chen, Ching-Chang. (2011) "The Absence of Non-Western IR Theory in Asia Reconsidered." *International Relations of the Asia-Pacific* 11: 1–23.

Fukuyama, Francis. (1992) *The End of History and the Last Man*. New York: Avon Books.

Gourevitch, Peter. (1978) "The Second Image Reversed: The International Sources of Domestic Politics." *International Organization* 32(4): 881–912.

Hasso, Frances. (2013) "Alternative Worlds at the World Social Forum 2013 in Tunis." *Jadaliyya*, May 1 (http://www.jadaliyya.com/pages/index/11396/alternative-worlds-at-the-2013-world-social-forum-) (Downloaded: December 3, 2013).

Lacassagne, Aurélie. (2012) "Cultures of Anarchy as Figurations: Reflections on Wendt, Elias, and the English School." *Human Figurations* 1(2). (http://quod.lib.umich.edu/h/humfig/11217607.0001.207/–cultures-of-anarchy-as-figurations-reflections-on-wendt?rgn=main;view=fulltext) (Downloaded: September 7, 2016).

Lam, Lai Sing. (2011) *The Romance of the Three Kingdoms and Mao's Global Order of Tripolarity*. Oxford: Peter Lang AG.

Ling, L.H.M. (2003) "Borders of Our Minds: Territories, Boundaries, and Power in the Confucian Tradition." In Margaret Moore and Allen Buchanan (eds), *States, Nations, and Borders: The Ethics of Making Boundaries*, 86–100. Cambridge: Cambridge University Press.

Ling, L.H.M. (2002) *Postcolonial International Relations: Conquest and Desire between Asia and the West*. London: Palgrave Macmillan.

Ling, L.H.M. (2014) *The Dao of World Politics: Towards a Post-Westphalian, Worldist International Relations*. London: Routledge.

Ling, L.H.M. (ed.) (2016) *India and China: Rethinking Borders and Security, India and China*. Ann Arbor: University of Michigan Press.

Ling, L.H.M. and Carolina M. Pinheiro. (forthcoming) "South-South Talk: Worldism and Epistemologies of the South." In L.H.M. Ling, Nizar Messari, and Arlene B. Tickner (eds), *Theorizing International Politics from the Global South: Worlds of Difference*. London: Routledge, forthcoming.

Marchand, Marianne and Anne Sisson Runyan (eds). (2011) *Gender and Global Restructuring: Sightings, Sites, and Resistances*. London: Routledge.

Miller, Manjari Chatterjee. (2013) *Wronged by Empire: Post-Imperial Ideology and Foreign Policy in India and China*. Stanford: Stanford University Press.

Minuti, Rolando. (2012) "Oriental Despotism." *EGO* (European History Online), May 3 (http://www.ieg-ego.eu/en/threads/models-and-stereotypes/the-wild-and-the-civilised/rolando-minuti-oriental-despotism) (Downloaded: December 1, 2013).

Nandy, Ashis. (1988) *The Intimate Enemy: The Psychology of Colonialism*. Delhi: Oxford University Press.

New York Times, The. (2013) *The Los Angeles Riots and Rodney King*. New York: New York Times Company.

Niou, Emerson M.S. and Peter C. Ordershook. (1987) "Preventive War and the Balance of Power: A Game-Theoretic Approach." *The Journal of Conflict Resolution* 31(3): 387–419.

Palumbo-Liu, David. (1994) "Los Angeles, Asians, and Perverse Ventriloquisms: On the Functions of Asia America in the Recent American Imaginary." *Public Culture* 6: 365–381.

Wendt, Alexander. (1999) *Social Theory of International Politics*. Cambridge: Cambridge University Press.

Waltz, Kenneth. (1979) *Theory of International Politics*. Reading: Addison-Wesley.

CONCLUSION

Uncontained worlds

Stephen Chan

The impulse of Huntington's "clash of civilizations" was that many "other" civilizations were both hostile and could not be understood. War or barricades against them were possible, but dialogue and negotiation not. Holding up Edward Said as Huntington's opposite (and opposed) number became an easy postcolonial device, almost a trope, but one of Said's essential points was that the "other" was not an enclosure. It partook in exchanges and in the giving and absorption of influences. It was dynamic and it changed. Its being open was key to its cosmopolitanism.

This was apparent in the opening chapter of *Culture & Imperialism*, a kind of expansion but also antidote to the one-dimensional interpretations of *Orientalism*. It was obviously part of an act of resistance, but it was also part of a process of change that occurs whenever two cultures intersect and interact. In a later interview, Said castigated the very postcolonial discipline he helped found by accusing it of "unhistorical anti-intellectualism." He committed himself to "a matrix of overlapping histories" and against "nativism or the idea of pure cultural essences" (Howe 2006: 61).

So that with the advent of "worlding" in IR, something long overdue, there must be cautions. Establishing the principle of different epistemologies, different cultural backgrounds, and different formative histories does not mean a principle that allows entry to something static. Not only is nothing static, nothing an intellectual and cultural museum piece, but only its most arrant chauvinistic expressions would wish it to be a revanchist and defensive circling of wagons labeled "not yours" and "not Western." It is not only at least partially Western – as the West is partially the parts of many others, Christianity and its Persian Zoroastrian influences being a case in point – but it contends within itself. No "world" is without debate, paradigmatic overthrows and contentions, arguments about modernity, and resizings of history.

Even in Europe, this has been evident throughout the twentieth century. The birth of Finland and the literal invention of a prehistoric literature; the transformation of

Csarist Russia into the Soviet Union and then its own transformation into today's Russia; Germany's waxing and waning and division through two world wars and a cold war; Turkey's struggle with itself as European, Asian, secular, Islamic, civilian, and military; and Yugoslavia's replacement by a problematic succession of smaller countries that suddenly speak their "own" languages and have certainly rewritten their own histories – are examples. These examples pale alongside the cataclysmic changes in thought and reinventions of culture that have occurred in the post-colonial realms of Africa (55 countries, each with its own reinvention and struggles for reinvention) and other developing nations.

It was Clifford Geertz, the pioneering anthropologist, who most certainly pronounced the necessity of appreciating different cultures differently – but that also means appreciating their wars and slaughters and rampaging corruptions differently. The problem with "worlding" is that it proposes itself as a moral modernity – but has within it many "immoralities."

These points are made clear or at least implicit in the chapters of this book. It is a series of Asian case examples with one chapter contrasting Turkey and Ethiopia. The African country of Ethiopia is the only state on the continent not to have been colonized. Its Christian religion has the oldest liturgies of any Christian order and is probably closest to that of the apostles. It is a nation with an ancient written language. It has always had close relations with its African neighbors but also with the Middle East on the other side of the Red Sea. The Queen of Sheba came from Ethiopia and traveled from there to Solomon's Israel. And Homer's great poem, the *Odyssey*, after the rubric, begins with the line: "Poseidon had gone to visit the Ethiopians worlds away."

The Hoffmann chapter on Ethiopia and Turkey, and their anti-imperialist cultures of resistance, serves great purpose both against a condescension towards Ethiopia (Mussolini's mistake) and a romanticization of the country (the mistake of the Rastas). In contemplating its recent history alongside that of Turkey, the chapter implicitly calls for similar future comparative work – but that work will be harder. One of the stock paintings that anyone can buy in the Ethiopian flea markets is of the clashes between the Ethiopian and Italian armies. Both have rifles and cannons. Both have Red Cross hospitals. But God's Christian angels and saints, particularly St. George, ride with the Ethiopians. In a curious way, the wars between the two were wars between cousins. They were very different but had much in common. The future difficulties will lie in case studies that appear opaque and are then interpreted as exotic. By "exotic," I mean precisely Said's original orientalism, but with the added piquancy or quaintness that, somehow, one could say (not without a bit of satire): *they have, the clever natives, learnt something from us – but how odd has been this learning.*

One of the book's most interesting chapters is that by Ching-Chang Chen on the Ryukyu Islands, conquered by Japan in the nineteenth century, with Okinawa at the heart of the archipelago. China sought to see the islands through a Confucian lens, but Japan through the eyes of a newly self-recognized Westphalian state with Westphalian interpretations of what was possible in international relations. The lingering Diaoyutai/Senkaku Islands dispute is a legacy of this moment of rupture between world systems. As a frequent visitor to Okinawa, I hasten to add that seeing the Ryukyu Islands as a territory defined in dyadic terms – Japan vs China – leaves out a peculiar but still compelling Okinawan narrative built around the self-views of the Sho dynasty; something that is still a strong cultural force in the Okinawan resistance to the proliferation of US bases on the islands.

The case of Taiwan as being also historically caught between China and Japan is made plain by Boyu Chen. But what is "Chinese" on Taiwan is composed of several generations of migration and settlement, some (as around Kaohsiung) with strong independence inclinations and others (around Taipei) with an openness towards an eventual negotiated reintegration with China. And what is "Chinese" stands often at odds with what is "aboriginal" – there being eight aboriginal MPs who have made it into parliament, but there being also an organized group that is in alliance with a chain of aboriginal societies that have organized themselves and stretch from Taiwan to New Zealand.

The chain of aboriginal alliances and links is like a trans-Pacific road, running across maritime and land configurations. Josuke Ikeda's use of the road metaphor, with its Confucian and Daoist implications of a moral way – but also with its sense of a future IR as one with linkages rather than self-centered and self-satisfied states that recreate themselves in order to reinforce themselves by recreating themselves in the cultures and states of others – is compelling. How then does the project of linkages occur?

This is where the book is at its most compelling. It offers not a series of solutions but a series of insights and *inside* accounts of the variables that must go into a new IR. What emerges is not a paradigm of "worlding" but a *program* of study for worlding to undertake. That program is clearly one of respect for other cultures but not one of ossification. It is, as L.H.M. Ling points out, one where Westphalia and romance live together. This is not an unusual or unprecedented conjuncture. Although Ling talks about the *Romance of the Three Kingdoms*, recent Eurocentric thought at its most decisive phase was not in fact about the triumph of the Enlightenment – but about the conjuncture of the Enlightenment with the romantic movement in literature, music and art.

Almost every foundation of European thought as it has come down to us from the seventeeth and eighteenth centuries onwards has had, as well as an epistemological foundation, a metaphysical one. Kant's categorical imperative, Hegel's spirit of history, and Rousseau's sense of nature are, none of them, actually rational. They are irrational devices deployed as motivating metaphors for a line of thought that then *becomes* rational and is accorded a realm of epistemology. It is polyvalent or, to use John Hobson's term, "polycivilizational," as well – in that the program must look at romance and rationality in many cultures, even as they change and the balance between them changes, and give the lie to the arch separations of Huntington and the Huntingtonians. This is the critical security studies envisaged by Pinar Bilgin.

I should reiterate one last element of the program. It must not exoticize. It is not to reformulate the Victorian idea of the "noble savage." That was a stereotype drawn from the Maori resistance to colonial land grabs, when Victorian writers were amazed at how chivalrous the Maori armies were. Those writers didn't investigate Maori culture any further, and their colonizing relatives still stole the land.

To this extent, the program is necessarily normative. To be recognized as noble but to be robbed in any case is not what is sought. At the same time, continuing with the subject of land, Robert Mugabe's use of a "norm" of cultural value residing in land as a justification for its seizure is also not what is sought, i.e. the program cannot be naïve as governments become canny and intellectual in their own program. And that poses one difficulty not yet covered in depth by the writers of this book: what happens as norms become constitutionalized – or not. The Iranian constitution is a proper constitution in the sense that it is a carefully articulated body of law and matrix for all laws. It is theocratic in the sense of enshrining constitutionally a clerical governance with clear institutions. But it also contains a huge number of exceptional clauses, where modernity requires a legal framework that simply cannot be theocratic. It is, if I might say so, an unholy mix of a constitution. But cultures and laws will be a potent and inflammable mix for some time to come. The Westphalian state proposes one problematique. Alongside it is the problematique of the constitutional state and that will be a nettle that future worlding must grasp.

References

Howe, Stephen. (2006) "An Interview with Edward Said." *Interventions* 8(1): 56–66.

INDEX

Page numbers in **bold** refer to figures, page numbers in *italic* refer to tables

50,000 MW Hydroelectric Initiative, India 38, 39

Abdulhamid II, Sultan 141
Aberystwyth School of Critical Security Studies 14, 20, 149
Acharya, Amitav 185
Adwa, Battle of, 1896 139, 143, 144
Africa 196
Africa Orientale Italiana 146n1
African Union 145
Agarwala, Jyotiprasad 60n3
Age of Imperialism/Age of Empire 104
agency 3, 33
Ahmed, Rafiul 2
aitia 129–31, **130**
Aksu, Esref 26, 33
Al-Azmeh, Aziz 19–20
All Assam Students Union (AASU) 51
Alliance of Civilizations 5
al-Qaeda 5
Anderson, T. 102
Angell, Norman 115
Anghie, Antony 6
anti-colonialism: and cultural traditions 168–9; and education 167–8; Ethiopia 137–9, 143–5; incompleteness of 169; pan-Africanism 144–5; pan-Islamism 141–3; the Philippines 162–9; social 139; state-centered 139; Turkey 137–9

anti-imperialist scientific racist international theory 111–3
anti-imperialist/anti-paternalist Eurocentric institutionalism 117–8
Appadurai, Arjun 49
Appiah, Kwame Anthony 30
Arab-Israeli conflict 143
Aristotle 129–31, **130**, 153
ASEAN 169, 170n2
Asia: definition 1; status 6
Asian Financial Crisis 173, 174–5, 180
Asian Infrastructure Investment Bank 6
Assam: Assam–Bangladesh border 49–52, 60n3; Bangladeshi numbers 52–5; Bengali-speaking Muslims in 48–60; Border Security Force 52; Brahmaptura River 50; British rule 54; *chars* 50; civil society organizations 61n22; contestation of citizenship 56–8; deportation movement 51; D-voters 56–8; ethnic cleansing 55; Hindu immigrants 57; immigrant subjectivity 52; indigenous people 57; Indo-Bangladeshi relations 58–60; infiltration issue 57–8; Line System 61n15; location 49–50; National Register for Citizenship (NRC) 56–7, 62n23; perceived threat of 49
Assam Accord, the 51, 56, 60n8
Assam Gana Parishad (AGP) 51
Assam Movement 55, 56
Atatürk, Mustafa Kemal 142, 146n4

Index

autochthony 58
Aydin, Cemil 6

Bacon, Francis 122
balance of power 97, 101
Bandung Conference 143, 185
Bangladesh 49, 68, 69; Assam–Bangladesh border 49–52, 60n3; Indo-Bangladeshi relations 58–60; national identity formation 72
Barker, Ernst 70
Beck, Ulrich 27, 31, 32, 34n2
beliefs 129
Benedict XVI, Pope 15, 17
Bengal, partition of 67
Bhabha, Homi K. 15, 173, 176–7, 181
Bhambra, Gurminder 19
Bharatiya Janata Party (BJP) 51–2, 55, 57
Bhattacharya, Sammujal 56–7
Bhutan 69, 71, 72
Bilgin, Pinar 2, 104, 197
Blair, James 111–2
Blaney, David 15
Bodoland Territorial Area District (BTAD) violence, India 56–7, 61n21
Boon, Vivienne 26, 30–1, 31
Booth, Ken. 20, 21
borders: Assam–Bangladesh border 49–52; Cosmopolitanism and 26, 31; fencing 49–50, 51, 52; fluid 1, 155; importance 1; militarization 52; partition politics 50, 52; porous 50; securitization 52
Bowden, Brett 6
Bright, John 115, 116
brotherhood 188, 190, *190*
Buck-Morss, Susan 17, 20, 20–1
Buddhism 153

Cao Cao enmity 187, *190*, 191
Capan, Zeynep Gulsah 3
capital-intensive mega-projects 38
capitalism 139, 150, 175
cartographic anxiety 49, 59
Catholicism 162–3
Celik, Y. 103
center, the 97
Central Electricity Authority (CEA), India 38
Chakravarti, K.C. 61n16
Chaliha, Bimala Prasad 50
Chan, Stephen 4
Chatterjee, Partha 74n1
Chatterji, Joya 50, 60n3
Chen, Boyu 3, 186, 197
Chen, C. 184

Chen, Ching-Chang 3, 196–7
Chen, Kuan-Hsing 1
Chen, Z.Y. 89
Chiang Kai-shek 86, 87
China: agency 113; conceptions of civilization 77; core interests 75, 83n6; Diaoyutai/Senkaku Islands dispute 3, 75–83, 184, 196–7; dispute with Imperial Russia 79; Ministry of Foreign Affairs 75; moral authority 76; "One Belt, One Road" (OBOR) policy 6; Qing Dynasty 75, 78, 82, 192n4, 192n7; relationships with Taiwan 86, 87, 88–9, 92–3; the Ryukyu crisis 76, 77, 77–81, 82, 197; Silk-Road initiative 6; Sino-Japanese diplomatic crisis, 1877 78; status in international hierarchy 76–7; Treaty of Trade and Friendship, 1871 80, 81; *Zongli yamen* 79, 80
Chinese School 151
Ching, Leo 89
Chong, Alan 3
Chong, J.I. 90
citizenship, contestation of 56–8
civic identity 25
civic nationalism 74
civil society, global 26
civilization 2; alternatives to concept 5; Chinese conceptions of 77; standards of 6
civilizational dialogue 2, 5–6, 13–21; critical security studies perspective 14, 20–1; epistemology 17, 20; as ethics 16–20; historical 17–8; interpretative struggles 16; and non-state referents 14–6; power/knowledge dynamics 15; problem of difference 15; role 13; short-termism 16
clash of civilizations scenario 5, 118, 195
Cobden, Richard 115–6
Cold War 137; Age of Imperialism/Age of Empire narrative 104; historiography 98–100; inevitability narrative 104; narratives 97–105; origin narratives 98–100, 100–3; pericentric narrative 102; revisionist narrative 101–2; structuralist narrative 102–3; Third World narrative 104; traditionalist narrative 100–1; Turkish foreign policy 3, 97–105, 142–3; turning points 99; Western-centrism 97–105
colonial dissection 67
colonialism 1, 74, 160–1, 161–2; civilizing mission 168; impact 164–7; and security 3
commercialism 117
competitive breeding 61n17

conceptual bridging 191
conditional agency 114, 114–5
Confucianism 153
conservative activism 123–4
conventionalism 125
Cos, K. 104
Cosmopolitanism 2, 25–33, 154; borders and 26, 31; core values 34n2; cultural/critical 30–2; definition 25–7; dilemmas 25, 27, 32–3; emphasis on consensus 33; global normative ethic 25; and human agency 33; and identity 27–30, 33; notion of power 30, 33; portrayal of 27–8; thick 28, 29; thin 28–9
Cox, Robert 98
Crimean War 115–6
critical security studies: Aberystwyth School perspective 14, 20; approaches 20; civilizational dialogue 14, 20–1; concerns 14, 21; literature 14
critical thinking 151
crossroads 149
cultural interactions, context 29
cultural linkages 1
cultural/critical Cosmopolitanism 30–2
cultural-realism 118
culture 160
Cushner, Nicholas 162
Cyprus 143, 146n6

Dallmayr, Fred 13
Daoism 153
Darfur 33
De Certeau, M. 100
decolonization 1, 104
defensive modernity 138
Delanty, Gerard 26, 30–1, 31
derivative agency 117
development 2, 104; capital-intensive mega-projects and 38; and environment 42–5
Diaoyutai/Senkaku Islands dispute 3, 75–83, 184, 196–7; causes 75–6; cyber discourse 90–3; East China Sea Peace Initiative 87; ethos of appropriateness 75; historical constitutional structures 76–7; the Ryukyu crisis 75, 77, 77–81, 82, 197; strategic value 75, 83n3; Taiwan and 3, 80, 83n4, 86–93
diaspora communities 70
difference, problem of 15
direct racial exterminism 113
diversity, IR scholarship 150
DuBois, W.E.B. 144
Duffy, Gavan 3
Duhem, Pierre 128–9

Eagleton, Terry 151
East Asia, international society 76–7, 82
East China Sea Peace Initiative 87
East Pakistan *see* Bangladesh
Eastern agency 109–18; within anti-imperialist scientific racist international theory 111–3; in anti-imperialist/anti-paternalist Eurocentric institutionalism 117–8; conditional 114, 114–5; emergence of discourse 109–10; within imperialist Eurocentric institutionalist international theory 114–7; within imperialist scientific racist international theory 113–4; levels of 109; within Orientalism 111–8; paradox of 109, 140
Eastern Other, the 2, 184–5
economic dependency 138
Electronic BBS Research Society 90–1
emancipation 20, 21, 31
empire of the mind 161–2
energy security 2, 36, 37, 42
Engels, Friedrich 167
English School, the 116
Enlightenment, the 18, 20, 151
enmity 186–7, *190*, 191
environment, and development 42–5
ethics, civilizational dialogue as 16–20
Ethiopia 3, 137–9, 140–1, 143–5, 196
ethnic expulsion 71
ethnic group, definition 69–70
ethnic identity 69, 70
ethno-nationalism 69–70
ethos of appropriateness 75, 83n7
Eurocentrism 2, 3, 97, 100–1, 103, 109, 180–1, 184–5, 191–2; anti-imperialist/anti-paternalist Eurocentric institutionalism 117–8; imperialist Eurocentric institutionalist international theory 114–7. *see also* Orientalism
Europe 83n8, 195–6
European Union (EU) 5, 27, 30, 32
Europeanization 30–1, 32

Facebook 90
fairness 27
Falk, Richard 13
falsificationism 125–7, 128
federalism 71
Feyerabend, Paul K. 127, 127–8
Finland 195
First World War 141–2; Gallipoli campaign, 1915 139, 141, 142
Francia, L.H. 162
friendship 186–7, 188, 190, *190*
Fukuyama, Francis 181, 184

Gaddis, J.L. 102–3
Gallipoli campaign, 1915 139, 141, 142
Gandhi, Rajiv 51
Ganguly, Rajat 69
Garvey, Marcus 144
Gati Infrastructure Limited 40
Geertz, Clifford 196
Gellner, Ernest 73
genocide 71, 169
Giddens, Anthony 73
Giese, K. 90
global energy security 36
global IR 149
global metabolism 155
global metamorphosis 155, 156
globalization 132, 174; high 49
Golden Dawn 34n4
Gong, Gerrit 6, 150
Gong, Prince 79–80
Goswami, A. 52–5
Gourevitch, Peter 184
governance, global 25, 32–3
Gramsci, A. 167
Grande, Edgar 31, 34n2
Grant, Ulysses S. 80
Great Britain, Cold War foreign policy 100, 102
Greater East Asia Co-Prosperity Sphere 151–2
green energy 36–45
Grovogui, Siba N. 19
Guha, Amalendu 54
Guillaume, Xavier 16–7

Habermas, Jürgen 20
Haile Selassie 144
Hale, W. 101
Halle, L.J. 100–1
Haytian Emigration Society 144
Hazarika, Bhupen 59
He Jing 78–9
He Ruzhang 78–9
Heidegger, Martin 28
Held, David 26
Hilferding, R. 117
Hindu nationalism 69
history 2; choices 98–9; conceptualization of 97, 98–100; non-European 140; turning points 99
Hitler, Adolf 116
Hobbes, Thomas 6, 26
Hobbesian enmity 186, *190*, 191
Hobson, J.A 110–1, 114, 115
Hobson, John M. 3, 17–8, 140, 197
Hoffman, Clemens 3, 196

homeland societies 70
Howland, D.R. 77, 81
human emancipation 122
human flourishing 122–3
human rights 19–20, 29, 30, 34n3
Human Rights Watch 52
Huntington, Samuel P. 5, 15, 18, 118, 195, 197
hybridities 1
hydroelectric power projects (HEPs), India 36–45
Hypermasculine- Eurocentric Whiteness 4

Ibn Battuta 153
ideas, movement of 3, 149–56
identity 15, 48, 155; civic 25; and Cosmopolitanism 27–30, 33; cross state 69; ethnic 69, 70; fluid 33; hybrid 32; national 3, 68, 73, 74n2, 87–90, 90–3, 94n2; national political 71–3; predatory 58–9; and security 2, 27–30, 33; transformation 31
identity-based politics 59
Ikeda, Josuke 3, 197
immigrant subjectivity 52
imperialism 1, 3, 104, 109, 114–7, 127
imperialist Eurocentric institutionalist international theory 114–7
imperialist scientific racist international theory 113–4
Inayatullah, Naeem 15
India 41–2; 50,000 MW Hydroelectric Initiative 38, 39; ACT (Affected Citizens of Teesta) 44–5, 46n17; *adivasis* 42; anti-colonial Muslim community 141–2; anti-dam organizations 44–5, 45n5, 46n17; Assam 48–60; Assam–Bangladesh border 48, 49–52, 60n3; Bangladeshi numbers 53; Bengali-speaking Muslim community 48–60; Bodoland Territorial Area District (BTAD) violence 56–7, 61n21; Border Security Force 52; British Raj 48, 54; capital-intensive mega-projects 38; Central Electricity Authority (CEA) 38; colonial dissection 67; conflicts with Pakistan 69; contestation of citizenship 56–8; development policies 42–4; displaced persons 43; economic growth 37, 42; economic liberalization 36, 38; Election Commission of India 56; Electricity Act (2003) 39; electricity sources 38; energy demand 36; energy policy framework 38–9; energy privatization 37, 39; energy resources 2; energy security 37, 42; Environment

Impact Assessment laws (2006) 41; Environment Protection Act (1986) 41; environmental compliance 42–4; ethnic nationalist movements 69; Forest Rights Act 42–3; green energy 36–45; hegemonies 54; Hindu nationalism 55; Hydel Schemes 40; hydroelectric power projects (HEPs) 36–45; Immigrants Act, 1950 60n7; Indo-Bangladeshi relations 49, 58–60; linguistic nationalism 68–9; Look East Policy 59; Ministry of Environment and Forests 41, 43; Ministry of External Affairs 49; Ministry of Petroleum and Natural Gas 43; National Environment Policy (2006) 41; National Forest Policy (1988) 41; National Hydroelectric Power Corporation (NHPC) 40; national identity 68; national political identity 71–2; National Water Policy (2012) 41; nationality movement 68; nation-building 67–8, 68–9; natural resource exploitation 37, 42–4; New Hydropower Policy, 2008 38–9; northeast HEP controversy 39–41; Northeastern (NE) region 45n2; Partition 61n18, 71; partition of Bengal 67; partition politics 50; Pasighat Proclamation on Power 39; Policy for Hydro Powe Development, 1998 38; Public Interest Litigation (PILs) 41; public-private partnerships (PPP) 42; the Radcliffe Line 50, 60n6; security 2; Sikkim 36, 37, 39–41; social equity 41–2; State Electricity Boards (SEBs) 39; Supreme Court of India 57, 57–8; urbanization 42; West Bengal 53
Indian Planning Commission 36
indirect racial exterminism 113
Indo-Bangladeshi relations 49
industrialization 73
insecurity 2, 14–6
inter-communal comity 71
interconnectivity 28
internal Other, the 2, 48–60
international hierarchy 75–6, 76
international law, Cosmopolitan 26
International Monetary Fund 6, 175
International Relations 4–6
International Rivers 40
international society: East Asia 76–7, 82; European 83n8
International Studies Association (ISA) 185
Internet 177
interpretative struggles 16
interstitial identities 15

Iqbal, Muhammad 67–8
Iran 198
Ireland, Alleyne 114
Islam, agency 113
Islamic nationhood 68, 72
Italy, invasion of Ethiopia 143–4, 145

Jacques, Martin 29
Japan: agency 113; annexation of Ryukyu 75, 77, 77–81, 82, 197; Diaoyutai/Senkaku Islands dispute 3, 75–83, 184, 196–7; imperialism 89; Meiji 75, 77–8; relationships with South Korea 178; relationships with Taiwan 86, 87, 89, 89–90, 92–3, 94n5; Second World War 151–2; Sino-Japanese diplomatic crisis, 1877 78; Treaty of Trade and Friendship, 1871 80, 81
Japanese Exchange Association 89
Jenkins, K. 98
Jones, Charles 27
Jordan, David Starr 112
justice 27

Kabasakal-Arat, Zehra 19
Kant, Immanuel 26, 117, 118, 123, 197
Kantian friendship 186, 188, *190*, 190
Kashmir 69
Kelly, Duncan 32
Khatami, Seyyed Mohammed 13
Kidd, Benjamin 113
Kim Dae-jung 175–6
King, Rodney 184, 192n3
Klilafat Organization 141
Kofman, Eleonore 28
Korea Tourism Organization 177–8
Korean Wave, the 4, 172–81; and the Asian Financial Crisis 174–5, 180; and economic recovery 175–6; films 177; historical background 172–3; impacts 177–9; and neoliberal globalization 174; origin of term 173; pop music (K-pop) 173, 177; scope 173–4; soft power 172; third space 173, 176–7, 181; TV drama 173, 176–7, 178
K-pop 173–4, 177
Kratochwil, Friedrich 16
Krishna, Sankaran 49, 59–60
Kuhn, Thomas S. 125–6, 127, 129
Kyoto School 151–2

Lakatos, Imre **123**, 123–4, 126–7, 128–9
Lam, P.E. 90
language: alternative 152–4; role of 154; translation 154

learning, role of 154
Lebow, Richard Ned 5
Lee, Jooyoun 4
Leffler, M.P. 102–3
legitimacy 87, 91–3
Lenin, V.I 117
Li, D.T. 89
Li Hongzhang 76, 79, 80–1, 82
Liberalism 27, 33
Lind, William 118
Ling, L.H.M 4, 154, 172–3, 175
literature, critical security studies 14
Liu Bei brotherhood 188, 190, *190*
Lockean rivalry 186, *190*, 190–1
logical positivism 125
Lu, G. 90
Lynch, Marc 13

McCormack, Tara 30
Mackinder, Halford 113
McSweeney, Bill 15
Mahan, Alfred 113
Malaysia 169
Maldives, the 70, 73
Maori culture 198
Marco Polo 153
Marshall Plan 99
Marx, Karl 115, 167
Mazrui, Ari 150
militarization, borders 52
Mill, John Stuart 115
Ministry of Environment and Forests, India 41
minorities, perceived threat of 49
Mishra, Binoda K. 3
modernity 2, 73, 140, 198
modernization 73
Mohajir movement 69
Mugabe, Robert 198
Mullan, C.S 54, 60–1n12, 61n13, 61n14
multi-ethnic states 70
multiple worlds 185
multiplicity 191

Nakamura, Hajime 154
Nath, H.K. 53
nation, definition 70, 73, 74n1
National Hydroelectric Power Corporation (NHPC), India 40
national identity 68, 73, 74n2, 87–90, 94n2; cyber discourse 90–3; political 71–3; and sovereignty 91–3
national security, internal Other and 52
nationalism 67–8, 73; anti-colonial 169; civic 74; linguistic 68–9; managing 70–1; religious 68

nationality question 71
nation-building 73, 74, 74n2; India 67–8, 68–9; Pakistan 68; South Asia 67
nationhood 2–3, 67
nation-state, the 67–74
NATO 143
natural nationalities 71–2
Nayak, Meghana 19
Nazi Germany 71
neo-colonialism 138
neoliberalism 174
Nepal 69, 71, 72
New Hydropower Policy, 2008, India 38–9
new imperialism 117
New International Economic Order (NIEO) 104, 185
Non Aligned Movement 104, 143
non-Western IR 150–2, 156
norms 153
Nussbaum, Martha Craven 29, 31
Nye, Joseph 172

Okinawa 80, 196–7
Organisation for Economic Cooperation and Development (OECD) 172
Organisation of Petroleum Exporting Countries (OPEC) 185
Oriental despotism 184
Oriental Other, the 184–5
Orientalism 2, 109, 195, 196; Eastern agency within 111–8; scientific racism *110*, 110–1, *111*
Other, the 150, 154, 155; Eastern 2, 184–5; internal 2, 48–60
Ottoman Empire 139, 140–2, 192n4

Pakistan: conflicts with India 69; national identity formation 72; national political identity 72; nation-building 68; Partition 71; religious nationalism 68
Palumbo-Liu, David 184
pan-Africanism 3, 138, 144–5
Pandey, Gyanendra 59, 60n2
pan-Islamism 3, 141–3
partition politics 50, 52
Pasha, Mustapha Kamal 17
Pasighat Proclamation on Power, India 39
paternalism 114–7
Pearson, Charles Henry 113, 118
periphery, the 97
Petito, Fabio 13, 15
Phanis, Urmila 70
Philippines, the 3, 160–9; anti-colonialism 162–9; Chinese community 163; Church and State relations 162–3, 166; cultural

traditions 168–9; education 167–8; historical background 162–4; Spanish colonialism 161, 161–2, 164–7; state building 164–7; US hegemony 161
Plato 153
pluralism 150
Policy for Hydro Power Development, 1998, India 38
political economy 112
political moments 151
political nationalities 70
political structure, accommodative 73
political trickster 189, *190*, 191
pop music (K-pop) 177
Popper, Karl 123, 124, 125–6
popular culture: films 177; the Korean Wave 172–81; and neoliberal globalization 174; pop music (K-pop) 173–4; soft power 172; third space 173, 176–7; TV drama 173, 176–7, 178
postcolonialism 139–40
postmodernism 127
post-Western IR 150–2, 156
power, Cosmopolitan notion of 30, 33
power/knowledge dynamics 15
pragmatism 129
predatory agency 113, 118
procedural justice 76
Putnam, Hilary 128

Quine, Willard Van Orman 128–9

R2P 30, 34n3
Rachman, Gideon 32
racism 3, *110*, 110–1, *111*, 116; anti-imperialist scientific racist international theory 111–3; imperialist scientific racist international theory 113–4
Rawls, John 27
Reade, W.W. 113
realism 127
reason 127–8
Reformation, the 18
Reformist Islam 20
regional world 185
Reinsch, Paul 111, 114
relativism 127–8
Reliance Industries 43
Renaissance, European 18
revolutionary activism 124, 125
Rigney, A. 100
Rijiju, Kiren 51
rivalry 186–7, 187–8, *190*, 190–1
Rizal, José 3, 160–9; and cultural traditions 168–9; and education 167–8; *El*

Filibusterismo, 160–1, 162, 164, 168–9; *Noli Me Tangere* 160–1, 162, 164, 165–7, 167–8, 168; political inclinations 167; socialization 163–4
road complex theory 152–3, 155
road-and-travel perspective 149–56, 197
Roh Moo-hyun 175–6
Romance of the Three Kingdoms, The 4, 185–6, 187–92, *191*
Roosevelt, Theodore 113
routine violence 48, 59, 60n2
Roy, D. 87–8
Rumford, Chris 25–7, 31
Rushdie, Salman 28
Russia, Imperial 79, 116, 196
Ryukyu crisis, the 76, 77, 77–81, 82, 197

Said, Edward 109, 110, 111, 138, 160, 195, 196
Saikia, Yasmin 58
Samaddar, Ranabir 52
Second World War 86, 151–2, 179, 180
secularism 71–2
securitization, borders 52
security 2; Aberystwyth School perspective 20; and colonialism 3; critical approach 14; and energy resources 2; and identity 27–30, 33; and imperialism 3; importance 1; non-reflexive approaches 16; short-termism 16; state-focused 16
Selbin, Eric 19
Self, the 150, 154, 155
Sen, Amartya 5, 18
Senkaku Islands. *see* Diaoyutai/Senkaku Islands dispute
September 11 2001 terrorist attacks 5, 13
Sever, A. 102
Shih, C.Y. 93
Shilliam, Robbie 19
Shim, Doobo 179–80
Shinde, Sushil Kumar 51
Shishido Tamaki 79–80
short-termism 16
Sidgwick, Henry 114
Sikkim 36, 37, 43; anti-dam organizations 44–5; Green Mission 41; HEP controversy 39–41
Silina, Everita 2
Silk Road, the 152–3
Silk-Road initiative, China 6
simplism 129
Singh, Rajnath 51
Sinha, S. K. 53
Sino-Japanese diplomatic crisis, 1877 78
Sino-Japanese War (1894–95) 81, 87

Smith, Adam 117, 118
social equity, India 41–2
soft power 172, 176
South Korea: and the Asian Financial Crisis 174–5, 180; Cultural Industry Bureau 174; cultural turn 173; economic recovery 175–6; entertainment companies 174; film industry 177; historical background 172–3; and neoliberal globalization 174; pop music (K-pop) 173–4, 177; popular culture 172–81; relationships with Japan 178; relationships with Taiwan 179; relationships with Vietnam 178–9; soft power 172, 176; state 174; third space 173, 176–7, 181; tourism 177–8; TV drama 173, 176–7, 178
sovereign hierarchy 76
sovereignty 1, 6, 73, 76, 87; ambiguity of 86; and national identity 91–3
Soviet Union 99, 101–3, 105n3, 117, 196
spaces of resistance: Ethiopia 137–9, 143–5; pan-Africanism 144–5; pan-Islamism 141–3; social 139; state-centered 139; Turkey 137–9
Spain 5, 161–7, 163, 164–7
Spencer, Herbert 112–3, 117, 118
Sri Lanka 69, 70, 71, 72
state-building 74n2
Stoddard, Lothrop 113, 118
Stoicism 26
Strange, Susan 150
strategic genius 188–9, *190*, 191
structural inequalities 27
Sudan 33
Sumner, William Graham 112, 117, 118
Suzuki, Shogo 6, 76, 78
Sypnowich, Chrýstýne 29
Syria 33

Tagore, Rabindranath 67–8
Taiwan: anti-Japanese sentiment 88–9; Chinese identity 86, 88, 88–9, 93, 94n2, 197; cyber discourse 90–3; Diaoyutai/Senkaku Islands dispute 3, 80, 83n4, 86–93; ethnic groups 93n1; historical background 86; Japanese-ness 88, 89–90, 93, 94n2; national identity 3, 87–90, 90–3, 94n2; relationships with China 86, 87, 88–9, 92–3; relationships with Japan 86, 87, 89, 89–90, 92–3, 94n5; relationships with South Korea 179; sovereignty 87
Tamils 69, 70, 72
Taras, Ray 69

Teesta Urja Limited (TUL) 40
telecommunications 132
terrorism: challenge of 13; September 11 2001 attacks 5, 13
Thailand 169
theories and theory choice 2, 121; conservative activism 123–4; conventionalism 125; crossroads 149; cultural traditions 132; falsificationism 125–7, 128; logical positivism 125; normative basis 122–3; practical considerations 129–31, **130**; pragmatism 129; predictive capacity 122; realism 127; relativism 127–8; scientific practice 125–6; simplism 128–9; theory characteristics 122; truth-relativism 128; typology **123**, 123; value trade-offs 122; verificationism 124–5, 128
third space 173, 176–7, 181
Third World 104
tourism 177–8
trans-cultural international studies, justification of 121–32; practical considerations 129–31, **130**; theory choice theories 121–9, **123**
translation, role of 154
transportation 132
travel perspective 149–56, 153–4
Truman, Harry S. 99, 102
truth-relativism 128
Turkey 5, 115–6, 196; background 137–9; civilizing mission 142; Cold War foreign policy 3, 97–105, 142–3; comparison with Ethiopia 3, 137–9, 140–1, 145, 196; Cyprus crisis 143, 146n6; democracy in 104; Gallipoli campaign 139; Gallipoli campaign, 1915 141, 142; inevitability narrative 104; Ottoman Empire 139, 140–2, 192n4; and pan-Islamism 141–3; pericentric narrative 102; revisionist narrative 101–2; structuralist narrative 103; traditionalist narrative 101; War of Independence (1919–1923) 142, 146n4
Turkkaya, A. 101
turning points, history 99
Twitter 90

ubiquitous narrator 189, *190*, 191
UN Year of Dialogue among Civilizations 5, 13
uncontainable worlds 4
United Nations (UN): membership 104; UN Year of Dialogue among Civilizations 5, 13

United States of America: black rights movement 145; Cold War foreign policy 98, 99, 100, 101–2, 102, 103; economic dominance 29–30; hegemony 86; and the Philippines 161; pop culture 30; September 11 2001 terrorist attacks 5, 13
Universal Declaration of Human Rights 19

Vasquez, John 127
Vatican, the 5
verificationism 124–5, 128
Vietnam 169, 178–9
Vitoria, Francisco de 156n2

Weiner, Myron 53
Wendt, Alexander 186–7, 188, 191
West Bengal 53
Western-centrism 2, 17–9, 97–105; rejection of 20
Westfailure 150–2
Westphalia, Peace of 6, 82, 161
Westphalian IR: 1, 4, 184–92; alternatives 185; cartographic anxieties 185, 188; comparison with *Romance of the Three Kingdoms, The* 185–6, 187–92, *191*; hegemony 184–5; Hobbesian enmity 186; Kantian friendship 186, 187, 188, 190; Lockean rivalry 186, 186–7; re-envisioning 185
white absence 184
white man's burden, the 114
White Paper on the Foreigners' Issue (Government of Assam) 51, 56
white world order 4, 6
Wight, Martin 76
Williams, W.A. 101
World Bank 6, 39
World Economic Forum (WEF) 185
World Social Forum (WSF) 185
worlding 196, 197
worldism 152, 154–5
Wyn Jones, Richard 20

Yao Wendong 81
Yellow Peril, the 113
Yugoslavia, former 33, 196

Zhuge rivalry 187–8, *190*, 190–1

Taylor & Francis eBooks

Helping you to choose the right eBooks for your Library

Add Routledge titles to your library's digital collection today. Taylor and Francis ebooks contains over 50,000 titles in the Humanities, Social Sciences, Behavioural Sciences, Built Environment and Law.

Choose from a range of subject packages or create your own!

Benefits for you
- Free MARC records
- COUNTER-compliant usage statistics
- Flexible purchase and pricing options
- All titles DRM-free.

Benefits for your user
- Off-site, anytime access via Athens or referring URL
- Print or copy pages or chapters
- Full content search
- Bookmark, highlight and annotate text
- Access to thousands of pages of quality research at the click of a button.

REQUEST YOUR FREE INSTITUTIONAL TRIAL TODAY — Free Trials Available
We offer free trials to qualifying academic, corporate and government customers.

eCollections – Choose from over 30 subject eCollections, including:

Archaeology	Language Learning
Architecture	Law
Asian Studies	Literature
Business & Management	Media & Communication
Classical Studies	Middle East Studies
Construction	Music
Creative & Media Arts	Philosophy
Criminology & Criminal Justice	Planning
Economics	Politics
Education	Psychology & Mental Health
Energy	Religion
Engineering	Security
English Language & Linguistics	Social Work
Environment & Sustainability	Sociology
Geography	Sport
Health Studies	Theatre & Performance
History	Tourism, Hospitality & Events

For more information, pricing enquiries or to order a free trial, please contact your local sales team: **www.tandfebooks.com/page/sales**

The home of Routledge books

www.tandfebooks.com